THE SCHOOL TO PRISON PIPELINE: THE ROLE OF CULTURE AND DISCIPLINE IN SCHOOL

ADVANCES IN RACE AND ETHNICITY IN EDUCATION

Series Editors: Joy Lawson Davis and James L. Moore III

Recent Volumes:

Volume 1: Black Male Teachers: Diversifying the United States' Teacher Workforce – Edited by Chance W. Lewis and Ivory A. Toldson

Volume 2: African American Male Students in PreK-12 Schools: Informing Research, Policy, and Practice – Edited by James L. Moore III and Chance W. Lewis

Volume 3: Gifted Children of Color around the World: Diverse Needs, Exemplary Practices, and Directions for the Future – Edited by Joy Lawson Davis and James L. Moore III

ADVANCES IN RACE AND ETHNICITY IN EDUCATION
VOLUME 4

THE SCHOOL TO PRISON PIPELINE: THE ROLE OF CULTURE AND DISCIPLINE IN SCHOOL

EDITED BY

NATHERN S. OKILWA
University of Texas at San Antonio, TX, USA

MUHAMMAD KHALIFA
Michigan State University, MI, USA

FELECIA M. BRISCOE
University of Texas at San Antonio, TX, USA

emerald PUBLISHING

United Kingdom – North America – Japan
India – Malaysia – China

Emerald Publishing Limited
Howard House, Wagon Lane, Bingley BD16 1WA, UK

First edition 2017

British Library Cataloguing in Publication Data
A catalogue record for this book is available from the British Library

ISBN: 978-1-78560-129-3 (Print)
ISSN: 2051-2317 (Series)
ISBN: 978-1-78560-128-6 (Online)
ISBN: 978-1-78714-342-5 (Epub)

CONTENTS

LIST OF CONTRIBUTORS

Brian Boggs	Michigan State University, USA
Joshua Bornstein	Felician University, USA
Felecia M. Briscoe	University of Texas San Antonio, USA
Christopher Dunbar	University of Illinois at Urbana-Champaign, USA
Decoteau J. Irby	University of Illinois at Chicago, USA
Andrea Kalvesmaki	University of Utah, USA
Muhammad Khalifa	University of Minnesota, USA
Hilary Lustick	Texas State University, USA
Nathern S. Okilwa	University of Texas at San Antonio, USA
Hugh Potter	Michigan State University, USA
Garth Stahl	University of South Australia, Australia
Joseph B. Tulman	University of the District of Columbia, USA
Brenda G. Valles	University of Utah, USA

DEDICATION

We dedicate this book to those students who struggle through the schooling process as well as those educators who advocate on their behalf. May schools be places of opportunity for all students and not just for some!

ACKNOWLEDGMENTS

A number of people, outside the editors and authors, contributed to the completion of this blind peer-reviewed book. As coeditors, we acknowledge, with great appreciation, the time and expertise of the reviewers listed below. Their substantive feedback to each author helped refine and improve the quality of the chapters presented herein.

Erin Atwood, Texas Christian University
Jason Brayden, University of Texas at San Antonio
Becky Cohen, Council of State Governments Justice Center, Austin, Texas
Heather Cole, University of Texas at Austin
Amanda Cordova, University of Texas at San Antonio
Brad Davis, University of Texas at Arlington
Barbara Pasey, University of Texas at Austin
Catherine Robert, University of Texas at San Antonio
Daniel Spikes, Iowa State University
Meagan Sumbera, A&M University

CHAPTER 1

INTRODUCTION AND OVERVIEW

Nathern S. Okilwa, Muhammad Khalifa and Felecia M. Briscoe

ABSTRACT

This introduction chapter provides context to the ubiquitous nature of school discipline disproportionality, which has morphed into what is now commonly known as school-to-prison pipeline (STPP). A sample of major studies on school discipline research is presented to highlight the breadth and depth of the impact of discipline disparity on racially, culturally, and linguistically diverse students, low-income students, and students with disabilities. We also address how the interaction between implicit or explicit racism and discipline policies and practices exacerbates STPP. We acknowledge the efforts made by school systems to reverse the STPP trend through interventions such as restorative justice and positive behavioral intervention and support (PBIS). We posit that principals and teachers are critical agents in reforming the pervasive STPP trajectory. Finally, this chapter provides a synopsis of the rest of the chapters contained in this book.

Keywords: School-to-prison pipeline; discipline disparity; racial and linguistic minorities; interventions; principals; teachers

The School to Prison Pipeline: The Role of Culture and Discipline in School
Advances in Race and Ethnicity in Education, Volume 4, 1–13

ISSN: 2051-2317/doi:10.1108/S2051-231720160000004002

The concern about discipline disparity by race/ethnicity, gender, socioeconomic status, and disability has increasingly become part of the academic discourse over the last decades. Major research studies have established the persisting nature of disproportionality in discipline (Fabelo et al., 2011; Losen & Gillespie, 2012; Skiba et al., 2011; Skiba, Michael, Nardo, & Peterson, 2002; Wallace, Goodkind, Wallace, & Bachman, 2008). In other words, minoritized students – such as Black, Latino, culturally and linguistically diverse (CLD) students, refugees and immigrants, and low-income students, among other subgroups – are more likely to be referred, suspended, expelled, and arrested while in school; moreover, they are more likely to be academically impacted by the disciplinary action that they endure. For instance, the 2011 landmark statewide study in Texas, "Breaking Schools' Rules," examined suspension and expulsion of nearly one million public secondary school (7–12 grades) students who were followed up for at least six years (Fabelo et al., 2011). The study established a number of important findings: approximately 60% of public school students were suspended or expelled, at least once, between grades 7 and 12; when students were suspended or expelled at least once, the likelihood that they repeated a grade, dropped out of school, and/or got involved in the juvenile justice system increased significantly; African Americans and students with disabilities were disproportionately suspended or expelled to a higher degree compared to their peers without disabilities; and suspension and expulsion rates varied with school. Another study by Losen and Gillespie (2012) found a disproportionately higher suspension rates for African Americans, 17%, in K12 schools compared to 8% for Native Americans; 7% for Latinos; 5% for Whites; and 2% for Asian Americans. Other findings of their study include the following: More than 13% of all students with disabilities were suspended, which is approximately twice than that of their peers without disabilities; more so, 25% of African American students with disabilities were suspended at least once in 2009–2010 school year; additionally, African Americans and students with disabilities were more likely to be suspended repeatedly in one school year. And a final consideration in the context of school suspensions is the strong link between low-income and CDL students. Low-income students, especially those who are also minoritized in other ways, are suspended from school more frequently than middle- and high-income students (Atkins et al., 2002; Skiba & Knesting, 2001).

Overall, the studies seem to suggest that *racially* minoritized students are most likely to bear the brunt of disproportionalities in school discipline. In their study "Race is Not Neutral," Skiba and colleagues (2011) examined office referrals of 364 elementary and middle schools and found that African American students are two times (elementary) and four times (middle school) likely to be referred to the office for problem behaviors than their White peers. In addition, for similar problem behaviors, African American and Latino students are more likely to be suspended or expelled than their White peers. These large-scale studies, outlined above, are only a sampler representation of many other studies that reveal the ubiquitous nature of discipline disparity in schools across the United States. The impact on educational and life outcomes of racially, culturally, and linguistically diverse students and students with disabilities is hard to ignore. The insidious part of discipline disproportionality is how the educational opportunities of some youth are squandered, and often these youth are funneled into the juvenile and criminal justice system. These realities gave birth to what we now know as the school-to-prison pipeline (STPP) phenomenon. Therefore, the purpose of this book is to highlight how the STPP has emerged through a complex interaction between the institutional culture of schools, discipline policies and practices, and the various agents (school leaders, teachers, students, and parents). To achieve this purpose, this book presents an examination of the scope and impact of STPP from a variety of perspectives: experiential testimonials from victims of STPP, systemic and institutional structures and cultures that bolster STPP, and a discussion on potential alternatives to disrupt STPP coupled with a measure of critique of the implementation of these alternatives.

THE CONSTRUCTION OF SCHOOL-TO-PRISON PIPELINE (STPP)

STPP has come to signify the pervasive pattern of students being pushed out of the mainstream educational contexts into increased contact or involvement with the juvenile justice system (Advancement Project, 2005; Children's Defense Fund, 2007; NAACP 2005; Wald & Losen, 2003). The NAACP Legal Defense Fund defines STPP as the "funneling of students out of school and into the streets and the juvenile correction system [perpetuating] a cycle known as the 'School-to-Prison-Pipeline', depriving children and youth of meaningful opportunities for education, future employment, and participation in our democracy" (NAACP, 2005, online). The interaction between implicit or explicit racism and discipline policies and practices exacerbates STPP. As previously stated, research indicates that African American students are more harshly punished than their White counterparts for similar violations, which leaves another explanation, that which is rooted in bias, of how discipline policies are implemented. As Witt (2007) notes:

> Some of the highest rates of racially disproportionate discipline are found in states with the lowest minority populations, where the disconnect between white teachers and black students is potentially the greatest. White teachers feel more threatened by boys of color. (www.chicagotribune.com)

In particular, the historical fear of African American masculinity among White Americans (especially White women) extends to the classroom and hence, negatively influences teacher perception and interaction with these students (Harry & Anderson, 1994). In their study about teacher–student racial matching efforts, Downey and Pribesh (2004) found that teachers (both White and African Americans) generally rated African American students as poorer classroom citizens, who exhibit more problem behaviors (e.g., argumentative, involved in fights, exhibiting anger) and lesser efforts in learning (e.g., the ability to be attentive, persistent with tasks, display of eagerness to learn) compared to White students in both kindergarten and eighth grade. Other studies indicate that White teachers view Black male students as older and less innocent than White male students (Goff, Jackson, Di Leone, Culotta, & DiTomasso, 2014). Such dehumanizing-biased perceptions of African American students underlie the immediate responses (reprimand or disciplinary sanctions) teachers meted out at any sighting of what teachers may consider aggressive or inappropriate behavior by African American boys.

In addition to the biased disciplining of students of color, the federal Gun-Free Schools Act of 1994, which mandated a one-year suspension for students who brought a firearm to school, heralded the implementation of "zero tolerance" in schools. According to Skiba and Peterson (1999), zero tolerance policies were meant to "deal out severe punishment for all offenses, no matter how minor, ostensibly in an effort to treat all offenders equally in the spirit of fairness and intolerance of rule-breaking" (p. 373). Despite the policies being "zero tolerance," it is clear that schools have a great discretion in how they interpret and implement the policies (Dunbar & Villarruel, 2004). Unfortunately, the wide net of zero tolerance policies have tended to catch and inequitably punish CLD students as well as students with disabilities for minor infractions such as shooting rubber bands, taking water pistols to school, pointing a finger in a game of cops and robbers, truancy, defiance, disrespect, chasing or running in the halls, and profanity (Cornell & Mayer, 2010; Skiba et al., 2002; Skiba & Peterson, 1999). Irby (2014) adds, the school discipline net has widened and as evidence shows, schools disproportionately apply it to African American and Latino students. There is further evidence to indicate that teachers more often refer African American and Latino students to the office for subjective discipline issues (e.g., defiance, disrespectful, argumentative) than they do for White students (Irby, 2014; Skiba et al., 2002). In comparison to White students, African Americans are subjected to more severe punishment for less serious infractions, which only aids to further isolate and alienate them from the educational process (Skiba et al., 2002). Isolation and alienation are often associated with increased school disengagement and eventual dropout (Balfanz, Byrnes, & Fox, 2013; Skiba et al., 2011). Often, African American and Latino students experience higher dropout rates than White students (Fine, 1991; Finn, 1989). Dropping out of school is a major warning sign of potential involvement with the juvenile justice system (Christle, Jolivette, & Nelson, 2005). All this suggests that it is not only a question of zero tolerance but a question of zero tolerance *for whom*? Clearly, zero tolerance policies criminalize minor infractions of school rules (more so for students of color), and the presence of police officers in schools has made the transition from student (school) to criminal (juvenile justice system) quite seamless. And indeed, racialized application of zero tolerance and other discipline policies take their toll on the academic success of CLD students. Isolation and alienation are often associated with increased school disengagement and eventual dropout (Balfanz et al., 2013; Skiba et al., 2011). Often, African American and Latino students experience higher dropout rates than White students (Fine, 1991; Finn, 1989). Dropping out of school is a major warning sign of potential involvement with the juvenile justice system (Christle et al., 2005).

EFFORTS TO REVERSE STPP TRENDS

Some schools and school districts are engaged in reform efforts in order to change persistent STPP trends. For some, it is a true acknowledgment of national discipline disproportionality and has a negative impact on students' future, whereas for others it is perhaps a response to the Office of Civil Rights mandate – to account for existing disproportionality and to take measures to correct it. Skiba et al. (2011) suggest that effective discipline systems rely on graduated or tiered models where serious consequences are reserved for serious offenses such as possession of illegal drugs, alcohol, or firearms, sexual battery and assault, physical attack, and hazing. Restorative justice and positive behavior intervention and support (PBIS) are two alternative approaches to zero tolerance discipline practices that are gaining momentum across the country. As much as these discipline alternative approaches have drawn interest from schools and school districts, there is increasing critique (Irby, 2014; Irby & Clough, 2013; Okilwa, 2015). For instance, restorative justice can be considered as an "after-the-fact" approach – a remedial approach – that is rooted in the criminal justice system with a focus on repairing harm caused by an offender and giving voice to the victim (Bazemore & Umbreit, 2001). Thus, this restorative justice was not originally used to restore justice to people who had been unfairly penalized by the criminal justice system. The criminal justice system is traditionally known to dispense consequences or punish wrongdoings. This is not oriented toward establishing and remediating its own wrongdoings or crime. Further discussion of restorative justice or discipline is presented in Chapter 6 of this book entitled "'What Are We Restoring?' Black Teachers on Restorative Discipline." With regard to PBIS, although it is a tiered program intended to manage behaviors according to severity, Irby (2014) suggests that if PBIS is not culturally responsive, then it will replicate the same disproportionate discipline. According to Irby, there is a tendency for the majority of CLD students and those with disabilities to be fast tracked to Tier 3 (most punitive level) of PIBS intervention. In addition, Skiba and colleagues (2011) suggest, discipline policies should encourage culturally responsive practices in order to create a positive school environment and climate for all students. The concept of culturally responsive pedagogy or teaching or practices is hailed as a critical component of bridging the learning processes and the experiences of most marginalized students (Gay, 2002a, 2002b; Ladson-Billings, 1995; Villegas & Lucas, 2002) with the potential of reducing the discipline disparity. In particular, culturally responsive teaching connects students' cultural knowledge, prior experiences, and performance styles to academic knowledge and intellectual tools in ways that legitimize what students already know (Gay, 2002a, 2002b). In essence, culturally responsive teaching activates students' funds of knowledge, thereby increasing academic engagement and achievement, which in turn alleviates problem behaviors. A further look at PBIS is presented in Chapter 7 of this book entitled "Can PBIS Build Justice Rather Than Merely Restore Order?" Thus, we wonder: Is PBIS meant to benefit schools or students? Can it be effective when being used by biased educators? And what elements are needed in PBIS to make it a culturally responsive intervention?

THE ROLE OF THE PRINCIPAL AND TEACHERS

The research suggests that a number of oppressive practices that contribute to STPP can be identified, reduced, and contested by strong leaders and leadership teams (Khalifa, 2012; Khalifa, Gooden, & Davis, 2016). Social justice-oriented school leaders have to understand that any reform effort needs to be consistent with the assumption that discipline disproportionality cannot be separated from pedagogical practices, teacher–student interactions, classroom management, curriculum design, school–family partnerships, and school programming (Cornell & Mayer, 2010). For example, the principal has to be intentional about their recruiting and hiring practices, targeting teachers who are oriented toward social justice. Discipline disproportionality often originates from teacher–student classroom interactions where most discipline referrals are first issued (Gregory & Weinstein, 2008, Skiba et al., 2002). Hiring right is not enough, teachers do not acquire cultural competence by accident; the school principal is obligated to provide relevant professional development to include topics on race and racism, culturally responsive pedagogy, etc. (Khalifa, 2011). Also, hiring efforts should seek to increase the ethnic and gender diversity of the teaching force. To the extent possible, the teaching force should reflect the student population that is increasingly becoming minority majority. Nationally, the teaching force is predominately White females. Advocates of "student's own-race teacher-pairing" point to the role model effect and the evidence that teacher's perceptions have an effect on student outcomes (Dee, 2004). However, Skiba and colleagues found discipline disproportionality at the administrative level as well (Skiba et al., 2011). Therefore, the need for educational leadership programs to emphasize social justice and produce a cadre of reform-minded leaders is paramount.

The Structure of This Book

In adapting zero tolerance-type polices, schools created a climate and culture grounded in intolerance for behavior deemed unacceptable within the school context. Acceptable school behavior has often been measured based on the values of the White middle class, thereby disenfranchising students from other culturally and linguistically diverse backgrounds. Nonconforming students find themselves caught in a cycle of exclusion through punitive and exclusionary practices of suspension and expulsion leading to problematic STPP. To achieve the purpose of this book, the chapters presented herein examine the critical aspects of the STPP phenomenon: Chapters 2 and 3 provide personal accounts of the impacts of STPP. Hearing from the adults (two Black men) and children (Chicano students), humanizes the alarming statistical references that often frame the scholarly research narrative. In Chapter 2 (The Indignities on Which the School-to-Prison Pipeline Is Built: Life Stories of Two Formerly Incarcerated Black Male School-Leavers), Irby presents narratives of two Black men who represent a population of people who are often talked about, but seldom heard from in the STPP research. To analyze their stories, Irby employed a framework that centers on understanding human dignity and the conditions, circumstances, and experiences that threaten it. In his analysis, he found that these men's sense of self was eroded by moments of personal loss, disposal, and ways that even well-intentioned people marked them "as problems." Consequently, these individuals engaged in disruptive and destructive behaviors. Irby concludes by discussing the importance of supplementing STPP research with Black boys' and men's first-hand accounts of their own experiences as a way of humanizing the primary subjects of this burgeoning area of education research. Similarly, in Chapter 3 (Resisting the School-to-Prison Pipeline Utilizing Guidance from the Frontlines: Chicano Student Experiences as a Source of Knowledge and Strength), Valles examines the impacts of STPP on Chicano students by focusing on the innovation of discipline policies and practices, students' personal experiences with STPP, and effective alternative practices to zero tolerance policies. Valles utilizes CRT and LatCrit frameworks to underscore the experiential knowledge that Chicano students contribute to conceptualizing ways of disrupting STPP. Particularly, Chicano students point to a praxis grounded in community to interrupt STPP and clear educational pathways.

As depicted in Chapters 2 and 3, school cultures, structures, and systems seem to continually perpetuate the harmful cycle of STPP. Chapters 4 and 5 present two uniquely different school contexts (the United States and the United Kingdom) and how they contribute to sustaining STPP. In Chapter 4 (Discipline and Punishment: How Schools Are Building the School-to-Prison Pipeline), Potter, Boggs, and Dunbar argue that the growth of punitive school discipline in American schools has created an inequitable system of school punishment that is reflective of the development of STPP and the establishment of an educational "total institution." The authors present data that exemplify the overreliance upon punitive school discipline in one urban school to address student behavioral problems. Potter et al. utilize the "total institution" theory of command and control of a population to conceptualize the impact of STPP. The authors argue for alternative and more effective measures of school discipline that school leaders can pursue to address the draconian treatment of Black and Brown boys in today's traditional public school environments. While in Chapter 5 (Pathologizing the White "Unteachable": South London's Working-Class Boys' Experiences with Schooling and Discipline), a South London context (the United Kingdom), Stahl presents a case of students from a White working-class background, who remain the lowest performing ethnic group with ominous implications on their long-term life chances. The author investigates how White working-class boys experience pathologization and deficit discourses in their schooling as they negotiate the discipline structures in three educational sites in South London (two state comprehensive schools and one pupil referral unit). Drawing upon empirical data from an in-depth sociological study of 23 White working-class boys, this chapter makes theoretical connections between how pathologization – both within the school and wider society – contributes to how these young men become constructed with and through deficit discourses contributed significantly toward low academic achievement. As often perceived, whiteness equates to power and entitlement; in the schooling contexts of this study whiteness was often socially constructed as undesirable and equated to low aspirations, stagnation, and anti-educational stances.

However, there are schools and school systems that are attempting to disrupt STPP – engaging in discipline reform. Restorative justice and PBIS are two of the predominantly school discipline reform interventions being implemented in school systems across the country. Chapters 6 and 7 acknowledge the potential in these two interventions, and they also provide a thoughtful critique that serves as a cautionary optimism in the effectiveness of these interventions. In Chapter 6 ("What Are We Restoring?" Black Teachers on Restorative Discipline), Lustick examines a group of Black teachers utilizing restorative discipline practices. Through interviews and observations, the teachers demonstrated Du Bois's theory of Double Consciousness: They recognized both the institutional dynamics of the school's discipline policy and the ways in which enacting the policy ultimately replicated traditional racial inequality. The teachers repeatedly challenged the relevance of restorative theory and practices to students whose everyday reality involved police injustice, community violence, and impoverished living conditions. Although the teachers recognized the potential of restorative discipline as a foundation for communication and trust building, they perceived its implementation as an immediate way to restore obedience in students and restore order in the school. In Chapter 7 (Can PBIS Build Justice Rather Than Merely Restore Order?), Bornstein presents a multicase qualitative study in which inclusive school leaders attempted to move their schools from the excessive use of suspension. In this effort they employed PBIS which they thought would be therapeutic rather than punitive. However, Bornstein argues that the PBIS system traded a disciplinary system of control for a medicalized system of restoring order. Unwanted behavior came to be defined as evidence of possible behavioral disability. Hence, the PBIS system exchanged one deficit identity of "disorderly" student for another of "disordered" student, subsuming other considerations of race, class, and gender identity. Based on the findings of the study, Bornstein proposes more liberatory practices for PBIS that interrupt dominant culture discourses of normal behavior and power, and hold promise for establishing justice rather than simply reinstating order.

Lastly, legislation is often meant to govern and protect the interests of citizens. For instance, disability laws were enacted to protect the rights of this vulnerable student population – student with disabilities. In Chapter 8 (A Systems Theory Analysis for Ending the School-to-Prison Pipeline: Using Disability Rights Laws to Keep Children in Schools and Out of Courts, Jails, and Prisons), Kalvesmaki and Tulman conceptualize STPP as a network of flows and feedback loops that connect the education and delinquency systems. The authors argue, this system is heavily biased to funnel students with disabilities, disproportionately from low-income minority families, away from productive educational outcomes to a path toward incarceration. Conversely, congress intended special education and disability rights laws to ameliorate injustice and ensure long-term positive outcomes for all students. Through a system's theory perspective, this chapter outlines the key leverage points inherent in disability rights laws, which can and should be activated to interrupt and reverse STPP. Many provisions within the law are overlooked or inadequately enacted within current educational practices. Kalvesmaki and Tulman present problem-solving strategies, rooted in the Individuals with Disabilities Education Act (IDEA) and other disability rights laws, for educators, juvenile justice advocates, and policy makers to use in order to provide educational opportunities for all students. Finally, in Chapter 9 (What We Can Do Right Now: What Needs Further Research?), Briscoe, Okilwa, and Khalifa draw upon the major ideas discussed in the seven preceding chapters to summarize what concerned educational stakeholders can do right now to disrupt the STPP. In essence, the authors compile and suggest a number of practical recommendations.

In summary, the current structure of school discipline is detrimental to the future of CLD students, low-income students, and students with disabilities. STPP has become a pervasive trajectory for far too many young people and has to be challenged and reversed. This book presents personal accounts, compelling data, and theoretical basis useful for stakeholders engaged with this issue. For instance, school personnel (e.g., administrators and teachers) will find the content of this book useful in understanding the theoretical underpinnings of STPP and hopefully to become vigilant about school discipline practices and proposed interventions, some of which create a new host of unintended consequences. Also, other stakeholders such as lawmakers may find this book informative in their efforts, from a legislative standpoint, to generate solutions that are considerate of the historic, economic, political, and social marginalizing factors that are part of the struggle of students with disabilities, CLD and low-income students.

REFERENCES

Advancement Project. (2005). *Education on lockdown: The school to jailhouse track*. Washington, DC.

Atkins, M. S., McKay, M. M., Frazier, S. L., Jakobsons, L. J., Arvanitis, P., Cunningham, T., & Lambrecht, L. (2002). Suspensions and detentions in an urban, low-income school: Punishment or reward? *Journal of Abnormal Child Psychology*, *30*(4), 361–371.

Balfanz, R., Byrnes, V., & Fox, J. (2013, January). Sent home and put off-track: The antecedents, disproportionalities, and consequences of being suspended in the ninth grade. Paper presented at the Closing the School Discipline Gap: Research to Practice Conference, Washington, DC.

Bazemore, G., & Umbreit, M. (2001). A comparison of four restorative conferencing models. In G. Bazemore & M. Umbreit (Ed.), *Juvenile Justice Bulletin*. Washington, DC: Department of Justice, Office of Juvenile Justice and Delinquency Prevention.

Children's Defense Fund. (2007). *America's cradle to prison pipeline*. Washington, DC: CDF.

Christle, C., Jolivette, K., & Nelson, C. M. (2005). Breaking the school to prison pipeline: Identifying school risk and protective factors for youth delinquency. *Exceptionality*, *13*, 69–88.

Cornell, D. G., & Mayer, M. J. (2010). Why do school order and safety matter? *Educational Researcher*, *39*(1), 7–15.

Dee, T. S. (2004). Teachers, race, and student achievement, in a randomized experiment. *The Review of Economics and Statistics*, *86*(1), 195–210.

Downey, D., & Pribesh, S. (2004). When race matters: Teachers' evaluations of students' classroom behavior. *Sociology of Education*, *77*, 267–282.

Dunbar, C., & Villarruel, F. A. (2004). What a difference the community makes: Zero tolerance policy interpretation and implementation. *Equity & Excellence in Education*, *37*(4), 351–359.

Fabelo, T., Thompson, M. D., Plotkin, M., Carmichael, D., Marchbanks III, M. P., & Booth, E. A. (2011). *Breaking schools' rules: A statewide study of how school discipline relates to students' success and juvenile justice involvement*. Council of State Governments Justice Center, New York, NY.

Fine, M. (1991). *Framing dropouts*. Albany, NY: SUNY Press.

Finn, J. D. (1989). Withdrawal from school. *Review of Educational Research*, *59*(2), 117–142.

Gay, G. (2002a). *Culturally responsive teaching: Theory, practice, & research*. New York, NY: Teachers College Press.

Gay, G. (2002b). Preparing for culturally responsive teaching. *Journal of Teacher Education*, *53*(2), 106–116.

Goff, P. A., Jackson, M. C., Di Leone, B. A. L., Culotta, C. M., & DiTomasso, N. A. (2014). The essence of innocence: Consequences of dehumanizing Black children. *Journal of personality and social psychology*, *106*(4), 526.

Gregory, A., & Weinstein, R. S. (2008). The discipline gap and African Americans: Defiance or cooperation in the high school classroom. *Journal of School Psychology*, *46*(4), 455–475.

Harry, B., & Anderson, M. G. (1994). The disproportionate placement of African American males in special education programs. A critique of the process. *Journal of Negro Education*, *63*(4), 602–620.

Irby, D. J. (2014). Trouble at school: Understanding school discipline systems as nets of social control. *Equity & Excellence in Education*, *47*(4), 513–530.

Irby, D. J., & Clough, C. (2013). Discipline philosophies and school culture: An exploration of teacher beliefs and school practices. Paper presented at the Annual Meeting of the American Educational Research Association, San Francisco, CA.

Khalifa, M. (2012). A re-new-ed paradigm in successful urban school leadership principal as community leader. *Educational Administration Quarterly*, *48*(3), 424–467.

Khalifa, M. A. (2011). Teacher expectations and principal behavior: Responding to teacher acquiescence. *The Urban Review*, *43*(5), 702–727.

Khalifa, M. A., Gooden, M. A., & Davis, J. E. (2016). Culturally responsive school leadership a synthesis of the literature. *Review of Educational Research*. doi:10.3102/0034654316630383

Ladson-Billings, G. (1995). But that's just good teaching! The case for culturally relevant pedagogy. *Theory into Practice*, *34*(3), 159–165.

Losen, D. J., & Gillespie, J. (2012). Opportunities suspended: The disparate impact of disciplinary exclusion from school. The Civil Right Project, The Center for Civil Rights Remedies, Los Angeles, CA.

NAACP. (2005). *Interrupting the school to prison pipe-line*. Washington, DC.

Okilwa, N. S. (2015). Racialized and gendered nature of school discipline: Are touted alternatives capable of making a lasting difference? *The National Journal of Urban Education and Practice*, *9*(2), 495–509.

Skiba, R. J., Horner, R. H., Chung, C.-G., Rausch, M. K., May, S. L., & Tobin, T. (2011). Race is not neutral: A national investigation of African American and Latino proportionality in school discipline. *School Psychology Review*, *40*(1), 85–107.

Skiba, R. J., & Knesting, K. (2001). Zero tolerance, zero evidence: An analysis of school disciplinary practice. *New Directions for Youth Development*, *92*, 17–43.

Skiba, R. J., Michael, R. S., Nardo, A. C., & Peterson, R. (2002). The color of discipline: Sources of racial and gender disproportionality in school punishment. *Urban Review*, *34*, 317–342.

Skiba, R. J., & Peterson, R. L. (1999). The dark side of zero tolerance: Can punishment lead to safe school? *Phi Delta Kappan*, *80*, 372–382.

Villegas, A. M., & Lucas, T. (2002). Preparing culturally responsive teachers rethinking the curriculum. *Journal of Teacher Education*, *53*(1), 20–32.

Wald, J., & Losen, D. (2003). Defining and re-directing a school to prison pipeline. Harvard Civil Rights Project, Cambridge, MA.

Wallace Jr, J. M., Goodkind, S., Wallace, C. M., & Bachman, J. G. (2008). Racial, ethnic, and gender differences in school discipline among US high school students: 1991–2005. *The Negro Educational Review*, *59*(1–2), 47.

Witt, H. (2007, September 5). School discipline tougher on African Americans. *Chicago Tribune*. Retrieved from http://www.chicagotribune.com/chi-070924discipline-story.html

CHAPTER 2

THE INDIGNITIES ON WHICH THE SCHOOL-TO-PRISON PIPELINE IS BUILT: LIFE STORIES OF TWO FORMERLY INCARCERATED BLACK MALE SCHOOL-LEAVERS

Decoteau J. Irby

ABSTRACT

In this chapter, I present narratives of two Black men who represent a population of people who are often talked about but seldom heard from in school-to-prison pipeline research. To analyze their stories, I employed a framework that centers on understanding human dignity and the conditions, circumstances, and experiences that threatened it. I found that their sense of self was eroded by moments of personal loss, disposal, and ways that even well-intentioned people marked them as "problems." I explore how their eroded sense of self led them to engage in disruptive and destructive behaviors. I conclude by discussing the importance of supplementing school-to-prison pipeline research with Black boys' and men's first-hand accounts of their own experiences as a way of humanizing the primary subjects of this burgeoning area of education research.

Keywords: Black males; dignity; gender; race; school discipline; school-to-prison pipeline

---

The School to Prison Pipeline: The Role of Culture and Discipline in School
Advances in Race and Ethnicity in Education, Volume 4, 15–39

ISSN: 2051-2317/doi:10.1108/S2051-231720160000004003

Scholars have written extensively about the complex racialized webs of legal, policy, and institutional processes that create linkages between schools and prisons, commonly referred as school-to-prison pipelines (Christle, Jolivette, & Nelson, 2005; Fasching-Varner, Martin, Mitchell, & Bennett-Haron, 2014). And rightfully so, Black and Brown youth are overpunished in schools, and today's punishment practices disproportionately funnel Black and Brown children and youth into these bureaucratic structures that facilitate the criminalization of school-aged youth (Mendez & Knoff, 2003; Monroe, 2005; Morrison & D'Incau, 1997). More broadly, Black males have long been subjected to criminalization in the United States (Muhammad, 2011) for a range of offenses related primarily to their racialized and gendered statuses. Zero tolerance and the school-to-prison pipeline advance a legacy of official and unofficial criminalization of Black boys and men (Muhammad, 2011).

Jenness' (2004) review of sociological studies of criminalization revealed that a number of factors foster and sustain the criminalization process over time. Among the factors are moral entrepreneurship and new professionalism, triggering events, interest group politics, social movements, the shape of political opportunities, and structural conditions. She argues that scholarship produced in the early 21st century considered these factors as ways to help more fully explain criminalization as a form of *state authorized social control* connected to larger processes of institutionalization and modernization. These included several approaches. A "classic approach" to understanding criminalization focuses on demography and exerting control over so-called problem populations. A definitional and political approach focuses on the emergence of formal mechanisms (policy and law) that label particular populations as in need of control. The current school-to-prison pipeline literature follows these sorts of sociological approaches that prioritize ideological (Giroux, 2003a; 2003b; 2001; Kupchik, 2009), structural (Irby, 2014; Verdugo, 2002), policy (Irby, 2013; Monroe, 2005; Reyes, 2006), and statistical analyses (Christle et al., 2005; Mendez & Knoff, 2003; Morrison & D'Incau, 1997) to understand its formation, maintenance, and deleterious effect of school–prison interactions on the educational lives of Black males.

Although sociological approaches to understanding the school-to-prison pipeline offer important insights into the ideological, political, structural, and policy underpinnings of this recent iteration of youth criminalization, this body of work would be strengthened by qualitative research that offers insights into the lived experiences of Black males and the ways they personally make meaning of their experiences. Laura's (2014) *Being Bad: My Baby Brother and the School-to-Prison Pipeline* offers a close example.

Laura (2014) presents the story of her brother Chris' transition from a boy who was enthusiastic about learning, to being diagnosed with a learning disability, misbehaving in school, and his eventual brushes with the criminal justice system and incarceration. Throughout, she points to teachers' and school leaders' missed opportunities to engage Chris as well as her families' desperate attempts to support her brother in his difficulties. Accounts such as that of Laura's (2014) contribute to the school-to-prison pipeline scholarship by challenging a body of research that conjures images of "nameless masses of black male bodies" being ushered out of school and into prison by focusing on the human beings – students, teachers, leaders, parents, and families – that are at the centerpiece of the school-to-prison phenomenon.

CHAPTER PURPOSE AND FRAMEWORK

In this chapter, I present two men's first-hand accounts of the school-based experiences that predated each of their eventual incarcerations. Deon and Aaron represent a population of people who are often talked about but seldom heard from in school-to-prison pipeline research. I conducted this research to better understand their educational lives, their interactions in and out-of-school circumstances, conditions, and experiences that played into their leaving school and eventual time in prison. My goal here is to offer humanizing accounts to supplement the current body of school-to-prison pipeline work that exists in the field of educational research.

I frame youth criminalization as a process that initiates the production of "criminal others" by systematically dispossessing youth of certain human and civil rights but more importantly their potential to grow and learn. My recurring refrain throughout this chapter is that criminalizing Black males is an affront that diminishes their sense of dignity. I focus primarily on the concept of noninherent dignity, an acquired condition of self-worth premised upon a person's condition, circumstance, and behavior (Hicks, 2011; Kateb, 2011; Michael, 2014; Rosen, 2012). Noninherent dignity is a relational concept. It is upheld or diminished in the context of social relations, reflects the nature of human relationships, and is best understood in terms of experiences, conditions, and moments of humiliation (loss) that diminish a persons' sense of equal status to that of his or her fellow humans. While the intrinsic dignity of humanity cannot be in any way diminished, failing to meet the educational needs of a person diminishes his or her ability to see his or her own humanity in relation to fellow humans. In other words, people can and do lose sight of their inherent worth and full human potential. Children and youth are especially vulnerable to these losses.

The dispossession of a young person's human potential, and the politics of containment and disposability that accompany it, threatens the dignity of humanity by failing to meet the moral and existential standard of stewardship associated with educating a child toward his or her fullest potential. Criminalization becomes particularly acute when a state authorizes systematic mistreatment of an entire population. This occurs through officially creating categories of "otherness" that enable people in positions of official power to act in ways that diminish an oppressed person's autonomy, rights to recognition, relational connections, ability to fulfill substantive needs, and strips away at his or her sense of self.

My hope is that readers think about not merely dismantling the school-to-prison pipeline but also challenging its very foundation – the indignities of Black males' experiences living in a deeply racist society that is in part produced by well-meaning social science researchers who contribute to a statistical discourse of Black male dysfunction by failing to collect and present Black boys' and men's first-hand experiences. I invite readers to consider three central features of the stories I present. First, Deon's and Aaron's stories feature moments when they came to see themselves *as problems* (as opposed to *having problems*). Second, their stories feature moments where each man remembered losing sight of his personhood and dignity. Third, experiences of containment and disposability (abandonment) were central phenomena that initiated, reinforced, and exacerbated their objectification and diminished sense of self.

RESEARCH PROCEDURES

My presentation of Deon's and Aaron's stories is my best effort to elevate their voices in a space where Black men's and boys' voices are hypermarginalized and too often lost in the statistical discourse that dominates the field. I conducted this research because I was interested in how each participant made sense of his drop out/stop out and eventual repeated periods of incarceration. I was specifically interested in their racialized and gendered experiences as Black men.

Introduction of Participants

At the time I interviewed Deon Davidson, he was in his mid-50s (Table 1). Deon spent most of his life in Philadelphia and "moved sort of around, pretty much back and forth to different parts of the city." He described his upbringing as "pretty good" and believed his mother moved around so much because she was "trying to find a good location for us to grow up." His mother and father got divorced when he was around the age of two. He explains that he was raised by 6–7 women in his household and believes that "growing up without a man figure or father potentially led to me being spoiled .... I got away with a lot." Deon grew up at a time when the City of Brotherly Love was what he described as gang-infested. As a teen, he was a victim of violence that left him severely injured. He eventually joined a gang to protect himself from the possibility of further harm, especially at the hands of White gangs that he encountered when his family relocated him to a "better" area of the city. Deon left school before graduating and soon after entered a vicious cycle of incarceration and recidivism.

At the time of the research interview, Aaron McNair was 40 years old and enrolled in a bachelor's degree program in counseling (Table 1). He aspired to earn a master's degree and eventually a Ph.D. He is an African American man who experienced a stint of incarceration for six years. He was on parol approximately five years before the interview. In introducing himself, he shared with me that addiction was a prevalent part of his life. His addiction took the form of substance usage and the vicarious experience of seeing family members' substance usage. He also confided that criminality had been a major part of his upbringing. He described many of his problems as stemming from "never having a relationship with a man whom I could trust enough to give me appropriate advice or advice that was life-altering or life-giving." He disclosed that "I've always had negative male influences. Unfortunately, those influences scared me away from those

Table 1. Participant Characteristics.

Name	Approx. Age	Approximate School Years	Primary City	Highest Educational Attainment
Aaron McNair	40	1974–1986	Wilmington, DE	Associate's degree
Deon Davidson	55	1959–1971	Philadelphia, PA	General equivalency diploma

things that would make me have a better quality of life." In the year leading up to the interview, Aaron worked with low-level offenders in jail facilities as an informal counselor. In these roles, he assisted with conflict resolution, offered informal counseling, and anger management using many of the techniques he learned during his incarceration.

I purposively selected Deon's and Aaron's stories from a larger pool of participants from whom I learned from. These men grew up in different cities at different time periods and had very different home lives and school experiences than other participants I interviewed. Neither of them was poor. Both had stable households. Relative to the general population of Black males I interviewed, Deon and Aaron displayed high levels of literacy and academic potential. Each eventually left school before graduating but later in life went on to earn an education equivalent to high school diploma or beyond. These characteristics were important because neither of them considered poverty, instability, or the academic demands of schools as impetuses for their lack of success in traditional school settings. I wanted to minimize those commonly referenced factors as variables of consideration. By holding these factors constant, it allowed me to consider other factors that played a role in shaping their educational trajectories.

DATA COLLECTION PROCEDURES

To collect Deon's and Aaron's stories, I conducted in-depth one-on-one interviews using a personal narrative approach (Riessman, 1993). I introduced the interview as a general conversation. In a series of audio-recorded interviews, I asked participants to "tell their stories." I asked them to discuss the role that key experiences in their childhoods, teens, and early adult lives played in their decisions to leave school and how these same experiences may have contributed to their eventual incarceration. I listened to the men tell their stories the way they each saw fit and asked probing and clarifying questions as needed to gain a deeper understanding of their narratives.

DATA ANALYSIS – MULTICASE ANALYSIS

I approached the analysis of participant narratives using a multiple-case study approach. Case study analysis is used to illuminate in detail the how and why of particular time and context-bounded phenomena. I treated each individual as a unique case, focusing on Aaron's and Deon's homes, neighborhoods, and school contexts as factors that shaped their school leaving and trajectory toward incarceration. I sorted the data using a combination of inductive and deductive coding procedures. My initial deductive codes stemmed from Jenness' (2004) contextual frames for studying criminalization as well as my own theoretical proposition that criminalization can be accomplished through containing, disposing, and objectifying conditions and experiences. Sample codes that I used to organize the data are shown in Table 2.

Table 2. Sample Codes Used to Categorize Data for Analysis.

Sample Codes	Sample Subcodes	Codes Applied at
Codes_Context	Demographic changes/ control of populations	Passages where participants described demographic changes or neighborhood or school composition that impacted their circumstances, conditions, or experiences
	Definitional and political processes	Passages where participants described their being legal, policy, or status changes that impacted their circumstances, conditions, or experiences
	Processes of globalization and modernization	Passages where participants described labor market conditions, structural forces that impacted their circumstances, conditions, or experiences
Code_Experience	Containment	Passages where participants described being contained or unable to leave or escape a circumstance, condition, or experience
	Disposability	Passages where participants described being disposed, abandoned, or alienated from a community, space or place, or web of relationships they deemed important to their sense of well-being
	Objectification	Passages where participants described being used or felt as though they were an object or instrument for someone else's use
Code_Loss	Erosion of identity	Passages where participants described losing a sense of some aspect of their identity
	Erosion of relationships	Passages where participants described losing relationships
	Erosion of safety	Passages where participants described losing a sense of physical, emotional, or psychological safety

To analyze the stories in light of the school-to-prison pipeline and criminalization writ large, I focused my analysis on the ways that participants recounted their experiences and treatment in relation to family members, neighborhood folks, schoolmates, and teachers. I was interested in moments of personal loss, disposal, and the myriad ways that people, even those well-intentioned, marked them as "problems." I also focused on the extent to which they internalized and challenged the problem labels and circumstances that could be used to justify or rationalize their containment, disposability, and dispossession.

RESEARCHER POSITIONALITY

I am a Black man. During the interview process and as a part of a year-long participatory research project, I developed a brotherhood with the participants. At the time of the project, I invited the participants to be my guests in an Urban Studies undergraduate class that focused on Black males. After the interviews, for a period of about three years, I maintained contact and met them over lunch or dinner to talk with the participants to gain further insights into their stories. I invited participants to cowrite chapters and articles (Drame and Irby, 2015). I also invited participants to present at local and regional conferences. My goal was to use my access and capital to connect participants to networks, opportunities, and access to spaces that they otherwise may not have the privilege to access. I considered it was important to have them directly share their experiences as free as possible. I also offered advice and resources related to educational opportunities.

I used a narrative approach and took the time to deepen my relationships with the participants because it allowed me to develop a more authentic and well-rounded understanding of the participants. The relational-oriented research method contrasts with traditional models of researching Black males, which risk pathologizing, objectifying, and obscuring their voices in a sea of disproportionality, risk ratios, and statistics. Although my remaining in contact was intentional and could advance my research, I did not intend it to merely serve professional purposes. I still remain in occasional touch with Aaron. I wanted to be a good person to these men. I chose to operate in a spirit of brotherhood. I wanted to demonstrate my commitment and appreciation for the individuals who invited me to learn about their lives (Drame and Irby, 2015), an appreciation that I maintain through this writing. I realize that having editorial power to share stories comes with great responsibility and stewardship. My goal is to present as accurate and as honest stories and analysis as possible. My hope is their voices come through. I use their language and draw heavily from their phrases and linguistic stylings. With these caveats in mind, I turn to a presentation of what Aaron and Deon taught me by sharing their stories.

PRESENTATION OF FINDINGS

Aaron's and Deon's stories are first-hand accounts that demonstrate the effects of the symbolic violence of racism, effects of dispossession, abandonment, and containment. More importantly, they are stories about young Black males' yearning for relationships and belonging in the midst of complex racialized lives. Both stories suggest the racialized terrain of school spaces presented major challenges that shifted each participants' views of themselves as having problems to being problems to not being worthy of dignified treatment. Their stories are windows into the roots upon which the school-to-prison pipeline was built and continues to thrive. In what follows I present each participants' story.

Deon's Story: Learning to Live with "Not Being Fine" and "Not Doing Good"

Deon grew up in a middle class neighborhood in Philadelphia and attended racially diverse Catholic schools in his elementary and middle school years. His parents and grandparents were active in his life. At home he was rarely disciplined and did not have an overwhelming sense of responsibility. The primary reason that he was disciplined or punished was because of bad grades. He believed that because he was young and lived in a household of women and girls, he had fewer responsibilities. As he explained when comparing his school life and home life:

> I was a problem in school because we had nuns who would [hit and beat students] and I would be outspoken, like 'you ain't hitting me, you ain't gonna put that ruler on me or crack me'. My parents would come to the school and say 'I don't know what's wrong with him, we ain't raise him to act like that'. The real reason was that I just didn't have a male figure to give me a view of how to behave and I knew I could get away with certain things.

Deon explained that early school-based incidents of outspokenness, defiance, and his refusal to allow the nuns and brothers to hit him led to referrals and suspensions that required his family members to constantly come to the school on his behalf. On one occasion, the school officials recommended that Deon be transferred to a boarding school run by the Order of Archdiocese and explains:

> I was what you would say a fairly average, C student. But I just had a lot of problems. At a very early age I had an identity crisis; most of the schools I went to, they were probably at the time predominantly white, but also blacks went there. I being a very light skinned black person had a lot of problems with both sides of the fence and it kind of derailed my scholastics in terms of me focusing in on my education. I found myself a lot of times fighting in school and *becoming a disciplinary problem*. Sometimes I didn't go to school. By the time I was in the 6th or 7th grade I was sent off to an institution … a reform school run by an Order of the Archdiocese which was the Jesuit Brothers. It was a corrective school. It was sort of, not like prison, but more like a reform school.

Deon regarded attending the reform school at age 12 as a major incident of life that damaged his relationship with his family and diminished his ability to identify with his inherent worth. It began with him feeling abandoned: "When I was sent there, I was hurt. I was angry with my family because I felt like they were sending me away and I was only 12 years old." The resentment and anger grew over the course of the two years he remained at the reform school.

Loss through Abandonment and Institutional Life

The reform school where Deon was sent was located on a 500-acre farm in rural area of Pennsylvania. Parents and family were allowed to visit once every two months. Although he described the academic offerings of the school as "on par," he regarded the school as very dangerous. He described living in fear of both other students and many of the Jesuit Brothers who ran the school. He feared physical violence from his peers. He feared physical and sexual abuse from the school staff and teachers. He told me that he got into a couple of fights and that the school was dangerous because "there was a lot of rivalry … guys from Washington, Detroit, New York, and even South Carolina. I saw guys do horrific things up there man. It's just kind of unimaginable for guys at that age to do that." Deon preferred to not share details of the acts he witnessed. Regarding the Jesuit Brothers' treatment of students, he was more forthcoming about the nature of violence and abuse, although not precise in describing specific incidents.

> Those Brothers didn't take no stuff. Their disciplinary actions were what I would call very abusive. They would beat us with paddles, hit us, or punch us. Here it is me and other 12, 13, 14 year old boys dealing with men that are 30 and 40 years old. There were Brothers up there doing things to students who were weak-minded or confused. They took advantage of them [sexually]. I actually use to be very nervous about it because I felt like I might be a target … I'm saying there was some stuff going on. So you know like what you hear today [about sexual abuse] about what's going on with people in those positions that deal with our youths? It's been going on.

Although he lived in fear, he explained that "a couple of people up there, two Brothers in particular, really helped me." Brother Joseph asked Deon the simple question "what's wrong?" and listened to his concerns. He became someone that Deon trusted and with whom he shared his fears and anxieties. Brother Joseph encouraged Deon to spend as many hours as possible on the farm whenever he was not in class. At the farm, his primary responsibility was tending to cows. He learned husbandry and developed an affinity for the animals under his care. The farm was an escape from the violence, rivalry, and abuse that plagued the school. Brother Matthew helped him academically with math, a subject that was difficult for him. He viewed both Brothers Joseph and Matthew as real crusaders who helped him and had no personal agenda. He viewed them in sharp contrast to the many Brothers who abused the students.

As Deon shared his story, he iterated repeatedly that the looming threat and vicarious experiences of abuse and first-hand experiences of violence made him so uncomfortable that it compounded "everything else that happened to me as far as my parents making the decision to send me there. I was really bitter. I was actually scared." When his parents and other students' families visited the school, the brothers made everything appear to be fine. He recalls the reoccurrence of the visits where the Brothers would say "he's doing fine, this that, and the other. And so I was like 'you got to be crazy. This place is crazy, I ain't fine. I ain't doing good up here'. I was having problems." Deon reflected on his belief that for the brothers making all seem well during family visits was a façade to ensure they upheld enrollment. It amounted to money. He explained that he had more fear of the school staff than the people in the communities where he and the other guys at the school lived before attending the school. His experiences lasted for two years. Each time his family visited and left, his resentment toward them deepened. He explained that he grew increasingly disenchanted because his family did not believe him when he told him about the school conditions. They continuously abandoned him.

Going Whichever Way the Wind Blew

Deon believed that he never had anyone in his life to help him with the early-age identity crisis that stemmed from his fair skin tone. The sense of disposal that he felt for being sent away and the deep feeling of abandonment crystalized during his two years of reform school. Moreover, the experience exacerbated his insecurity about his skin complexion and hair texture. He left the school very angry. He explained "when I came back I had a lot bitterness toward them [my family]." To make matters worse, his mother remarried a police officer while he was away. He developed "an animosity toward him [step father] and then my mom because it seemed like he wanted me out of the way after I returned home." In reflection, he clarified. "I'm not saying he was a bad person. [Looking back] it was probably an odd or weird situation for him as well. He wasn't a bad guy … he was not an affectionate person, and that's really what I probably, as a young man, was yearning for, you know what I'm saying." He further revealed that by the time he left reform school and entered high school "my [biological] father was so caught up in his second marriage with a woman who already had children" that he never got the male affection that he wanted or needed.

In high school, Deon's disregard for school worsened. He pointed to his exposure to the civil rights movement and the widespread access to ideas about racial and economic injustice as a tipping point that escalated his unrest and disdain for school teachers, administrators, and White students. He became interested in the Fruit of Islam and Black Panther Party: "having an identity crisis, I joined a lot of movements, north, east, west, and south. Whichever way the wind blew because I wanted to belong. A lot of changes were taking place in terms of racial unrest. So, you know with these new ideas, I begin acting out with a lot of the Brothers." During his 9th grade year, he was kicked out of Catholic school and eventually attended public school. It was around his 10th grade year that he started skipping school and involving himself in a negative lifestyle.

During his 12th grade year, he attended a high school dance in an area of town occupied by a rival gang. He got into a fight and was stabbed by one of his rivals. The stabbing left him physically unable to attend school for "quite some time, while mending and getting my health back together." He explained that by the time he started attending school he had still not dealt with his anger issues, which were exacerbated because he physically could not play sports. By then he lost focus on school. Soon after, he started to affiliate with a street gang in an effort not to get hurt again. Although he attended school until the 12th grade, he never finished the last year. He recalled that hanging out with a gang not only offered protection but also "an introduction to chemical dependency. I used to drink wine. I was still in school but I was going to school intoxicated, running around and messing with girls, fighting, and so on. So I didn't graduate."

Aaron's Story: Learning He "Ain't Worth It"

Aaron attended public schools throughout his K-12 experience. In his elementary years, he attended segregated schools. In secondary grades, he attended a diverse high school where he described the population as "the predominant race was white, second African American, and then foreign exchange students and students from various demographic backgrounds." Instead of outright feelings and experiences of abandonment and loss as was the case with Deon, Aaron articulated his losses as a series of experiences that eroded his sense of self-worth leaving him "deep down, just hurting." The hurt manifested in rage and by 10th grade Aaron was a habitual substance user.

Aaron grew up splitting his early years between northern New Jersey and Wilmington, Delaware. He grew up in "a fire and brimstone type of house [where] you do something wrong, they pulling out leather belts and going to town." It was also "one of those families where the men were always doing all the dirt under the sun and the women were always going to church to pray for them." He considered himself a beneficiary of growing up in a family of praying women. He described his childhood as profoundly influenced by his mother whom he repeatedly characterized as brilliant and caring, but who was also an alcoholic. Despite her alcoholism, he continually spoke about the positive impact that his mother had on his life. One pivotal moment he recounted was when his mother entered a relationship with a drug dealer. This relationship caused her to grow distant from him and his siblings as his mother fell deeper into addiction. It was at the ages of eight or nine when he began becoming *a behavioral problem*.

He regarded the lack of a meaningful male role model as a major factor that shaped his lack of school success. He explained "I've never had an intimate relationship with a man where I could trust him enough to give me appropriate advice that was life-giving or life-altering." The absence of a loving and emotionally present male figure was salient given the unsafe neighborhood where he came of age. He described the challenge of getting to and from school as a constant fight:

> [As I reflect] I got four distinct snapshots of my days. One, I wake up to the serenity of my mom spending time with me, praying to me, encouraging me and talking to me.

> Two, I walk out the house and I got to go through this jungle [neighborhood] to get to the school. Three, I get to school and I'm in this beautiful setting, blissful playground. That snapshot ends. Four, I got to run back through the jungle to get home … by the time I would get to school I would be so emotionally drained, I didn't feel like [being at] school.

He informed me that his accounts of the neighborhood differed from his mother's recollections. She considered their neighborhood to be of middle class. He concedes that by surface appearances, it was. Firemen, elected officials, and other working and professional people lived in the area. But despite the neighborhood's middle class residential profile, it none-the-less had a criminal element in it [and] the same stuff that was happening in the projects poured into the neighborhood. The difficulty of walking 10 blocks to get to school remains a point of contention. He recounted to me his explanation to his mother and sister: "My mom to this day doesn't see it that way, nor does my sister, because well, you haven't experienced none of it." With time, the emotional exhaustion of getting to school dampened his enthusiasm to complete his work. He found it difficult to be present in mind. His teachers found his lack of willingness to complete his assignments perplexing. And his experiences both at home and school did little to enhance his self-worth.

How Aaron Learned He "Ain't Worth It"

Aaron described school as a place of refuge and explained that his early school years were exciting: "I had a bridled enthusiasm every time I got As. I really used to go to school feeling I'm a superior student and trying to compete. I really got my thrills off of that – school was good. School was it." Except for occasional challenges in math, Aaron faced little difficulty meeting the academic demands of school. He explained that one of his earliest clear recollections of school was when his 5th grade teacher, a 60-year-old White woman whom he described as enamored with him, held several parent conferences with his mother, trying to get him into a few gifted programs.

Aaron explained that although he was enthusiastic early on, his enthusiasm and giftedness were not reciprocated or acknowledged by adults within his household: "All I can remember is man, coming home with report cards with straight As or As and Bs type report cards and like, no response. Like they [family members] would act like 'okay, alright'. And I'm stunned like huh?" He expected a greater sense of enthusiasm and praise at least to match his own enthusiasm. Ironically, he recalled that he did get a response when he earned a low grade. He recounted one story in detail:

> I remember the first time I ever got a D and an F. Seventh grade. I was so scared to come home with the report card. They [mother and her boyfriend] were going to snap. So I took a typewriter, filled in the F with a B. I did all that. I changed the transcript. And somehow, they [parents] came to the school and actually got my official transcript and wild out on me man. I was like 'I don't believe this' and I think that was around when school just changed. I started getting expelled for fighting because I definitely lacked coping skills for what was going on in my household. And people were pressing me because they could see my potential. But underneath the mask, I had this uncontrolled anger brewing in me.

By 7th grade, Aaron was attending school primarily to keep his mother off of his back. It was also around this time that his close relationship with his mother began to wane. Her relationship with her eventual long-term boyfriend (described above) played a substantial role in eroding his relationship with his mother.

Before 7th grade, Aaron's family consisted of his sister, mother, and stepfather. He described his stepfather as an extremely intelligent guy but as very emotionally distant so much so that Aaron was afraid to approach him for help or to ask for advice. Given the difficulties Aaron experienced traveling to and from school, he sought his stepfather's advice on multiple occasions but his stepfather's answers were cold: "I didn't feel like I had his attention. There was no eye contact. There was no body language that showed me he was present. Nothing." He explains why his emotionally distant stepfather created problems for him:

> I was the type of child that needed to be able to talk and ask questions, to feel any degree of comfort. He [stepfather] was the fire and brimstone type of guy, where he just preached. I would do stuff to nitpick with him which made it difficult for the family to function well. When I started getting into trouble, my stepfather would just beat me or lock me in a room to punish me. It would just be funny to me. And I brooded to the point that I developed this hatred for him. I didn't even have anger. I had an unrelenting hatred.

Aaron even pointed to his stepfather as an impetus for him growing to disdain and underperform in school. He acknowledged that his stepfather would tell him he loved him. But Aaron didn't feel the words meant anything. His stepfather's actions and distance were too off-putting to make his words convincing. When helping him with homework, his stepfather did the best he knew how but he could not meet Aaron's unique learning needs.

> My stepfather only knew one way of learning, which was auditory. So he thought he could just explain it once and I would get it. I'm not an auditory learner. I'm a visual learner. Of course, I didn't know at that age what type of learner I was. When I asked

for more help or additional explanations the look that came over my stepfather's face scared me away.

He eventually stopped asking his stepfather for help. His favorite teacher, an African American man also did not understand his learning needs. His teacher Mr. Anderson would try and try to help him understand math. Aaron recalled thinking as a child "I still don't get it. I started to feel like I was retarded or something ... it got to the point where when Mr. Anderson tried to engage me I was like 'I ain't worth it'." Aaron responded to these difficulties by acting out in defiance, especially when his school-based struggles spilled over into his home life:

I could make one mistake and he [stepfather] would ride me. I just got to the point where I was insolent. I didn't care. If I got into a fight, I got into a fight. It didn't make any difference to me. I would sit at the dinner table and sneer at him and grin at him. I would think to myself, he ain't going to hit me because my mom is here. As sick as it sounds, it gave me a sense of empowerment. I was like "what you going to do?" It definitely affected my ability to perform in school and be a student. In fact, I wasn't a student when I came to school man. I was a ball of anger.

Losing Identity and Learning to Not Belong

Aaron's mother eventually divorced his stepfather (for several years, stepfather would come and go). But by that time, Aaron's sense of self was diminished, in part because of his interactions (or one could argue lack thereof) with his stepfather. A few vivid memories that Aaron recounted drove the point home. In 9th grade, at his new high school Aaron started to hang out with the jock crowd. He took interest in a range of sports, including swimming and football. As his interest increased he found a sense of positive identity as a student athlete; his behaviors and academic performance changed for the better. Yet, during the crucial time of identity reformation, he experienced a debilitating loss to his sense of racial and gender identity. The event happened at a swim meet but spilled over into his home.

A profound memory is I'm on an AAU swim team. It's kind of a bicultural – African-American, European-American, different nationalities. We go to a small town in Pennsylvania. It's the first time I've ever felt racism (although I didn't know what it was at the time). I could just feel, getting off the bus, like the way people were looking at us, that we just weren't welcome. Because I really hadn't had a positive man in my life, I was kind of insecure about my body. I'm at that age, I'm like 13, 14. I've sprouted up a little bit. I have big buttocks. I have on speedos. I'm already feeling uncomfortable with this tension I feel that I don't understand. The gun pops for us to dive into the water. I dive in and I was so anxious and so emotionally distraught, I almost drowned. I get out and I just remember this [white] girl looking at me, like, "they don't even

> belong with us." The way the girl looked at me it just felt like something inside of me just cracked. Swimming was the only thing nobody could take from me at the time. But after that point, I just slowly moved away from swimming.

Aaron suffered a sense of loss in terms of his athletic identity as a swimmer. But he also called into question his racial and gender identities, his sense of belongingness. After the episode, he had no one to turn to who could help him make sense of the experience. This outlet would have likely enabled him to recover from the sense of loss he felt.

He explained further that his swim coaches were two White women. Even they in their naiveté were as "caught off guard" as the students were by the swim meet's racist undercurrents. He thinks back that the coaches "lacked the ability to communicate to [the swim team] what happened." He believed a father figure would have been ideal to help him process the trauma of what he considered a racist environment and emasculating experience. But he explained he was unsure "how I could go into a household where I have such a distant man being my stepfather and explain, 'I feel like maybe I got emasculated today?'" Instead of forging a new or emergent identity that was supportive of his school success he maintained a sense of loss. In fact, he quit swimming altogether.

After he stopped swimming, he turned to football. And he found he was good at this sport too: "I was killing it on the field. I was a freshman and I really was playing well." But it all spiraled downward one day when his stepfather offered him his opinion of his athletic pursuits:

> When I came home after a game one evening, he just looked at me and said "you're just another nigger trying to use sports to get out the ghetto." I was just looking at this cat like, how can you make a comment about something you never even seen me do? Like, what's good with you? I didn't even really get that upset. I just looked at him bewildered and went up the steps thinking to myself "this dude is crazy." The strange thing is my enthusiasm to play sports just left after that day. I would play half-heartedly, I wouldn't show up to practice, and I wouldn't practice hard.

Shortly after this incident, his stepfather, who treated his mother the same way, left home and his mother finalized a divorce with him. At around this same time, Aaron's mother solidified her relationship with her long-term boyfriend, a drug dealer, whom he adored. He explained "I know that guy loved me, I really do. He would just say certain loving and encouraging stuff to me and it may only be a short phrase from him, but the intensity of how he expressed it. Like, he cared you know what I mean?" But what Aaron did not realize early is that his mother's boyfriend's lifestyle would cause his mother's substance usage to escalate.

Losing His Mother's Unrelenting Support

Without his mother to stay on his back, Aaron started gaining exposure to "the criminal element" and drinking. He kept the secret of what was going on in his household close as he learned early that his family lived by the code what happens in this house stays in this house. Even with his deep disdain for his stepfather, Aaron regarded his mom's new boyfriend, not his stepfather, as the person who was most impactful in terms of his turning and going the wrong way. He explained the changing situation:

> The relationship with my mother's boyfriend started off good man. Dude was really alright. Everything was peachy. And then it was like, yo man, somebody took my family from me. He turned my mom and sister against me. At the time my mother was getting high, I don't know about anything [related to signs of drug use]. Then all of a sudden I start finding coke straws in the house, quills [i.e. cocaine; heroin; methamphetamines], and it's like I don't really know what any of this is. I had seen people high on drugs, but I had never physically seen drugs and paraphernalia like that.

By 10th grade, the support and encouragement Aaron's mother offered him in his academic and athletic pursuits dwindled. He did as little as possible to achieve school success. He continued to play sports. But getting high became a priority. He encountered a couple of teachers who believed in him but it was primarily only related to academic achievement in their respective class, not beyond it. He continued to attend school because he was worried if he did not attend his mother would come looking for him. While he was physically present, he was not emotionally present. His behavior improved because he learned to not act out as a means to hide his substance use. Although he described his high school environment as one that might have prepared him to go to college, he was too far gone in terms of low self-regard. His teachers passed him but he did not understand why. When he did do work, he would excel: "I'd get an A on one paper and then fail four straight." He explained "I never had that trusted relationship with an educator where the relationship and interaction was just not merely about me being in class, but also about 'okay, what's going on with you?'" When his mother sent him to a therapist, he flipped over the therapists' desk and walked out. He never returned again. He explained that to protect himself, he "took the approach where I'm going to hurt people before they hurt me." He experienced loss in both settings. He also never had the relationship to counter the losses he experienced.

What is clear from Aaron's story is that he did not view his school and home life as separate. But looking back he refused to let schools off the hook for his disengagement. He recalled that teachers struggled to engage African Americans despite the diversity of the schools' student population.

The classes within the building were segregated. By the time he entered his large high school, he considered himself a face in the crowd of approximately 2,000 students: "there was never anybody in front of me who made me feel like I could *be anything*. No one stopped me and said 'what's going on with you? You need to explain some things – matter of fact I'm going to call your parent'. Nobody ever did that. Ever."

DISCUSSION

As boys and young men, Deon and Aaron encountered interlocking experiences I refer to as early indignities of criminalization. They experienced disposal (abandonment), containment, violence, and loss of relationships that primed them to not see value in their selves. These experiences had the ultimate effect of dispossessing them of their full potential. To different extents, Deon and Aaron suffered moral and existential losses (Kateb, 2011). At young ages, they both felt like nobodies.

Deon's story demonstrates the experiences that he adapted to and his eventual ability to "not be fine" and to "not do good" were learned in the context of his experience at reform school. Aaron's story differs in that he learned he "ain't worth it" at home and at school. For both men, the people in their life made their best attempts to help. After all, Deon's family's decision to send him to reform school, at the urging of school personnel, was an attempt to help him by taking "expert" advice. But for all of their efforts, parents, teachers, coaches, and others never attended to either boys' identity needs in the context of a racist society. Deon was an adult before he grappled with his skin color. Aaron was an adult before he discovered his learning needs. As both of them note, few sought to relate to them on an emotional level as human beings who yearned for deep affection. No one actively cultivated their ability, in the context of affectionate male relationships, to forge positive identities that dignified their being and doing in the world.

Noticing Dignifying Spaces and Places

The participants described feelings of alienation, abandonment, and fear as immediate responses to their experiences of *being sent* or *relegated to* what they regarded as either overtly or subtlety hostile environments. These places included their schools, homes, and neighborhoods. These include places and spaces many would characterize as "good" for them such as private schools, college prep high schools, and athletics programs. The experience these sites offer are critical to understand. Relegating Black boys to spaces and places that send them messages, however subtle, that they are unwanted continues to be a pressing problem.

Aaron's swim meet, a seemingly positive experience, became a containment experience. From the moment he arrived, he knew he didn't belong and the events that transpired and anxiety that resulted had a profound impact on his life. With the right educators who were attuned the indignities he and other students could potentially encounter, he could have been forewarned and prepared to cope with the racialized setting before the swim meet occurred. Instead he was humiliated at the event and felt abandoned even well after it was over. In the absence of a school that would take on this sort of dignity-preserving and enhancing work, his home would have been a supportive place of refuge to process his experience and begin recovering from the harm of what he described as a "racist and emasculating" experience. Deon's experiences at reform school speak volumes to the harm that a "reform" environment did to him. At the reform school, he found solace on the farm and by "wandering around." Wandering reflected Deon's agency to find a place in his relatively constrained reform school world.

Unfortunately, the official disciplinary policies that schools adopt such as quarantining, giving tickets, and the soft punishment of writing Black boys off as "not worth it" makes school yet another experiential place of containment. The other option is to cultivate spaces that make Black boys feel wanted and loved by prioritizing deep relationships, warm and demanding expectations, and positioning Black boys with problems closer rather than farther away from the school's academic and relational resources. Schools are too often places where boys are conditioned to accept their lot in a world where they have no place. At worst, Black boys are conditioned to believe as if they are nobodies. These connections were not lost on Aaron and Deon who readily identified where and when they learned they were nobodies. They also recalled who the culprits of their indignities were, the words they spoke, and the (in)actions these adults engaged that eroded their senses of self.

Noticing Dignifying Relationships

Overexposure to containment experiences resulted in an eroded sense of dignity. And it also led to relational losses. Deon and Aaron associated their physical containment with fear of violence, lack of control and autonomy, and damaged relationships that led to emotional and psychological distance from other human beings. In fact, both Aaron and Deon came to *prefer* having no relationships at all. The cost of this preference was on the one hand the loss of potential for healthy and beneficial relationships. On the other hand, they filled their void of healthy relationships with unhealthy ones and substance abuse. Aaron's methods for achieving this was to "hurt people before they hurt him." Both men decreased their reliance on human relationships and increased their reliance on drugs and alcohol as a sort of replacement. In Aaron's case, his increased substance use (a thing-oriented relationship) improved his school-based behaviors and compelled him to fly under the radar of his teachers. His teachers passed him based on his willingness to not disrupt class or invite conflict. This tacit agreement grounded their teacher–student relationship.

Understanding the relational dimensions of Black boys' containment and isolation from affectionate adults who are attuned to their dignity needs is critical. Both cases bring to bear the important role that people who are assumed to be "good", such as Brothers, stepfathers, or well-intentioned teachers, play in extending or denying dignifying experiences to Black boys. Aaron's coaches did not possess the skills to help him make sense of his feeling of isolation and abandonment. Adding insult in injury, he lived in a home environment with a stepfather who would and could not support him academically, athletically, or emotionally.

The common outcome of their containment experiences and inabilities to escape a place at a particular time resulted in feelings of hurt, anger, depression, and loss. Externalizing behaviors that reflected both men's attempts to not be contained included withdrawal from relationships and interests, engaging more willfully in physical confrontations, and disrespecting others and authority in an attempt to not be hurt. Yet, both Deon and Aaron were balanced in their understanding that the people in their lives were human beings with flaws as well. Deon acknowledged this by observing his mother's husband was a good guy who found himself in an awkward situation, responsible for developing a relationship with a teenage boy who had recently returned from reform school. Aaron acknowledged his stepfather expressed his love for him with words, tried to help him with his homework, and offered advice. Yet, Aaron remained critical of his stepfather's hell and brimstone methods. Mr. Anderson's efforts failed because his math teacher was not attuned to his learning style or the home issues that impaired his ability to be fully present in mind while at school. Being locked in his room for bad grades and having a teacher repeat a problem solution over and over using the same method did little to develop a healthy sense of self.

Deon's and Aaron's senses of self-worth diminished further, and they grew estranged from the people in their lives that indeed deemed them worthy of love and life and who acted on these beliefs by treating them with dignity. Their most acute relational dispossessions occurred when the women who loved them so much were all but stripped from their lives at formative stages of their development. Deon lost his connection with his family, mostly women who nurtured him during his time at reform school. Aaron lost his mother and sister to his mother's drug dealing and supplying boyfriend while he was in high school. After these losses Aaron and Deon sought relational connectedness in the streets among peers and negative adult influences. In the context of these relationships, each of them developed addictions and engaged in criminal lifestyles that harmed themselves, loved ones, and communities.

Throughout the process, they made people around them miserable. They beat up their school-aged peers. They disrespected teachers. They came to school high and intoxicated. They refused to comply with authority figures. They disrupted their classmates' learning. They made teachers' and principals' efforts to educate them more difficult than anyone would wish for any decent educator or adult for that matter. Most tragically, neither Deon nor Aaron worked toward their full potential. How could they have done so given their experiences?

Disposability as the Root of the Pipeline

Deon's and Aaron's stories serve as reminders that dismantling the school-to-prison pipeline is a noble, yet not fully a sufficient cause. The roots of the pipeline are founded in the disposability of Black boys. The school-to-prison pipeline extends and compounds the notion of Black boy disposability. It compounds the myriad challenges that impede Black boys' life prospects in the United States as reflected in Deon's and Aaron's narratives.

If one concedes that the school-to-prison pipeline is merely a new state-sanctioned manifestation of racist policies that push Black males out of school, that diminishes Black males' participation in formal labor, and that casts Black males as unembraceable, it becomes plausible that the pipeline is a symptom rather than a root problem. In short, a sole focus on the school-to-prison pipeline, without sufficient accounts of Black males' direct experiences, masks the potential for new oppressive forms to emerge even if and when the current pipeline falters. Simply put, if the pipeline is dismantled, something new is likely to take its place, a sanctioned mechanism for containing Black boys' bodies and minds.

For now, the school-to-prison pipeline literature is organized largely around research projects and studies that present data showing disproportional punishment and treatment of Black boys. Although grounded in social justice orientations and critical perspectives, the school-to-prison pipeline literature offers few counter-narratives that unmask the deep-seated and pervasive marginalization that Black boys experience across the numerous domains that shape their school-aged years. What I hope to have done with this chapter is to offer an approach to deepen the scholarship that is produced on this critical topic. Specifically, qualitative research studies that center Black males' voices, experiences, and stories are critical levers that can do more to illuminate the dimensions of degradation and humiliation that Black boys experience in their school age years than theory-based and quantitative research alone. With this in mind, it is critically important to not lose focus on life and educational experiences of Black boys and to invest as much energy into teaching to Black males' dignity and humanity as it is to critiquing the policies and structures that sweep them into the pipeline when schools fail them.

CONCLUSION

The purpose of this chapter was to present glimpses into the early life experiences of two Black men whose containment experiences and subsequent behaviors might be used to support the sort ideological justifications that foster overly punitive school cultures, climates, disciplinary policies, and practices. Progressive educators and scholars must challenge both the historical development and contemporary maintenance of punitive disciplinary frameworks by recognizing that school-to-prison pipelines are built on traumas and dispossessions experienced by Black boys and men. Social science research plays a role in the process. The near absence of Black males' voices in academic research paradoxically objectifies the very subjects for whom school-to-prison pipeline scholars advocate. It distances the research from the human beings for whom it is supposedly intended to support.

Centering the voices, stories, experiences, and perspectives of Black men and boys, as I have made my best attempt to do here, reveals that the degradation of Black men and boys is rooted in their assumed disposability. One lever to dismantle the pipeline is to focus on creating dignifying experiences in schools (Hantzopoulos, 2016). This is a matter of improving climate, culture, and of course academic programming and instruction. School leaders and teachers must engage in the critical work of agitating, arousing, and inspiring students (Camangian, 2015) to see themselves as humans and agents of change who have tremendous potential to act as stewards for the their fellow human beings, communities, and environments.

REFERENCES

Camangian, P. (2015). Teach like lives depends on it: Agitate, arouse, and inspire. *Urban Education*, *50*(4), 424–453. doi:10.1177/0042085913514591

Christle, C., Jolivette, K., & Nelson, C. (2005). Breaking the school to prison pipeline: Identifying school risk and protective factors for youth delinquency. *Exceptionality*, *13*(2), 69–88.

Drame, E., & Irby, D. (2015). *Black participatory research: Power, identity, and the struggle for justice in education*. New York, NY: Palgrave MacMillan.

Fasching-Varner, K., Martin, L., Mitchell, R., & Bennett-Haron, K. (2014). Beyond the pipeline and toward an educational and Penal Realism. *Equity and Excellence in Education*, *47*(4), 410–429. doi:10.1080/10665684.2014.959285

Giroux, H. (2003a). Racial injustice and disposable youth in the age of zero tolerance. *International Journal of Qualitative Studies in Education*, *16*(4), 553.

Giroux, H. (2003b). Zero tolerance, domestic militarization, and the war against youth. *Social Justice*, *30*(2), 59–65.

Giroux, H. A. (2001). Mis/education and zero tolerance: Disposable youth and the politics of domestic militarization. *Boundary*, *28*(3), 61–94.

Hantzopoulos, M. (2016). *Restoring dignity in public schools: Human rights education in action*. New York, NY: Teachers College Press.

Hicks, D. (2011). *Dignity: Its essential role in resolving conflict*. New Haven, CT: Yale University Press.

Irby, D. (2013). Net-deepening of school discipline. *Urban Review: Issues and Ideas in Public Education*, *45*(2), 197–219.

Irby, D. (2014). Trouble at school: Understanding school discipline systems as nets of social control. *Equity and Excellence in Education*, *47*(4), 513–530. doi:10.1080/10665684.2014.958963

Jenness, V. (2004). Explaining criminalization: From demography and status politics to globalization and modernization. *Annual Review of Sociology*, *30*, 147–171.

Kateb, G. (2011). *Human dignity*. Cambridge, MA: The Belknap Press of Harvard University Press.

Kupchik, A. (2009). Things are tough all over: Race, ethnicity, class and school discipline. *Punishment and Society*, *11*(3), 291–317. doi:10.1177/1462474509334552

Laura, C. (2014). *Being bad: My baby brother and the school-to-prison pipeline*. Teaching for Social Justice Series. New York, NY: Teachers College Press.

Mendez, L., & Knoff, H. (2003). Who gets suspended from school and why: A demographic analysis of schools and disciplinary infractions in a large school district. *Education & Treatment of Children*, *26*(1), 30.

Michael, L. (2014). Defining dignity and its place in human rights. *The New Bioethics*, *20*(1), 12–34. doi:10.1179/2050287714z.00000000041

Monroe, C. (2005). Why are "bad boys" always Black? Causes of disproportionality in school discipline and recommendations for change. *The Clearing House*, *79*(1), 45–50. doi:10.3200/TCHS.79.1.45-50

Morrison, G., & D'Incau, B. (1997). The web of zero-tolerance: Characteristics of students who are recommended for expulsion from school. *Education & Treatment of Children*, *20*(3), 316.

Muhammad, K. G. (2011). *The condemnation of blackness: Race, crime, and the making of modern Urban America*. Cambridge, MA: Harvard University Press.

Reyes, A. (2006). *Discipline, achievement, race: Is zero tolerance the answer?* Lanhan, MA: Rowman and Littlefield Education.

Riessman, C. K. (1993). *Narrative analysis*. Qualitative Research Methods Series. No. 30. Newbury Park, CA: Sage.

Rosen, M. (2012). *Dignity: Its history and meaning*. Cambridge, MA: Harvard University Press.

Verdugo, R. (2002). Race-ethnicity, social class, and zero tolerance policy: The cultural and structural wars. *Education and Urban Society*, *35*(1), 50–75.

CHAPTER 3

RESISTING THE SCHOOL-TO-PRISON PIPELINE UTILIZING GUIDANCE FROM THE FRONTLINES: CHICANO STUDENT EXPERIENCES AS A SOURCE OF KNOWLEDGE AND STRENGTH

Brenda G. Valles

ABSTRACT

The school-to-prison pipeline is a booming pipeline that is the cause for alarm. Increasingly, this pipeline includes more of Chicano males, and this dynamic is reflected in low rates of high school graduates going to college contrasted with the growing number of Chicanos in the juvenile justice and court systems. This study focuses on the impacts of the school-to-prison pipeline on Chicano students. Furthermore, utilizing a CRT and LatCrit framework, this study centers the experiential knowledge that Chicano students contribute to conceptualizing ways of disrupting the school-to-prison pipeline. Themes of this study include the following: (1) Chicano student experiences with the school-to-prison pipeline, (2) innovation of discipline policy and practice, and (3) effective alternative practices to a

The School to Prison Pipeline: The Role of Culture and Discipline in School
Advances in Race and Ethnicity in Education, Volume 4, 41–64

ISSN: 2051-2317/doi:10.1108/S2051-231720160000004004

zero tolerance framework. Through this, Chicano students point to a praxis grounded in community to clear educational pathways and interrupt the school-to-prison pipeline.

Keywords: Chicano students; school-to-prison pipeline; school discipline policies

Chicano/Latino male students are disappearing from the educational pipeline. According to the National Center for Educational Statistics (2016), by the age of 16, Chicano[1]/Latino male student enrollment drops dramatically compared to their other male counterparts. For about the last 30 years, Chicano/Latino students have had among the highest push out rate[2] from middle and high school (NCES, 2016). There are some deep educational issues that have an impact on Chicano student lives. Chicano students face aggressive systemic attacks that negatively impact their educational attainment and higher education access. By way of school discipline policies such as zero tolerance, Chicano students' experience of being pushed out of school, are excluded from educational settings, tracked into juvenile court and detention (school-to-prison pipeline), criminalized, and among other attacks emotionally traumatized. The school-to-prison pipeline has become increasingly punitive over the last 20 years since zero tolerance policies were introduced, and it has framed a leading backdrop for the education crisis of Chicano students today.

This educational context for Chicanos begs the question, where is the love for Chicano students? It is critical to the educational success of Chicano students that we as educators, educational leaders, researchers, and policy makers, sisters, brothers, and members of the community pay careful attention to the school-to-prison pipeline. One way to further understand and best address the school-to-prison pipeline is to engage Chicano youth that have had direct experience with these policies and practices for informed guidance and direction. As such, this study seeks to understand and identify ways to disrupt the impact of the school-to-prison pipeline on Chicano students. By drawing on interviews of young Chicano men, utilizing their experiential knowledge, I arrive at policy and practical implications that can begin to identify and disrupt the destructive patterns at play with the school-to-prison pipeline by making schools revolutionary loving educational spaces.

REVIEW OF RELEVANT LITERATURE

The school-to-prison pipeline has been facilitated by the alignment of school discipline policies and practices with a zero tolerance framework (Wald & Losen, 2003). School discipline policies include referrals, suspensions, and expulsions (Raffaele Mendez, 2003; Reyes, 2006). However, the broader zero tolerance framework fueling the school-to-prison pipeline includes practices that are outside the direct discipline purview and includes school security measures such as school resource officers, strip searches, metal detectors, and surveillance cameras (Dohrn, 2001; Eisenbraun, 2007; Rios & Galicia, 2013; Theriot, 2009). This zero tolerance framework or approach creates a more punitive educational environment (Hyman & Perone, 1998; Raffaele Mendez & Knoff, 2003; Rios & Galicia, 2013; Skiba, Michael, Nardo, & Peterson, 2002) and facilitates the relationship between schools and juvenile justice systems (Reyes, 2006) such that the result is the school-to-prison pipeline. Derived from the Safe Schools Act and Gun Free Schools Act that took shape under President Clinton in 1993, these policies were initially created with the intention of keeping schools safe from violence, guns, and promote order and civility of students (Gun Free Schools Act of, 1993). However, the result has often been that of a heightened sense of student victimization (Hyman & Perone, 1998) and hypercriminalization (Rios, 2007).

The entire system of school discipline under zero tolerance policies is increasingly set up to address students with stringent responses that can have immediate legal implications on the student (Dohrn, 2001; Rios & Galicia, 2013; Skiba, et al., 2002; Townsend, 2000). The way these policies link to the prison pipeline is they frequently include police infractions such as class C misdemeanors. These types of citations require court hearings and fines, depending on the punitive nature of the citation they can also result in arrest, and juvenile incarceration (Reyes, 2006); citations that require court hearings are one way the zero tolerance framework relates schools and students to the criminal justice system (Casella, 2003; Osher, Magee Quinn, Poirier, & Rutherford, 2003; Raffaele Mendez, 2003; Verdugo, 2002). The school-to-prison pipeline is a direct result of the zero tolerance framework grounded in stringent legal approaches to address school violence reduction rather than drawing from educational pedagogical approaches or models (Devine, 1996; Eisenbraun, 2007; Hyman & Perone, 1998; Larson, 1994). Across the United States, Chicanos have a one in six chance of being incarcerated as a child (Children Defense Fund, 2008), indicating the high rates of incarceration and how the juvenile court system facilitates the incarceration rate growth through punitive approaches.

The school-to-prison pipeline exists as a result of zero tolerance and the development of school discipline policies over the last two decades (Skiba, et al., 2002; Verdugo, 2002). We know that there are real and severe implications from these policies, particularly for the male students of color (Casella, 2003; Children's Defense Fund, 2008; Skiba, et al., 2002; Reyes, 2006; Noguera, 2008). This study focuses primarily on the implications of the school-to-prison pipeline on the Chicana/o community (Rios & Galicia, 2013; Reyes, 2006; Noguera, 2007; Valles & Villalpando, 2013). There are also long-term academic implications for students that become caught in the pipeline (Casella, 2003; Raffaele Mendez, 2003; Rioss, 2007). For instance, students experience a hypercriminalization (Rios, 2007), harsher and more punitive responses for male students of color (Raffaele Mendez, 2003). This harsher punishment is further compounded by double jeopardy, meaning students cited with a disciplinary infraction will be punished at school either with suspension or expulsion and will also be punished through the court system and have court hearings, fines, or even incarceration, all for the same offence and therefore experience harsher and double the punishment for an infraction (Reyes, 2006). Additionally, there is a lack of transparency and communication in the disciplinary process between the school and student's family. For instance, the disciplinary process often requires a communication protocol such as due process, thereby providing families accurate documentation and communication from the school. However, while this type of due process should be a part of the process of suspensions and expulsions, often, as was found in this study, this is not the case and families find out about expulsions after the fact.

Overall, the pattern of racial/ethnic disproportionality of school discipline infractions for male students of color remains steady (Skiba, et al., 2002), as does an increased growth for students in the juvenile justice system (Raffaele Mendez, 2003). Examining the zero tolerance framework in schools, with the growth in the juvenile justice system, leads us to a clearer sense of the school-to-prison pipeline. However, coupled with the educational implications as a result of the school-to-prison pipeline (Valles, 2015), this matter of discipline in schools becomes a crisis for males of color (Children's Defense Fund, 1975; Fenning & Rose, 2007; Reyes, 2006).

The Rationale for Urgency: Why This Crisis Matters

This study was conducted in the mountain west in a region where the state demographics are quickly changing. Utah, the site of this study, is now considered a "gateway state" due to the doubling of the Latina/o population over the last 15 years – primarily with Latinas/os of Mexican heritage (Kochhar, Suro, & Tafoya, 2005; Perlich, 2008; Singer, 2004). The reason the school-to-prison pipeline is a matter of crisis and urgency is that while the state demographics shift to about a 13% Latina/o (over 70% of these being of Mexican heritage) (US Census, 2010), students are not graduating at a rate their demographic is growing. In fact, Chicano males are not graduating middle school or high school, much less reaching university-going rates that reflect their growth in the school system (Villalpando, 2010). There is even a differential rate of graduation and postsecondary access for Chicana/o and Latina/o students when disaggregating by gender (Utah State Office of Education, 2015). Chicanos graduate at lower rates from middle and high school than their female counterparts and access higher education at even lower rates (Harvey & Anderson, 2005; Saenz & Ponjuan, 2009).

The students being pushed out of educational settings and being channeled into a school-to-prison pipeline as a result to zero tolerance framework are ending up populating the prison system and feeding the prison industrial complex (Casella, 2003). Most incarcerated Chicanos are of college age (Harrison & Beck, 2002), and the Chicano demographic is the fastest growing prison population. Moreover, Chicanos have the lowest educational background of all federally incarcerated males (Jackson, 1997). These facts speak to the urgency and severe crisis this presents.

The Role of Gender: Centering Chicanos

This gendered achievement gap negatively impacts male students. For Chicano students, the educational attainment figures drop 15.9% from the level of achievement of their female counterparts (Villalpando, 2004). In addition, Chicana students fare better on national exams (Quin, 2005), have higher grades, and earn more with a BA than their male counterparts (Wortham, 2001). All the while, Chicanas receive fewer discipline infractions (US Department of Education Office of Civil Rights, 2004), are placed in special education at lower rates (Glennon, 1995), and are incarcerated at lower rates than their male counterparts (Reyes, 2007). This growing gender gap for Chicana/o students does not mean female students of Chicana/o and Latina/o backgrounds no longer face educational barriers nor does this suggest we no longer focus on female students as they continue to be an underrepresented group in higher education (Eberle-Sudre, Welch, & Nichols, 2015). Rather, this gap between Chicana and Chicano students shines light on the importance of focusing on Chicano (male) students, in particular, to better understand how to address the school-to-prison pipeline.

THEORETICAL FRAMEWORK

I apply a CRT and LatCrit framework to examine discipline policies and how race, racism, dominant ideologies, and various aspects of Chicano identities are reflected in the larger discourse of discipline within this study. A CRT and LatCrit lens serves to challenge notions of objectivity, racial neutrality, and deficient perspectives of Chicano students embedded within discipline policies and practices. CRT poses the following core set of tenets: (1) the centrality of racism and the intersections with other forms of subordination (Solórzano & Delgado Bernal, 2001); (2) a challenge to dominant ideologies such as objectivity, meritocracy, colorblindness, race neutrality (Solórzano & Yosso, 2001); (3) a commitment to social justice (Lynn & Parker, 2006); and (4) the centering of experiential knowledge through counterstories and narratives (Delgado, 1989; DeCuir & Dixson, 2004).

Too often, the voices of Chicano students experiencing the school-to-prison pipeline, or succumbing to schooling environments that are tangled in a punitive zero tolerance discipline framework, is missing (Fenning & Rose, 2007; Harvard Civil Rights Project, 2000; Raffaele Mendez, 2003; Skiba & Rausch, 2006). Although absent from the majority of scholarly conversations about zero tolerance and the school-to-prison pipeline, Chicano students are not absent from being a part of these. Delgado (1995) reminds us that we live in a socially constructed reality and from this our "patterns of perception become habitual" whereby we will decide what we accept as reality and what we will not (p. 66). By telling their stories and offering their lenses to the reader in this chapter, Chicano students are able to challenge the "habitual" narratives accepted around the school-to-prison pipeline.

This study utilizes CRT to focus on the experience of Chicano students and understand their experiences with the school-to-prison pipeline as "sources of strength" (Solorzano & Yosso, 2002). The voices and experiential knowledge of Chicano youth that have experienced some aspect of the school-to-prison pipeline position them as knowledge holders, and further as producers of knowledge (Bell, 1987; Delgado, 1995; Delgado Bernal, 2002; Solorzano & Delgado Bernal, 2001; Solorzano, Villalpando, & Oseguera, 2005). Centering Chicano students as knowledge holders and producers talks back to and challenges dominant discourse and existing hegemonic stories surrounding Chicano students within the zero tolerance framework (Bell, 1987; Cook, 2013; Delgado, 1995; Ladson-Billings, 2000; Solorzano & Yosso, 2002). Wing (2003) posits that the traditional mode of scholarship focusing on the production of knowledge from the academy, however noting that this is not where marginalized communities will develop ways to address the oppression faced (p. 6), rather CRT and LatCrit scholars urge us to create spaces for marginalized communities to tell their stories and draw from their expertise to work toward achieving social justice and transformation (Elenes & Delgado Bernal, 2010, p. 65). In this way, Chicano students will name their own reality and speak to the ways in which they experience the school-to-prison pipeline (Delgado, 1995).

The combination of LatCrit and CRT is necessary for a more holistic examination of Chicano students and the school-to-prison pipeline. LatCrit speaks to other identities and cultures and their intersections (Hernandez-Truyol, 1999). It also explicitly addresses pan-ethnicity and transnationality (Hernandez-Truyol, 1999); language, phenotype, and immigration (Solórzano & Delgado Bernal, 2001); and religion, sexuality, and poverty (Iglesias & Valdes, 1998). LatCrit provides a framework that describes the school-to-prison pipeline on Chicano students while accounting for the historical context of Chicanas/os in public schools. It is helpful to have a framework to interrogate the school-to-prison pipeline through student narratives. Portillos, Gonzalez, and Peguero (2012) argue that Chicana/o students' "experiences are set within a context of racialized space where criminalization is one possible outcome of school" (p. 171).

CURRENT STUDY

This chapter is drawn from a larger mixed-method study. The section analyzed here is a qualitative piece examining a set of in-depth interviews through a CRT and LatCrit lens. These interviews construct a counternarrative that shifts the dominant understanding that may exist to describe Chicanos impacted by the school-to-prison pipeline, in some ways, that it creates space for their stories where it has too often been missing. Chicano students use their voice to tell their stories and offer their understanding of discipline in schools by offering a narrative that puts their lens on the reader (Bell, 1987; Delgado, 1995). The overarching question guiding the narratives was, "how did you experience discipline in school?" This question led to students discussing a variety of aspects of their schooling experience such as discussing their experiences in the classroom, their identity, the school-to-prison pipeline, and the criminalization they experienced as a result of these policies and practices. Additionally, students began to allude to ways in which the school-to-prison pipeline could be disrupted.

In this study, the experience Chicano students had with school-to-prison pipeline is maintained as valid knowledge that contributes to the academy (Wing, 2003) and as unique sources of strength (Solorzano & Yosso, 2002). As such, this propelled me to focus this chapter on what they offer as guidance on how to challenge and remedy the impact of the school-to-prison pipeline.

Methodology

This study focuses on drawing from Chicano students and their experiential knowledge and strength to inform approaches to disrupt and push back against the school-to-prison pipeline. To do so, the research question this chapter addresses is what guidance do Chicano students offer for challenging and remediating the impact of the school-to-prison pipeline? The interview data in this study are presented here in a narrative format. In other words, study participants tell their stories from their perspective and experiences. This use of narrative can be transformative, empowering, and raises the individual's consciousness while opening up opportunity for social action (Bell, 1987; Delgado, 1989; Freire, 1970). The narratives in my study push back on the "dominant gaze" as a form of resistance to hegemony and in an effort to work toward social transformation (Bell, 1987; Cook, 2013; Martinez, 2002; Ladson-Billings, 2000).

The students who participated in this research told stories that counter and challenge the dominant story about them as Chicano students (Delgado, 1989). Delgado (1995) described stories told by marginalized people such as Chicano students in their study as down-to-earth and "underdog" stories, further stating that because reality is socially constructed, it is important to hear the stories from those who are often not heard – in this case, Chicano students (p. 65).

Collectively, the narratives in this research create space to tell their stories and realities of their experiences with the school-to-prison pipeline. These stories of Chicanos in the school-to-prison pipeline are frequently told from a dominant view and deficit standpoint. In this study, counter storytelling allowed me to understand how participants responded to disciplinary policies and practices, within the school-to-prison pipeline, through their own narratives. Ladson-Billings (1995, p. 413) calls the research participant the "knower," – which was the basis for selecting this format. Delgado Bernal (2002) notes, Chicana/o students are creators of their own knowledge and the best fit to recount their narratives.

Data Source

To address this research question, three in-depth interviews were conducted with young Chicano males that had experienced some aspect of the school-to-prison pipeline. The participants in this study included three Chicano males (Sandino, Cesar, and Oscar) who attended public school in Utah, the site of this study. The study participants were identified from a local community organization that works to promote community empowerment and education. All participants were over the age of 18 at the time of the interview and experienced disciplinary infractions at some (or various) points in their schooling. Additionally, two were pushed out of the school system and one was incarcerated as a juvenile. The broader study includes a quantitative analysis, with a sample from two school districts, looking at discipline patterns and educational effects through a logistic regression, and a hierarchical linear model.

SITUATING THE SCHOOL-TO-PRISON PIPELINE

This study was conducted in the mountain west state of Utah, a politically conservative and predominantly white location, with couples with the ever-growing[3] official representation of Chicana/o students in schools to provide a context for how discipline plays out within a zero tolerance approach (Perlich, 2002). Additionally, part of what makes this state context unique is the dominant culture of "niceness" that permeates all institutions including the state legislature and schools; this "niceness" culture is laden with deficit thinking of perspectives and cultural understandings that fall outside of this norm (Aleman, 2009). For instance, in the Utah context of "niceness" a Chicano student would be to blame for being expelled (for a nonviolent infraction such as "disobedience") under a zero tolerance discipline framework (Valencia, 1997). Furthermore, this backdrop informs the way this zero tolerance framework in school has led to the development of the school-to-prison pipeline.

The majority of zero tolerance disciplinary infractions male students of color face are for nonviolent offenses (Casella, 2003; Noguera, 2008; Raffaele Mendez, 2003; Reyes, 2006; Skiba, et al., 2002), rather than punishing what was once considered to be adolescent behavior (Reyes, 2006). These studies (Casella, 2003; Children's Defense Fund, 1975; Dohrn, 2001; Raffaele Mendez, 2003; Reyes, 2006; Skiba, et al., 2002; Valles, 2013; Verdugo, 2002) indicate that most of these zero tolerance infractions are cited for very subjective and nonviolent offenses such as "disrespect," "disobedience," or being perceived as potentially "dangerous." Furthermore, of these offences treated like violent infractions under the zero tolerance approach in schools, male students of color can expect to be treated with harsher punishments for the same infraction of their white counterparts and can expect to see an increase in likelihood of suspension in the following year of their education once they are suspended once (Raffaele Mendez, 2003; Valles, 2013). This chapter navigates this Utah school-to-prison pipeline to unpack the ways students experienced these policies and practices and what lessons they glean from their knowledge, strength, and experience.

Salient Themes and Guiding Voices

For this chapter, I choose to reflect on three salient themes from interviews with Cesar, Oscar, and Sandino that are central to the goal of this chapter. These themes include the following: (1) the Chicano student experiences with the school-to-prison pipeline, (2) innovation of discipline policy and practice, and (3) effective alternative practices to a zero tolerance framework.

Cesar, Oscar, and Sandino are the guiding voices of this study. Although all three of the participants belonged to a community organization at the time of these interviews, they were all very unique in their experience with the school-to-prison pipeline and had different perspectives of discipline policies and practices and the zero tolerance approach in schools. The students all attended schools at different times and none were born in Utah; however, they all moved to Utah at a very young age. Below, I briefly introduce each student that participated in this study.

Cesar considers himself a community activist. He was born in the bay area but moved to Utah when he was very young. Cesar has two children, is married, and works full-time with computers. He aspires to graduate with a bachelor's degree in Computer Science. English was his second language and learned later in life that he has a learning disability. Cesar was the eldest of the participants and graduated from high school in a traditional high school setting.

Oscar was the youngest participant. He was born in southern California and moved to Utah at a very young age. Oscar was pushed out of school and attended an alternative high school, and he was struggling to find a steady employment. Oscar was believed to be a recently arrive immigrant from Mexico by his teachers even though he was born in southern California. He was also believed to be a gang member by his teachers, although he did not affiliate himself with a gang.

Sandino was also born in southern California but also grew up in Utah from a very young age. Sandino was a youth organizer and also a community activist. He was pushed out of high school and attended an alternative high school and the local community college. Sandino joined a gang and explained that he joined a gang because of friendships he made while he was suspended and needing a support system.

Before examining the ways Cesar, Oscar, and Sandino frame the themes of (1) the Chicano student experiences with the school-to-prison pipeline, (2) innovation of discipline policy and practice, and (3) effective alternative practices to a zero tolerance framework, I invite you to put on the lenses of one of the students in the following narrative.

A Moment through Sandino's Eyes

Imagine that you are a high school student and begin your routine morning the way you would on any other weekday. You wake up, very likely you do so very begrudgingly, and you shower, get dressed, find your books and put everything into your backpack. You begin to walk to school, it isn't very far so you walk the 20 minutes every day. You show up to school, see some friends and say "hi," and feel pretty good about today. Then, imagine that suddenly the school security guard confronts you and he quickly grabs your shirt and says, "Hey, where do you think you're going?" You're confused and caught by surprise, say, "class, where else?" You are immediately escorted to the Vice-Principal's office, where he calls the campus police officer to join you all. All of a sudden, you are in his office and not sure what is going on.

When the police officer joins the Vice-Principal and the security guard that flagged you, you are asked by the Vice-Principal, "What are you doing on campus?" You respond, nervous and confused, "going to class." What follows is not uncommon; you are informed by the Vice-Principal, "the police-officer will be escorting you off campus because you are no longer a student at this school." You have been expelled and were allegedly mailed a letter, which, neither you nor your family received. You are asked to stay off the school grounds and it is suggested you go to the local alternative high school if you want to continue with your education. You are given a copy of the letter you are to expect in the mail and you are never alerted of this risk. You never saw it coming. There is no way to petition this, or inquire more, or seek advocacy. Even if you knew about any advocacy, or it even existed, you have already been expelled. You are the one who has to notify your parent.

While this might sound like a stretch or fiction as counterstories often do (Delgado, 1995), this is what happened to both Sandino and Oscar. Both were expelled from school without prior notice and ended up attending an alternative high school education.

Experiences with the School-to-Prison Pipeline

Cesar, Oscar, and Sandino offer their experiences with the school-to-prison pipeline and school discipline under a zero tolerance framework. These experiences span along a spectrum of exposure to the zero tolerance framework. In some cases, participants describe the way in which they were criminalized or treated as less than, and in other instances, they describe being incarcerated as a youth.

Sandino recalls how he was expelled and the absence of communication between the school and his parents.

> When they kicked me out they didn't even tell me, they just sent me a letter that said "your records have been dropped from Rocky Mountain High School and they are sending you to the alternative school." They didn't even tell my parents. I remember I got the letter and I went to my friend's house cause he lived close, "hey dog I'm going to the alternative high school" and he's all like, "I'm going too!" They didn't even tell us they just sent us out a letter ...I was fifteen at the time. (Sandino)

He was asked to leave and had to call his mother to let her know. She left work, picked him up, and they drove to the alternative high school to proceed with enrolling him. Sandino had aspirations to go to graduate school and wanted to study economics.

Sandino developed relationships with friends he made when he was suspended and in his neighborhood. He described how he was lonely and did not have many friends since they were all in school. These new friends he made were all gang-affiliated and he quickly found himself seeking their support and joining a gang himself. During this time, he was involved in a fight. Sandino was arrested as a result of this altercation, and coupled with his gang involvement he showed up in a gang member database, and was arrested and charged more severely for the fight.

Appearing in juvenile court and being processed into the juvenile detention facility for incarceration had long-term effects he goes on to share. Namely, he describes the deep emotional ways that youth are affected through the process of being incarcerated as a child.

> Once you get locked up, you just don't really care anymore. Like, that's some of the most degrading stuff and even for young kids and I know for a fact that juvenile corrections is way less bull***t than prison or than jail … but like, at the same time, the stuff they do to you there …. They [juvenile detention centers] are preparing you for prison. They are not there to help you out; they are preparing you to feel like a piece of s***. (Sandino)

This experience Sandino goes through parallels what Rios (2007) describes as "multispatial criminalization," that is, that male youth of color – particularly Latinos and Blacks – are "hypercriminalized" in that they are criminalized in multidimensional layers and multiple social settings such as in school. A way this notion of multispatial criminalization has long-term implications is when students internalize this treatment and react from it. Another student describes how after years of being hypercriminalized or treated like a gang member and targeted, he began to accept this and own those perceptions of him.

> If you think I'm a f*** up, if you think I'm a gang banger, if you think I am the type of person that is going to graffiti up the school, then f*** it, I'll do it, and I'll do it bigger and better than you ever think …. It's like no matter what I do, I'm always going to be treated like s***. So, I might as well do what I want to do. (Cesar)

In retrospect, Cesar says he realized that he was doing damage to his own future and life by feeling the need to prove himself and states, "You don't stop and think and process, like hey, this is affecting my people." His ways of resisting were at times what Smith, Yosso, and Solorzano (2007) refer to as maladaptive or self-damaging. However, at the same time, he is cognizant that those feelings derive from deficit perceptions of who he is as a Chicano, stating, "I think it's [the internalization of deficit views] self-made. Not by us but by the teachers and the administration. I think they created the problem." In the last statement where Cesar says, "I might as well do what I want to do," he is recognizing what often occurs to Chicano students when they experience the school-to-prison pipeline – they internalize the negative stereotypes and assumptions about who they are that they receive from their environment (Rios, 2007).

These maladaptive resistance practices have long-term academic and professional effects. Oscar, a student who was also frequently suspended and eventually expelled to an alternative high school, talked about how going through that process affected his lack of interest in pursuing college or any formal schooling.

> I don't care. I don't need it. I don't need that kind of s*** in my life. I don't need anybody giving me any negativity. That's what I thought about myself, it was like, f*** – if they don't care about me then I'm not going to care about me. (Oscar)

Oscar internalized the treatment he received from his teachers and the curriculum from his high school. This experience affected his performance at school and his future. He began to resist these feelings in maladaptive ways. Oftentimes, students of color can resist in ways that are self-destructive and, even more dangerous, internalize the treatment they receive and believe it as a way of resistance and defiance. They do so as a result to the lack of support and respect they experience from school officials (Solórzano & Delgado Bernal, 2001; Yosso, Ceja, Smith, and Solorzano, 2009).

In reflection, students describe a violent and aggressive climate in schools. They spoke of the hypercriminalized environment and to the extent to which they internalize and begin to believe that stock story about themselves (Delgado, 1995). These experiences shaped their futures as adults and their emotional reflections spoke to the damage they experienced as a result to the school-to-prison pipeline.

Innovative Policies and Practices

Here Cesar, Oscar, and Sandino all reflect on ways their disciplinary experience could have been different. They draw on their experience to discuss ways in which we can reconsider relating with young people in school rather than the zero tolerance framework. This section offers guidance from participants for ways schools can push back against the school-to-prison pipeline.

While Sandino, Oscar, and Cesar were all suspended and experienced different forms of the school-to-prison pipeline, they were all conscious of working with community in ways that describe how engaging in praxis can be a way to enact resistance. Solórzano and Delgado Bernal (2001) call this type of resistance a transformative resistance, in that they experienced a "*conscientization*" or a critical awareness brought on by social justice awareness, critical self-reflection, and praxis, *conscientization*-driven action (Freire, 1970; Valdes, 1996).

The spaces that allow for transformational resistance (Solórzano & Delgado Bernal, 2001) can occur in the classroom. In these cases, resistance was fostered with the student's involvement with communities that they felt safe in and played roles that differed from those imposed on them in school. Sandino, Oscar, and Cesar were leaders and activists in the community.

> They underestimate what kids really know. The kids know the problems they are going through, they know the struggle. They might not be able to articulate it as good as adults, but listen to them, I think the legislators need to listen to them. They [legislators, policymakers, and school officials] don't understand that what youth need is to be encouraged and loved, and to be accepted in order to keep going and succeed. Giving the youth a sense of belonging and understanding and pride of who they are … instead of having to learn who they are from music, TV images, and media images that they have nothing to do with really. (Cesar)

Cesar echoed Freire's (1998) *Pedagogy of Freedom*, where Freire urges educators "To listen to the student's doubts, fears, and incompetencies that are part of the learning process. It is in listening to the student that I learn to speak with him or her" (p. 106). He also points out that students need "to be encouraged and loved," this is another element of praxis that can occur in the classroom but often students seek elsewhere for it or what resembles that encouragement and love they seek.

Duncun-Andrade and Morrell (2008) describe this love Cesar refers to, as "revolutionary love" as a love that is about not giving up on students and taking tremendous courage for us as educators, educational leaders, advocates, scholars, researchers, etc. to exercise this form of love with students in under-represented communities (p. 187). Revolutionary love "looks like endless dedication, an unyielding belief in the brilliance and potential of every student, and the commitment to stop at nothing to get students to learn (p. 187)."

Freire (1970) describes this form of love as liberating for the oppressed and argues that it is a commitment and dialogical, in other words working from a place of love will result in reciprocity (p. 89). This revolutionary love that Duncan-Andrade and Morrell (2008) and Freire (1970) discuss is the foundation to praxis. Praxis here is grounded in community addressing the school-to-prison pipeline from a place of love for students.

The participants in this study all suggested practices that would be tied to praxis in this way.

The young men here also described the ways praxis can be simple, accessible in schools, and a practice that already exists in some educational spaces (Duncun-Andrade & Morrell, 2008). Oscar goes on to describe a peaceful campus climate and positive student–teacher relationships that he experienced while at the alternative high school.

> Teachers that give you respect, just treat you like actual human beings like an adult or anything like that – students themselves treating themselves with respect and they start becoming more adults to me. They're not like in [the regular high school] how you get treated like you're a piece of s***. (Oscar)

He discusses a reciprocal learning environment and credits this with also enhancing his educational experience at that school,

> In [the alternative school] we all go together. Teachers learn from us and we learn from them … teachers are so down to earth that they will learn from you too, they will teach and learn at the same time … it's not that they tell me [the curriculum or their approach is reciprocal], it's that you notice it. (Oscar)

The sense of support from his new teachers at the alternative high school permitted Oscar the latitude to focus on his academic achievement rather than the hostility he experienced from his educators at his previous school. The relationships between teachers and students also impact student–student relationships (Pizarro, 2005; Valenzuela, 1999). Although it is noteworthy that Oscar identifies pedagogical practices educators can utilize that are drawn from a place of care and respect (Duncan-Andrade & Morrell, 2008), it is important to note that alternative schools are not typically a strong bridge for increased access to college and the particular school Oscar and Sandino note is a rare instance of this dynamic. Once students of color are labeled and pushed out to alternative self-contained school programs, they experience extreme difficulty in returning to a regular high school, and this form of push out becomes another mechanism utilized within the school-to-prison pipeline (Casella, 2003; Fenning & Rose, 2007, p. 543).

Students described deep interest in communication and a humanized approach in schools. They suggest that teachers can get to know them and develop meaningful relationships with them. They also discuss ways their educational interests could have manifested differently if they had different approaches to discipline. Remarkably, most of their innovative approach was grounded in a desire for mutual respect.

Effective Alternatives

Today, Chicanos face triple the school discipline rate and double the expulsion rate of their White counterparts (Valles & Villalpando, 2013; Valles, 2015). It is of grave importance to focus on understanding the ways to eliminate the school-to-prison pipeline and growth of the prison industrial complex to save the lives of Chicano youth. Evidence suggests that school discipline policies can be racially biased, subjective, unequally distributed, and unfair frameworks to target specific groups of people, and further, that school discipline policies do not make schools safer or nonviolent spaces (Casella, 2003; Reyes, 2006; Skiba et al., 2002; Valles & Villalpando, 2013). Knowing these policies and practices are subjective, it can be inferred that they can be disrupted, changed, and addressed.

In their interviews, students outlined the characteristics necessary for having revolutionary loving educational spaces. They identified fundamental ways that schools can utilize to interrupt the current school-to-prison pipeline needing educational spaces to be reciprocal, respectful, loving, encouraging, peaceful climates, positive relationships, acceptance, and the opportunity to develop a sense of self. Together, these characteristics would form a context that would support transformational resistance for students. For instance, reflective work through professional development for educators and educational leaders focused on deficit thinking and the intersectionality of identities could result in a powerful step in working toward a revolutionary loving educational space. Students develop transformational resistance when they are engaged with community and they are able to develop leadership skills; this can come from incorporating critical service-learning and self-reflection. These efforts are examples all the study participants point to in order to develop transformational resistance and revolutionary love in school. In this dynamic, that is praxis.

We, as educational researchers and educators, must recognize the knowledge and expertise of Chicano students and seek their guidance and leadership in understanding ways to address policies and practices that support school-to-prison pipeline. This chapter calls on their experiential knowledge as a source of informative data that can be applied to school discipline policies in real and tangible ways. This is beautifully articulated by Cesar when he describes the way educational policy makers might address the school-to-prison pipeline when he says, "They don't understand that what you need is to be encouraged and to be loved, and to be accepted in order to keep going and succeed." He goes on to describe his interest in being taught about his history and background and connects this to self-esteem and pride, which he believes would have made a difference for him. Student-centered projects could address this in the classroom as an example of how this might be achieved.

Rios and Galicia (2013) point out that schools have the capacity to change and transform, to spaces of learning and empowerment rather than pushing students out of school and perpetuating deficit thinking (p. 63). Sandino, Cesar, and Oscar also agree that schools can change and direct us to a praxis of revolutionary love and transformational resistance as a vehicle to work around the skewed discipline policies. Furthermore, Fujimoto, Garcia, Medina, and Perez (2013) suggest additional tangible approaches to consider in an effort to move in a direction of revolutionary love and transformational resistance. Fujimoto et al. (2013) propose that schools work to develop collaborative relationships with the surrounding community and focus on partnerships between community and school (and beyond) and in doing so, move toward an asset-based approach (Yosso, 2005, p. 93). Many schools are beginning school-community gardens as a way to develop collaborate relationships with the surrounding communities. These projects are often funded and supported in partnership with local businesses and community members.

IMPLICATIONS

There seems to be a disconnect between the practices employed in school to promote "safe" learning spaces and the actual development of "safe" learning spaces for Chicano students. If we draw from their experience and strength, we can learn that Chicano students in this study experience a very harsh and punitive disciplinary reality in schools. We also glean that they desire respectful and humane relationships with their teachers and school staff. Finally, Cesar, Oscar, and Sandino propose a different way to relate to students that is one grounded in a framework of love and praxis of care instead of the hostility they experienced.

The findings in this study lend themselves for the applied use in schools today. The students in this study identified key ways to push back on the school-to-prison pipeline, and they offered accessible and applicable ways of doing this. Educators and educational leaders can draw on the findings of this study and begin by engaging with students, open up communication with the student population impacted by school discipline policy at the most disproportionate rates, and draw from the experiential knowledge on what school discipline is like for them at their respective schools and/or districts. From their perspectives, establishing communication between educational leaders and students and their communities is the key.

One of the most significant findings in this study was about students feeling respected and cared for. Although ambiguous, establishing a sense of communication can begin to identify what would address a caring and respectful space for each respective educational environment. In this study, Cesar, Oscar, and Sandino identified a desire for connection and a more humanized and respectful relationship with their teachers. They were able to point out what it did and did not look like. This will likely differ by educational settings but dialogue between educators, educational leaders, and students can be part of a strong beginning. Professional development for educators and educational leaders to work on deficit thinking, harmful assumptions, and identity intersectionality are part of a strong beginning. Building a meaningful and collaborative relationship with community can facilitate transformational resistance practices. Furthermore, connecting with surrounding communities can support students and school leaders in developing a praxis-based approach to empower students and address disciplinary concerns. Developing school-community connections can foster a transformative resistance rather than a self-defeating one, as the participants suggest. Lastly, the study participants urge the reader to re-evaluate pedagogical approaches in their school for the broader school implications this can have on climate of the school.

Ways of redefining our educational backdrop do not have to come with expensive consultants or curricular practices. It can also come in accessible methods. Although I am not suggesting these efforts are easy, or efficient, I believe relying on experiential knowledge can begin to guide us on the issue of the school-to-prison pipeline. Let us take note from the participants in this study and create more spaces where we learn from youth and their experiences to guide how classroom relationships function toward a transformative learning space.

NOTES

1. In this study Chicano or Chicanos represent male students of Mexican, Mexican American, and/or males of Mexican origin or heritage. The use of Chicano/Latino is inclusive of all Spanish-speaking backgrounds.
2. The NCES description of this data labels students as drop-outs; this study does not use that language and recognizes the institutional responsibility in students

not in school, and thus uses the term, "push out." See Burciaga, Pérez Huber, and Solorzano (2010) for more on this.

3. Please note that there has been diverse populations (indigenous peoples, Mexicans, Japanese, and others) inhabiting the territory Utah was founded on for thousands of years before the current occupants and before it became a formal state (Aleman, 2009; Perlich, 2002; Solorzano, 1998).

REFERENCES

Aleman, E. (2009). Through the prism of critical race theory: *Niceness* and Latina/o leadership in the politics of education. *Journal of Latinos and Education*, *8*(4), 290–311.

Bell, D. (1987). *And we are not saved: The elusive quest for racial justice.* New York, NY: Basic Books.

Burciaga, R., Pérez Huber, L., & Solorzano, D. (2010). Going back to the headwaters: Examining Latina/o educational attainment and achievement through a framework of hope. In E. Murillo, S. Villenas, R. Galván, J. Muñoz, C. Martínez, & M. Machado-Casas (Eds.), *Handbook of Latinos and education: Theory, research, and practice* (pp. 422–437). New York, NY: Routledge.

Casella, R. (2003). Zero tolerance policy in schools: Rationale, consequences, and alternatives. *Teachers College Record*, *105*(5), 872–892.

Children's Defense Fund. (1975). *School suspensions: Are they helping children?* Washington, DC: Author.

Children's Defense Fund. (2008). *The State of America's Children.* Washington, DC: Author.

Cook, D. A. (2013). Blurring the boundaries: The mechanics of creating composite characters. In M. Lynn & A. D. Dixson (Eds.), *Critical race theory in education handbook.* New York, NY: Routledge and Taylor & Francis Group.

DeCuir, J. T., & Dixson, A. D. (2004). "So when it comes out, they aren't that surprised that it is there": Using critical race theory as a tool of analysis of race and racism in education. *Educational Researcher*, *33*(5), 26–31.

Delgado, R. (1989). Storytelling for oppositionists and others: A plea for narrative. *Michigan Law Review*, *87*, 2411–2441.

Delgado, R. (1995). *Critical race theory: The cutting edge.* Philadelphia, PA: Temple University Press.

Delgado Bernal, D. (2002). Critical race theory, LatCrit theory, and critical raced-gendered epistemologies: Recognizing students of color as holders and creators of knowledge. *Qualitative Inquiry*, *8*(1), 105–126.

Devine, J. (1996). *Maximum security: The culture of violence in inner-city schools.* Chicago, IL: The University of Chicago Press.

Dohrn, B. (2001). "Look Out Kid/It's Something You Did": Zero tolerance for children. In W. Ayers, B. Dohrn, & R. Ayers (Eds.), *Zero tolerance.* New York, NY: The New Press.

Duncan-Andrade, J., & Morrell, E. (2008). *The art of critical pedagogy: possibilities for moving from theory to practice in Urban schools.* New York, NY: Lang Publishing, Inc.

Eberle-Sudre, K., Welch, M., & Howard Nichols, A. (2015). *Rising tide: Do college grad rate gains benefit all students?* The Education Trust.

Eisenbraun, K. D. (2007). Violence in schools: Prevalence, prediction, and prevention. *Aggression and Violent Behavior*, *12*, 459–469.

Elenes, C. A., & Delgado Bernal, D. (2010). Latina/o education and the reciprocal relationship between theory and practice: Four theories informed by the experiential knowledge of marginalized communities. In E. G. Murrillo, S. A. Villenas, R. Trinidad Galván, J. Sánchez Muñoz, C. Martínez, & M. Machado-Casas (Eds.), *Handbook of Latinos and education: Theory, research, & practice* (pp. 63–89). New York, NY: Routledge.

Fenning, P., & Rose, J. (2007). Overrepresentation of African American students in exclusionary discipline: The role of school policy. *Urban Education*, *42*(6), 536–559.

Freire, P. (1970). *Education for critical consciousness*. New York, NY: Continuum Publishing.

Freire, P. (1998). *Pedagogy of freedom: Ethics, democracy, and civic courage*. New York, NY: Rowman & Littlefield Publishers, Inc.

Fujimoto, E., Garcia, Y., Medina, N., & Perez, E. (2013). Alternatives to the school-to-prison pipeline: The role of educational leaders in developing a college-going culture. *Association of Mexican-American Educators*, *7*(3), 85–95.

Glennon, T. (1995). Race, education and the construction of a disabled class. *Wisconsin Law Review*, 1237–1338.

Gun Free Schools Act of 1993, S. 854, 103rd Cong. (1993). Retrieved from ProQuest Congressional Database.

Harrison, P. M., & Beck, A. J. (2002). *Prisoners in 2001*. Washington, DC: Bureau of Justice Statistics.

Harvard Civil Rights Project. (2000). *Opportunities suspended: The devastating consequences of zero tolerance and school discipline*. National Summit on Zero Tolerance, Washington, DC.

Harvey, W. B., & Anderson, E. L. (2005). Minorities in higher education: 2003–2004. Twenty-first annual status report. American Council on Education, Washington, DC.

Hernandez-Truyol, B. E. (1999). Latina multidimensionality and LatCrit possibilities: Culture, gender, and sex. *Miami Law Review*, *53*, 811–829.

Hyman, I. A., & Perone, D. C. (1998). The other side of school violence: Educator policies and practices that may contribute to student misbehavior. *Journal of School Psychology*, *36*, 7–27.

Iglesias, E. M., & Valdes, F. (1998). Afterword-religion, gender, sexuality, race and class in coalitional theory: A critical and self-critical analysis of LatCrit social justice agendas. *UCLA Chicano – Latino Law Review*, *19*, 503–588.

Jackson, K. (1997). Differences in the background and criminal justice characteristics of young black, white, and Hispanic male federal prison inmates. *Journal of Black Studies*, *27*(4), 494–509.

Kochhar, R., Suro, R., & Tafoya, S. (2005). *The new Latino South: The context and consequences of rapid population growth*. Pew Hispanic Center.

Ladson-Billings, G. (1995). Toward a theory of culturally relevant pedagogy. *American Educational Research Journal*, *32*(3), 465–489.

Ladson-Billings, G. (2000). Racialized discourses and ethnic epistemologies. In N. K. Denzin & Y. S. Lincoln (Eds.), *Handbook of qualitative research* (2nd ed., 257–277). Thousand Oaks, CA: Sage.

Larson, J. (1994). Violence prevention in the schools: A review of selected programs and procedures. *School Psychology Review*, *23*, 151–164.

Lynn, M., & Parker, L. (2006). Critical race studies in education: Examining a decade of research on U.S. Schools. *The Urban Review*, *38*(4), 257–290.

Martinez, T. A. (2002). The double-consciousness of Du Bois and the "Mestiza Consciousness" of Anzaldúa. *Race, Gender & Class: An Interdisciplinary Journal*, *9*(4), 158–176.

Noguera, P. (2007). How listening to students can help schools improve. *Theory into Practice*, *46*(3), 205–211.

Noguera, P. (2008). *The trouble with Black boys: ...And other reflections on race, equity, and the future of public education*. San Francisco, CA: Jossey Bass.

Osher, D. M., Quinn, M. M., Poirier, J. M., & Rutherford, R. B. (2003). Deconstructing the pipeline: Using efficacy and effectiveness data and cost-benefit analyses to reduce minority youth incarceration. In J. Wald & D. J. Losen (Eds.), *New direction for youth development: Deconstructing the school-to-prison pipeline* (pp. 91–120). San Francisco, CA: Jossey-Bass.

Perlich, P. (2002). *Utah minorities: The story told by 150 years of census data*. Bureau of Economic and Business Research, University of Utah, Salt Lake City, UT.

Perlich, P. (2008). Utah's demographic transformation: A view to the future. *Utah Business and Economic Review*, *68*(3).

Pizarro, M. (2005). *Chicanas and Chicanos in School: Racial profiling, identity battles, and empowerment*. Austin, TX: University of Texas Press.

Portillos, E., Gonzalez, J. C., & Peguero, A. A. (2012). Crime control strategies in school: Chicanos/as perceptions and criminalization. *Urban Review*, *44*(2), 171–188.

Quin. (2005). *Proceedings from the unacknowledged crisis: Latino makes and higher education*. Los Angeles, CA.

Raffaele Mendez, L. M. (2003). Predictors of suspension and negative outcomes: A longitudinal investigation. *New Directions for Youth Development*, *99*, 17–33.

Raffaele Mendez, L. M., & Knoff, H. M. (2003). Who gets suspended from school and why: A demographic analysis of schools and disciplinary infractions in a large school district. *Education and Treatment of Children*, *26*(1), 30–51.

Reyes, A. (2006). *Discipline, achievement & race: Is zero tolerance the answer?* Washington, DC: Rowman and LittleField.

Reyes, A. (2007). The criminalization of student discipline programs and adolescent behavior. *St. John's Journal of Legal Commentary*, *21*(1), 73–110.

Rios, V. M. (2007). The hypercriminalization of Black and Latino male youth in the era of mass incarceration. In M. Marble, I. Steinberg, & K. Middlemass (Eds.), *Racializing justice, disenfranchising lives*. New York, NY: Palgrave Macmillan.

Rios, V. M., & Galicia, M. G. (2013). Smoking guns or smoking & mirrors? Schools and the policing of Latino boys. *Association of Mexican-American Educators*, *7*(3), 53–66.

Saenz, V. B., & Ponjuan, L. (2009). The vanishing Latino male in higher education. *Journal of Hispanic Higher Education*, *8*(1), 54–89.

Singer, A. (2004). *The rise of immigrant gateways*. Washington, DC: Brookings Institution.

Skiba, R. J., Michael, R. S., Nardo, A. C., & Peterson, R. (2002). The color of discipline: Sources of racial and gender disproportionality in school punishment. *The Urban Review*, *34*, 317–342.

Skiba, R., & Rausch, M. (2006). School disciplinary systems: Alternatives to suspension and expulsion. In G. Bear, K. Minke, & A. Thomas (Eds.), *Children's needs III:*

Understanding and addressing the developmental needs of children (pp. 87–102). Bethesda, MD: National Association of School Psychologists.

Smith, W. A., Yosso, T. J., & Solórzano, D. G. (2007). Racial primes and Black misandry on historically White campuses: Toward a critical race accountability in educational administration. *Education Administration Quarterly*, *43*(5), 559–585.

Solórzano, A. (1998). Struggle over memory: The roots of the Mexican Americans in Utah, 1776 through the 1850s. *Aztlán*, *23*(2), 81–118.

Solórzano, D. (1998). Critical race theory, racial and gender microaggressions, and the experiences of Chicana and Chicano scholars. *International Journal of Qualitative Studies in Education*, *11*, 121–136.

Solórzano, D. G., & Delgado Bernal, D. (2001). Examining transformational resistance through a critical race and LatCrit theory framework—Chicana and Chicano students in an urban context. *Urban Education*, *36*, 308–342.

Solórzano, D. G., & Yosso, T. J. (2001). Maintaining social justice hopes within academic realities: A Freirean approach to critical race/LatCrit pedagogy. *Denver University Law Review*, *78*(4), 595–621.

Solórzano, D. G., & Yosso, T. (2002). Critical race methodology: Counterstorytelling as an analytical framework for education research. *Qualitative Inquiry*, *8*(1), 23–44.

Solorzano, D. G., Villalpando, O., & Oseguera, L. (2005). Educational inequities and Latina/o undergraduate students in the United States: A critical race analysis of their educational progress. *Journal of Hispanic Higher Education*, *4*, 272–294.

Theriot, M. T. (2009). School resource officers and the criminalization of student behavior. *Journal of Criminal Justice*, *37*, 280–287.

Townsend, B. L. (2000). The disproportionate discipline of Black learners: Reducing school suspensions and expulsions. *Exceptional Children*, *66*(3), 382–384.

U.S. Census Bureau. (2010). *State quickfacts: Utah*. Retrieved from https://www.census.gov/quickfacts/table/PST045215/49/accessible

U.S. Department of Commerce, Census Bureau, Current Population Survey (CPS). Population 3 to 34 years old enrolled in school, by sex, race/ethnicity, and age group: Selected years, 1980 through 2014.

U.S. Department of Education, National Center for Education Statistics. (2016). The condition of education 2016 (NCES 2016-144), Status dropout rates.

U.S. Office of Civil Rights. (2004). Table 07A/08A student enrollment, students participating in gifted and talented programs, students enrolled in and needing LEP programs, and incidents of student discipline.

Utah State Office of Education. (2015). Annual report.

Valdes, F. (1996). Forward: Latina/o ethnicities, critical race theory and post-identity politics in postmodern legal culture: From practices to possibilities. *La Raza Law Journal*, *9*, 1–31.

Valencia, R. (1997). Conceptualizing the notion of deficit thinking. In R. R. Valencia (Ed.), *The evolution of deficit thinking: Educational thought and practice*. London: The Falmer Press.

Valenzuela, A. (1999). *Subtractive schooling: US-Mexican youth and the politics of caring*. New York, NY: SUNY Press.

Valles, B. (2015). *Educational impacts of discipline policies on Chicano students in Utah: A mixed method critical race theory and LatCrit analysis*. Unpublished doctoral dissertation. University of Utah, Salt Lake City, UT.

Valles, B., & Villalpando, O. (2013). A critical race policy analysis of the school-to-prison pipeline for Chicano males. In M. Lynn & A. D. Dixson (Eds.), *Critical race theory in education handbook* (pp. 260–269). New York, NY: Taylor & Francis.

Verdugo, R. R. (2002). Race-ethnicity, social class, and zero tolerance policies: The cultural and structural wars. *Education and Urban Society*, *35*(1), 50–71.

Villalpando, O. (2004). Practical considerations of critical race theory for Latino/a college students. In Ortiz, A. M., (Ed.) *Addressing the unique needs of Latino/a students, new directions for student services. No. 105*. San Francisco, CA: Jossey-Bass.

Villalpando, O. (2010). Latinos/as in higher education: Eligibility, enrollment, and educational attainment. *Handbook of Latinos and education*. New York, NY: Routledge Press.

Wald, J., & Losen, D. (2003). Defining and redirecting a school-to-prison pipeline. *New Directions for Youth Development*, *99*, 9–15.

Wing, A. K. (2003). *Critical race feminism: A reader*. New York, NY: NYU Press.

Wortham, S. (2001). Gender and school success in the Latino diaspora. In S. Wortham, E. Murillo, & E. Hamann (Eds.), *Education, policy, and the politics of identity in the new Latino diaspora* (pp. 117–141). Westport, CT: Ablex.

Yosso, T. J. (2005). Whose culture has capital? A critical race theory discussion of community cultural wealth. *Race Ethnicity and Education*, *8*(1), 69–91.

Yosso, T. J., Ceja, M., Smith, W. A., & Solorzano, D. (2009). Critical race theory, Racial microaggressions, and campus racial climate for Latina/o undergraduates. *Harvard Educational Review*, *79*, 659–690.

CHAPTER 4

DISCIPLINE AND PUNISHMENT: HOW SCHOOLS ARE BUILDING THE SCHOOL-TO-PRISON PIPELINE

Hugh Potter, Brian Boggs and Christopher Dunbar

ABSTRACT

In this chapter, we argue that the growth of punitive school discipline in US schools has created an inequitable system of school punishment that is reflective of the development of the school-to-prison pipeline and the establishment of an educational "total institution." Current school discipline practices negatively affect student academic growth in the classroom as a result of an increase in suspensions and expulsions. Data in this chapter exemplify the overreliance on punitive school discipline in one urban school to address behavioral issues and also further expand on the concept of school-to-prison pipeline using the "total institution" theory of command and control of a population proposed by Goffman (1961). We argue that there are more effective measures of school discipline and seek to provide alternate possibilities for school leaders to address the draconian treatment of Black and brown boys in today's traditional public school environments.

Keywords: Discipline; punishment; school-to-prison pipeline; total institution theory

---

The School to Prison Pipeline: The Role of Culture and Discipline in School
Advances in Race and Ethnicity in Education, Volume 4, 65–90

ISSN: 2051-2317/doi:10.1108/S2051-231720160000004005

US Attorney General Eric Holder stated, "*Ensuring that our educational system is a doorway to opportunity – and not a point of entry to our criminal justice system – is a critical, and achievable, goal*" (Holder, 2011 as cited in Dunbar, 2015). No truer words have been spoken, with respect to how government, law enforcement, academic, and community leaders should respond to what is an unprecedented increase, as seen in the national school suspension data provided by the Office for Civil Rights from 2002 to 2012, in the removal of Black and brown boys from traditional public schools. Suspensions and expulsions have left a trail of tattered lives of children who have been sent to alternative schools – schools that simply serve as "holding tanks" until their inevitable trek to youth detention centers and eventually adult incarceration facilities (Dunbar, 2015).

This chapter examines the similarities between Goffman's (1961) cultural and organizational thesis and its primacy and application in today's urban school environments. There are too many instances where children are suspended or expelled from schools as a result of violations to the school's code of conduct, which result in the application of draconian measures that serve only to displace children, viewed as disruptive, from the school that they attend. These children are sent to alternative schools as "*temporary holding tanks*" or released, unsupervised by adults who are unable to oversee the actions of the students while suspended, into the general community (due to their exclusion from school because of suspension) until their inevitable run-in with law enforcement. We argue that there exists a thin line between the behavior of public school administrators, with respect to suspensions and expulsions, and the practices of the juvenile authorities. In fact, we argue that the policies and subsequent behaviors, when filtered through Goffman's theory of a total institution, mirror each other. This is explained in three areas:

1. *Theoretical Lens* – One cannot help but see the cultural and organizational similarities between schools and prisons. In sociology, a prison would be referred as a "total institution." Goffman (1961) defines this as a place or residence cut off from a larger community (by choice or force) where a routine life is ordered and administrated. In general and traditional society, schools and prisons share a similar relationship with respect to authoritarian structures; negative reinforcements for violating social norms; loss of individual autonomy; constrained access to rights exercised by the wider community outside of the institutionalized group; no control over decision-making, input, or processes; and set times, routines, and counts for attendance, food, and regimented activities

(Boggs & Dunbar, 2015). The concept that schools are total institutions is often overlooked, but the concept of total institution provides a bridge, to make a concrete transition from the school institution to the prison institution, and a framework for further investigation.

2. *Current Research* – School discipline has risen to the forefront of US educational debate as seen in the number of studies that identify discipline disparities for different populations (particularly for African Americans) within schools, which also document the overall ineffectiveness of the dominant current model of discipline used within schools. School districts across the nation (Skiba & Peterson, 1999; Smith, 2015) have implemented expansive zero tolerance policies for a multitude of what were previously mundane violations to the student's code of conduct (e.g., insubordination or disorderly conduct) under the auspices of making school a safe place for the nation's children. At the height of implementation, 79% of US schools, in the 1996–1997 school year, had implemented zero tolerance policies (Kang-Brown, Trone, Fratello, & Daftary-Kapur, 2013). Unfortunately, school districts charged with enforcement of the mandate have misguidedly imposed draconian measures that exceeded the law's intended purpose by suspending students for infractions that had in the past, been handled by school personnel. What has resulted is a dramatic increase in the number of students suspended/expelled who are left on their own without a viable means to acquire an education. What is more alarming is that a disproportionally higher number of the most vulnerable population of Black and brown children fall victim to this ill-advised policy. As zero tolerance policies have been implemented in US schools, the impact of subjective punishments leading to exclusion (as seen in this chapter) from schools to the criminalization of student misbehavior represents a system of punishment that is broken and harming the overall educational process in the United States.
3. *Case Study of School Disciplinary Data* – Current school discipline procedures and protocols in schools across the United States reflect an alarming increase, as exemplified later in this chapter, in the use of exclusionary discipline for students who violate a school's code of conduct. We examine the discipline data for the 2012–2013 school year of five different schools located within the same Midwest urban district during a single school year to assess and analyze the implementation of a student's code of conduct. We focus on the incidence of exclusionary discipline including the removal of students from the classroom environment by suspensions and expulsions and the number of subjective

punishments (e.g., insubordination or disorderly conduct) that result in exclusion. Due to the limitations of the data available, this chapter examines the overall incidence of school discipline for a single year and does not disaggregate the punishment of students on an individualized basis but looks at the overall discipline distributed during the course of the school year. The primary unit of analysis for this examination is the overall number of student incidences involving exclusionary punishment. This study aligns with the numerous other studies around this topic and provides an important insight into the discipline practices within an urban school setting during the course of a school year.

We conclude this chapter with policy recommendations to positively impact school climate and dismantle the production of school-to-prison pipeline. We propose that the adjustment of the school climate from a punitive, reactionary system to a proactive system of behavioral modification by restorative justice or other form can improve the overall school climate. We also argue, as others have before us, that the school-to-prison pipeline is a byproduct of punitive discipline practices in US schools (Dunbar, 2015). Our recommendations also address the need for future measures and research to examine discipline and the school-to-prison pipeline.

THEORETICAL LENS: SCHOOLS AS TOTAL INSTITUTIONS

The concept of a total institution in the sociological context is not a new one. As a point of fact, it has been a theory used since Erving Goffman introduced the term in 1957 while studying mental hospitals and prisons. However, what is new is its application to schools and, in particular, to describe the urban school setting and the conditions that create the school-to-prison pipeline (Boggs & Dunbar, 2015). To build on this theoretical lens in the school context, it is important first to define the term. As Goffman (1961) argues, "A total institution may be defined as a place of residence and work where a large number of like-situated individuals, cut off from the wider society for an appreciable period of time, together lead an enclosed, formally administrated round of life" (p. xiii).

In his original work, Goffman (1961) divides this theory of a total institution into five specific types, of which K-12 education (aside from boarding schools) is not included. The first type includes institutions that have been established to care for those who are considered unable to care for themselves, such as orphans, the aged, and indigent (Goffman, 1961). The second type includes institutions for those who are unable to care for themselves, but also are considered to be an unintended threat to society in some form, such as sanitariums for contagious diseases or mental hospitals. The third type includes institutions for those deemed to be intentional dangers to society, such as jails, prisons, and prisoner of war camps (Goffman, 1961). The fourth includes those institutions established "to pursue some work like task and justifying themselves only on these instrumental grounds," such as army barracks and boarding schools (Goffman, 1961, p. 5). And, finally, the fifth type includes those institutions established "as retreats from the world even often serving also as training stations for religious," including abbeys, monasteries, convents, and other cloisters (Goffman, 1961, p. 5).

Goffman argues that traditional public schools lacked (at least schools of the 1950s) the residential component of this concept. This is why boarding schools are considered as a total institution by his definition but public schools are not. However, we argue, with exception to the residential component of the total institution theory, most of today's urban public schools fit this paradigm. Schooling and its function in society have changed since his original writing, especially with the overall deterioration of many major US cities (Boggs & Dunbar, 2015). However, in later works, Goffman (1961) argues that the purpose of residency is not about residency at all but about the establishment of a barrier between the member of the institution and the "wider world" (p. 45). When we consider that completing a high school education has been deemed by society as a basic prerequisite for entry into the workforce or further educational advancement, then not completing a K-12 education (or alternative) is a barrier to successful entry into society. Therefore, schools meet the goals of a total institution in that it "create[s] and sustain[s] a particular kind of tension between the … [wider] world and the institutional would and use[s] this persistent tension as leverage" (Goffman qtd. Frank, 2002, p. 44).

Building on this, for an entity to be considered as a total institution there are several additional key features or characteristics that it must exhibit. First and foremost among these is involuntary membership (Goffman, 1961). With a struggle to get students to attend schools that are considered to be struggling or in crisis, typically in urban areas, and compulsory attendance and truancy laws driving attendance, membership in schooling is involuntary (in the sense students do not want to attend). Second, members of a total institution "are compelled to carry out most or all of their activities in the company of virtual strangers" (Frank, 2002, p. 45).

Students in school are grouped by age and grade and may or may not have any prior relationship with the individuals with whom they are grouped – at least not at the beginning of their journey in the institutional environment. Third, life within a total institution is organized, regimented, and controlled by a single governing authority or established organization (Boggs & Dunbar, 2015; Frank, 2002; Goffman, 1961). This would include when meals are served, activities and ceremonies occur, routines are created and observed, and when staff and members of the total institution may come and go.

Finally, total institutions are characterized by their use of authority, specifically to reward and sanction. This would include the establishment of what Goffman (1961) refers to as "house rules," which are essentially the formal rules for the members of the institution to follow, and these rules are usually explicit. There are also informal rules that members of the staff can use to grant privilege to some members of the institution for their preferable behavior. To some degree, authority and the right to discipline are given over to staff of school (Goffman, 1961). In addition, "the authority of corrective sanctions is directed to a great multitude of items of conduct … constantly occurring and constantly coming up for judgment; in brief, authority is directed to matters of dress, deportment, social intercourse, manners and the like" (Goffman, 1971, p. 247). In the context of a school, these matters have little to do with the actual education of students but still result in disciplinary action. This is followed by misbehaviors extending into other aspects of one's participation in activities of the institution, which may be unrelated to the original action. For example, a student's behavior in class may affect their eligibility to play an extracurricular sport.

When we consider the act of schooling and the characteristics of a total institution, there is a clear theoretical lens to place schools, beyond just boarding schools described by Goffman in the 1950s, in the framework of a total institution. This theoretical lens might not be overly subscribed to in middle class suburban school areas where there is often more curricular flexibility and instruction is focused on critical thinking skills. However, the manifestations of this theory are evident in low-performing, high-poverty schools that are generally located within urban areas with a high minority population where there is generally a strong focus on behavior and rote skills. These characteristics of total institutions represent a stark reality to their schooling experience. Viewing schools as total institutions helps us to better understand the conditioning and socialization processes that occur in many urban schools for direct transition of students into the prison system. Through the creation of routinization, schools are setting the groundwork and the experiential knowledge that foreshadows the draconian punitive legal system that many students encounter later in life. The process by which schools condition students by mirroring the characteristics of a total institution, especially in urban areas, reflects the manner in which educational systems come to train minority students for entry into the legal system as adults.

CURRENT RESEARCH

The staggering increase in subjectively based punishments as a result of the expansion of zero tolerance school discipline policies exemplifies how the current model of school discipline is broken. This policy ultimately led to students being excluded from schools and to an overall criminalization of student misbehavior. If the current model of school punishment continues, then there is a potential for significant harm to occur in the overall educational experience for many students in school across the United States. This is especially true for students of color. Historically, one purpose of discipline policy within a school was to establish a sense of order and to establish the overall security expectations within schools (Gregory, Skiba, & Noguera, 2010; Losen, 2013). Discipline policies have also been conceived of and implemented within schools to provide explicit codes of conduct that ordered movements and societal interactions of students (Hirschfield, 2008), aligning with Goffman's (1961) house rules concept. Although these functions of discipline policies are theoretically sound, current empirical research suggests that the policies are ineffective in addressing day-to-day student misbehavior and actually produce negative long-term effects for students, particularly for students of color. School discipline policies are becoming increasingly punitive in nature (Fowler, 2011) and have significant effects on the families of students, involved in school discipline proceedings, who are forced to adjust their lives to provide care and oversight for students who have been punished by schools (Losen, 2013).

School discipline policies that rely on exclusionary punishments also have considerable effects on the students who lose valuable instructional time in the classroom (Losen & Skiba, 2010). The current trend in discipline policy, a path of exclusion and removal, has also been linked to an increased likelihood that students will come into contact with the judicial system in what is known as the "school-to-prison" pipeline (United States Department of Justice & United States Department of Education, 2014). The historical attempt to establish order, structure, and overall safety in schools through zero tolerance policies has failed to achieve the goals that motivated the initial creation of discipline policy and is an overall failure as a "behavioral intervention" process (Raffele Mendez & Knoff, 2003).

Zero Tolerance Laws

Modern US zero tolerance school discipline codes emanate from the 1994 Gun Free Schools Act (GFSA) that was signed into law by President Clinton and these zero tolerance discipline policies have been bolstered by a number of high-profile violent incidents in schools across the country, such as the Columbine and Newtown school shootings. The GFSA, "mandated that each state must pass legislation that requires a one year expulsion for any student who brings a firearm to school in order to receive federal education funding" (Dupper, 2010, p. 17). Following the federal implementation of the GFSA, schools across the country began to expand the zero tolerance school discipline policies and produce extrapolations of the zero tolerance approach from illicit drugs to student actions that are less serious (e.g., insubordination and disorderly conduct) in a concerted effort to establish order and structure with schools.

The term zero tolerance grew out of the federal criminal policies (outside of education) that were established by the federal government to target the burgeoning illicit drug epidemic in the United States during the 1980s (Skiba & Peterson, 1999). The initial aim of the use of zero tolerance policies within educational settings was to make schools safer (Raffele Mendez, 2003) by establishing a set of predetermined consequences of infractions committed by students, regardless of the overall severity of the action by students (Brownstein, 2010). As the use of zero tolerance policies expanded in schools across the country, the definition of the zero tolerance came to include a multitude of actions beyond the scope of the GFSA, including drugs and alcohol (Brownstein, 2010) as well as truancy, tardiness, and "vague catch-all categories such as insubordination and disrespect" (Dupper, 2010, p. 18). The increasing application of zero tolerance policies in schools can be seen as establishing a sense of authoritarianism and fear within the school. Skiba and Peterson (1999) argue that the implementation of zero tolerance policies has been used to cast a broad net that not only establishes specific punishments for those in violation of the code of conduct but also, more importantly, is used to send a message to potential violators as well. Pedro Noguera (as cited in Skiba & Peterson, 1999) argues that the primary function of harsh punishments within the zero tolerance framework is not to alter the behavior of students but is a way in which schools can promote and establish the overall power of school authorities over the student body.

Empirical research on the consequences of the application of zero tolerance policies in schools and the "get tough on crime" approach to regulating student behavior has shown that the implementation of these unalterable concrete punitive actions for student infractions has increased the risk that violators of a school's code of conduct will have contact with the juvenile justice system (Monahan, VenDerhei, Bechtold, & Cauffman, 2014), will have lower test scores for students (Dunbar, 2015), and will lead to a substantial increase in the number of suspensions and expulsions of students for small and trivial offenses, such as disorderly conduct and insubordination (Skiba & Peterson, 1999). Dunbar (2015) reports that the harsh punishments, incurred as a result of strict adherence to zero tolerance discipline policies, have "failed to make our schools safer. In fact, research has shown just the opposite. Overly punitive practices can actually be harmful to student outcomes" (p. 10). Skiba and Peterson (1999) have argued that, "we lack solid evidence to support the effectiveness of harsh policies in improving school safety" (p. 8). Although explicit evidence of the effectiveness of zero tolerance policies is hard to locate, the impact of the policies on increased use of exclusionary punishment in schools is readily available.

Exclusionary Punishments

The use of exclusionary punishments (punishment that removes a student from the learning environment for an extended period of time: from 1 to 20 days) is a common type of disciplinary action taken in schools today. The two specific types of exclusionary punishments are suspensions and expulsions. Skiba and Sprague (2008) define suspension as a relatively short-term removal of a student from a school for disciplinary action and expulsion as a procedural removal of a student for a longer period of time. According to Losen (2013), the purpose of exclusionary punishment for students is to accomplish three specific goals:

1. To improve students' behavior in the future
2. To deter others from misbehaving
3. To create a positive learning environment for other students.

Although the effectiveness of these exclusions is questionable, it has become evident that their use has grown in the recent years. The number of suspended or expelled students has nearly doubled in the recent decades, from 3.7% in 1974 to 7.1% in 2006 (Brownstein, 2010). During the 2005–2006 school year, more than three million school children were suspended and over 100,000 students were expelled from US schools (Brownstein, 2010). Students, historically, were suspended or expelled from school for serious offenses, but according to Monahan et al. (2014), suspensions and expulsions are now being applied to far less severe incidents, such as disobedience, truancy, and insubordination. The overall expansion of exclusions based on subjective interpretations should be of significant concern for school leaders and communities today.

The increase in the use of exclusionary punishments has been shown to lead to decreased instructional time in the classroom for students (Losen, 2013) and an overall reduction in the opportunity to learn (Losen & Skiba, 2010). The educational impact of an increase in suspensions and expulsions has been shown to not only cause delays in the development of reading skills (Arcia, 2006) but also has been linked with an increase in school avoidance by students (United States Department of Justice & United States Department of Education, 2014). Additionally, the incidence of exclusionary punishments for students has been shown to produce an increase in the rate of repeat suspensions for students (Brownstein, 2010), and there has also been an increase in substance abuse by students who have been subjected to exclusionary punishments (United States Department of Justice & United States Department of Education, 2014). Finally, the practice of suspension and expulsion in schools has been shown to lead to an increased likelihood of a student to drop out of school later in their academic lifetime (Losen & Skiba, 2010) and an overall decrease in the school's achievement capacity (Arcia, 2006). In their entirety, the broad spectrum of negative outcomes associated with exclusionary discipline has left scholars and school officials questioning the overall effectiveness of exclusionary punishments for schools and students.

Dupper (2010) has provided research that has explicated the inability of exclusionary punishments to reduce the incidence of misbehavior. In addition, researchers have not found whether exclusionary punishments cause any form of deterrence for students to participate in activities that lead to punitive actions by school officials (Bock, Tapscott, & Savner, 1998; Raffele Mendez, 2003). Furthermore, Raffaele Mendez (2003) found that the use of exclusionary punishments has not been shown to be effective for any particular subgroup of the school's population. According to

Losen and Skiba (2010), exclusionary punishments did not improve the school climate either. It is apparent from research that the use of exclusionary punishments for misbehaving students is increasing, and there is little evidence of its effectiveness in reducing the overall incidence of misbehavior in schools. Instead, research suggests that exclusionary discipline is disruptive to the learning process, not just in urban schools, but also across the entirety of the educational spectrum.

Of particular interest, is the effect of disproportional discipline on African American students. Black youth represent only 17% of the population of US schools; however, Black students account for 32% of all students suspended from schools (Raffele Mendez & Knoff, 2003). Using longitudinal data from the Office for Civil Rights, it is clear that this trend of disproportionate impact is continuing for African American males as per the most recent data publication for the 2011–2012 school year showing that African American males are subjected to suspension more than their White counterparts per capita. Dupper (2010) reported that African American students are suspended "2.8 times the rate of white students in 2002 and 3.1 times the rate in 2006" (p. 10). The disproportionate rate of school punishment for African American students, as has been shown above, has significant effects on the ability of the students to progress academically and socially within the schooling system as it is set up today.

Criminalization of Misbehavior

It can be argued that the growth of zero tolerance policies in schools, from elementary to high schools, has been accompanied by an increase in the criminalization of students and student behaviors. Skiba and Peterson (1999) posit that by relying on zero tolerance policies in schools today, we are creating a model of schooling that demonstrates to students that in order to maintain order in schools, students must relinquish or suspend their own rights and liberties as citizens and acquiesce to the expected norms of the school administration, if our schools are to be safe and orderly. The reliance on zero tolerance policies also privileges the concept that the primary goal of school discipline, specifically exclusionary punishment, is to deter and incapacitate (Hirschfield, 2008) misbehaving students in order to maintain a civilized and orderly learning environment for other students.

These school disciplinary practices socially norm students to be participants in the criminal system after matriculating out of school, thereby laying the framework for school-to-prison pipeline for some students.

The existing system of punishment in schools across the United States comes to serve as a training ground for students to acculturate themselves to the existence and reality of the criminal justice system that many of the students will face soon after exiting the school house doors. As a result of the implementation of a stringent, procedural code of conduct that is more about the literal offense than the nature of the offense (Hirschfield, 2008), schools are increasingly mirroring an authoritarian system without regard for the potential of a corrective action by the school leadership. As Dunbar (2015) insists, "discipline today is decidedly punitive rather than corrective" (p. 10). The end result of this criminalization of the school environment is that, as Hirschfield (2008) bluntly puts it, "trouble-making students are more likely to be defined as criminals – symbolically, if not legally – and treated as such in policy and practice and society" (p. 80).

Discipline Data: A Case Study in Minor Infractions

Our research and investigation examined the disciplinary actions of a specially created state reform school district of chronically low-performing schools. This district was composed of 12 urban schools from a large Midwestern, postindustrial city. The data is from the 2012 to 2013 school year and resulted in several important and noteworthy findings. These findings provide evidence that the implementation of harsh, punitive punishments for behavioral violations has resulted in a significant number of students being removed from schools for what were once considered as minor infractions. The data used in the present study highlight three specific characteristics related to school discipline:

1. That in these five schools studied, discipline related to violent acts was an uncommon occurrence.
2. Exclusionary discipline was used quite frequently to address minor students' misbehavior.
3. Discipline for subjective infractions by the students, those infractions that have a high level of discretion in their application, was most frequently imposed punishments in the schools used for this study.

Together, these three findings help to illuminate the issues and concerns about the use of harsh punitive discipline protocols in schools today for transgressions that traditionally were dealt within the classroom by teachers.

Riva Ridge School District

Riva Ridge[1] is an urban Midwestern school district with a unique organizational structure that is composed of 12 schools. There are six high schools (grades 9–12), four elementary schools (kindergarten to eighth grade), and two academies (kindergarten to ninth grade). As can be seen in Table 1, in the district there were 8,682 students (www.mischooldata.org) during the 2012–2013 school year. The district was predominately African American, representing 95.08% of the student body with the remaining 4.92% of the student body made up of Hispanic (2.63%), White (1.38%), Asian and Pacific Islander students (0.73%), American Indian (0.09%), multiethnic (0.08%), and Native Hawaiian Islander students (0.01%). The gender breakdown for the school district is 52.89% males and 48.1% females. For this study, due to the limitations of data available, we focus on two high schools and two elementary schools.

Demographic data for the two high schools in this study have been shown in Table 2. The first high school in this investigation, Liberty High School, had a population of 1,110 students, of which 50.99% were males and 49.01% were females during the 2012–2013 school year. At Liberty High School, African American students constituted 99.19% of the student body, 0.27% of the students were Hispanic, 0.36% of the students were White, 0.09% of the students were American Indian, and another 0.09% of the students were multiethnic. The second of the two high schools, Hemlock High School, had a student population of 923 students, of which 50.49% were females and 49.51% were males. Of these students, 99.35% were African American, 0.22% of the students were White, 0.22% of the students were Asian and Pacific Islander, 0.11% of the students were American Indian, and 0.11% of the students were Hispanic.

Table 1. Riva Ridge School District Demographics.

Riva Ridge school district demographics total student population	8,682		
Gender distribution	Males: 52.9%	Females: 48.1%	
Ethnic distribution	African American: 95.08%	Hispanic: 2.63%	White: 1.38%
	Asian and Pacific Islander: 0.73%	American Indian: .09%	Multiethnic: .08%
	Native Hawaiian Islander: 0.01%		

Table 2. High School Demographic Data.

	Liberty School	Hemlock High School
Population	1,110	923
% Male/% female	50.99/49.01	49.51/50.49
% African American	99.19	99.35
% Hispanic	0.27	0.11
% White	0.09	0.22
% American Indian	0.09	–
% Multiethnic	0.09	–
% Asian and Pacific Islander	–	0.11

Table 3. Elementary School Demographic Data.

	Simba Elementary	Boomer Elementary
Population	363	430
% Male/% female	47.11/52.89	51.16/48.84
% African American	98.07	99.3
% Hispanic	–	–
% White	–	0.47
% American Indian	0.28	0.23
% Multiethnic	–	–
% Asian and Pacific Islander	1.65	–

The demographic data for the elementary schools (Table 3) share similar characteristics as that of the high schools. The first elementary school in the study, Simba Elementary, had a total student population of 363 students, 52.89% were females and 47.11% were males. In the school, African American students composed 98.07% of the student body with Asian Pacific Islander students representing 1.65% of the students and American Indian students making up 0.28% of the total population. The second elementary school, Boomer Elementary, had 430 students during the 2012–2013 school year. Of these 430 students, 51.16% were males and 48.84% were females. Again, African American students composed the majority of the student body with 99.3% of the students, White students represented 0.47% of the students and 0.23% of the students were American Indian.

According to the Michigan Department of Education data (www.mis-chool.data), there were 223 faculty members in the Riva Ridge School District during the 2012–2013 school year. Of these 223 faculty members (Table 4), there were 114 White teachers (51.1%), 92 African American teachers (41.3%), eight Asian teachers (3.6%), seven Hispanic teachers (3.1%), and two American Indian/Alaskan Native teachers (0.9%).

Although the teacher corps (Table 5) was balanced between White and African American teachers, it was not representative of the majority of African American school district, school, or local community population demographics. The 2010 United Census Bureau reported that in the city, the population was 82.7% African American, 7.8% White, 6.8% Hispanic, 2.2% multiethnic, and .04% American Indian.

Although the distinction between the demographic makeup of the community and the school does not immediately correlate or cause a disparate outcome in student punishment, it is important to note the cultural differences between faculty and student population. It would also be of great interest for further research to illuminate the importance of demographic differences in the educational disciplinary actions of schools, although it is not the focus of this chapter.

Table 4. Riva Ridge School District Faculty Demographics.

	Number	Percent
Overall # of faculty in district	*223*	*100*
White	114	51.1
African American	92	41.3
Asian	8	3.6
Hispanic	7	3.1
American Indian/Alaskan Native	2	0.1

Table 5. Demographic Data for Where Riva Ridge School District Is Located.

African American	82.7%
White	7.8%
Hispanic	6.8%
Multiethnic	2.2%
American Indian	0.04%

Violent Offenses by Students

One of the greatest concerns related to school safety and the overall learning environment for students is the possession and use of weapons in schools. In 1994, President Clinton signed into law the GFSA. This act was designed to keep schools safe from weapons by mandating an expulsion for students found to be in possession of or using a weapon in school. The act has also been used as a foundation for many zero tolerance policies in school districts. However, when analyzing the data in this study, the use or possession of a weapon represents a minute portion of the overall punishments meted out. Including all of the listed infractions related to weapons, from the possession of a gun, a knife, or any other item used as weapon, the district administered only 49 infractions among 12,279 total infractions, as shown in Table 6. Furthermore, as seen in Table 6, it is clear that when considering the number of infractions for each of the schools, violent offenses happen relatively infrequently. Across all schools, disciplinary action for weapons represented a very small fraction of all offenses. Each individual school unit's issuance of punishment was less than 1% of all infractions.

Within the district, of the 49 total incidents that were related to a weapon of any kind within the school, however, only four were for students

Table 6. Number of Infractions Related to Violent Offenses.

School	Total Number of Infractions for Weapons	Percentage of all Infractions (%)	Percentage of All Exclusionary Infractions (%)	Total Number of Infractions the Led to Exclusions
Riva Ridge School District[a]	49	.39	.46	10,452
Hemlock High School	5	.51	.71	709
Liberty High School	11	.78	.90	1,219
Simba Elementary	2	.20	.23	880
Boomer Elementary	1	.10	.10	714

[a]The four schools listed here do not comprise the entirety of the district.

who were in possession of a gun. Of the four incidents in which guns were involved, the referrals were for students in the fourth, fifth, eighth, and eleventh grades. Knives were the most common weapon that was brought to schools, with 24 incidents during the course of the 2012–2013 school year. Riva Ridge School District's definition of a knife includes any knife of any size or blade length and includes box cutters or "any instrument which has been altered to be used as a weapon in a manner similar to a knife such as a letter opener or file" (p. 16). Students in high school were punished more often for possession of knives than elementary/middle school students with 19 incidents in high school compared to five in the elementary/middle schools. There were 11 other instances with an object other than a gun or a knife that was in possession of students that was categorized as a violent offense. In all, there were 49 instances where students were in possession of a weapon, but there were only 10 instances, out of 12,279 total infractions for the district in which a student was subject to a school action for the actual use of a weapon representing a very small percentage of all infractions, .08%.

School violence in any form is unacceptable, especially when it occurs at the scale and severity of Sandy Hook or Columbine. However, it is also important to be cognizant of the relatively few incidents that occur of such magnitude. As is evident in the above data, incidents of violent acts in schools comprise a very small percentage of the overall number of disciplinary incidents in a school system. However, it is evident from the data that, like society in general, minor and less aggressive forms of behavioral incidents that are contrary to the code of conduct in schools produce a considerable impact on the individuals. In essence, it is not the severity of the incident that results in separation of the student from the school but the overall desire to use punishment as a form a remediation. As such, schools and society operate as a total institution that is structured and operated to reward those who abide by the rules and severely punish those who run even slightly askew of acceptable behavior.

Exclusionary Punishments

An exclusionary punishment was defined by the Riva Ridge School District as any punishment that prevents the student from being physically present in the classroom. These exclusionary punishments include in-school suspensions (which preclude the students from attending actual class periods but mandate their attendance in school), short-term suspensions (1–3 days of physical removal), and long-term suspensions (5–20 days). Not included in the results of this study are punishments that did not indicate a final decision by the school. These omitted punishments included recommended expulsions, administrative transfers (the forced transfer of a student to another school), any suspensions that were pending when the data were culled by the district, and any punishments that were pending a rescheduled hearing for the students. The total number of exclusionary punishments for the school district in this study was 10,452 for the 2012–2013 school year.

These 10,452 exclusionary punishments represented 85.2% of the entire set of punishments meted out during the course of the 2012–2013 school year within the school district. Of these 10,452 total exclusionary punishments, 83.4% were in the form of short-term suspensions, 13.5% were in-school suspensions, and 3.1% were long-term suspensions. Of the short-term suspensions, 3,044 (29.1% of all infractions) suspensions were for subjective offenses, which are categorized as insubordination and disorderly conduct. Another 2,126 short-term suspensions were handed out to students who were truants and had accrued 10 unexcused absences. The trend, as you can see in Table 7, shows that exclusionary punishments were a common form of punishment used in the district and were most common in one elementary school, representing 93.15 of all punishments.

At Boomer Elementary school, where 93.1% of all punishments handed out were exclusionary in nature (where the students were precluded from participating in the educational opportunities taking place in the classroom), 414 of the exclusionary punishments were in-school suspensions. Of the 414 in-school suspensions, 322 were for either insubordination ($n=99$) or for disorderly conduct ($n=223$). Another 22 referrals were for verbal abuse (name calling, racial or ethnic slurs, or derogatory statements aimed

Table 7. Exclusionary Punishments by School Unit during the 2012–2013 School Year.

School Unit	Number of Exclusionary Punishments	Percent of All Punishments for the School Unit (%)
Riva Ridge School District	10,452	85.0
Hemlock High School	709	73.5
Liberty High School	1,219	86.7
Simba Elementary	880	89.2
Boomer Elementary	714	93.1

at another person) and another 18 referrals were for fighting but not severe enough to cause an injury to either of the involved party.

Subjective Infractions in the Code of Conduct

The final piece to this study is the investigation into the use of exclusionary punishments for students who violated the two subjective categories of the code of conduct of the school district: insubordination and disorderly conduct. Of the 51 individual categories of infractions, these two categories (insubordination and disorderly conduct) were the most open to the discretion of the school leadership team (defined as any principal, assistant principal, or other disciplinary leaders) who came in contact with the student who exhibited a behavior not in line with what the school or the teacher deemed to be appropriate for the school. In the code of conduct handbook, insubordination is defined as:

> A student will not ignore or refuse to comply with directions or instructions given by school authorities. Refusing to open a book, write an assignment, work with another student, work in a group, take a test, or perform any other class or school-related activity not listed herein, refusing to leave a hallway or any other school area, or running away from school staff when told to stop all constitute insubordination.

The other punishment that fell within the subjective category was disorderly conduct. Disorderly conduct, as defined in the code of conduct handbook is:

> A student will not harass others or misbehave in a manner that causes disruption or obstruction to the educational process. Disruption caused by talking, making noises, throwing objects or otherwise distracting another constitutes disorderly conduct. Behavior is considered disorderly if a teacher is prevented from starting an activity or lesson, or has to stop instruction to address the disruption.

These two offenses, both of which are discretionary and are dependent on the perspective of the administrator (who may not be representative of the dominant ethnicity population of the students and therefore represent a bias in the distribution of subjective punishments to students), represent a large number (Table 8) of the infractions that were recorded during the 2012–2013 school year.

Throughout the school units within this study, as seen in the district-wide data for Riva Ridge School District, exclusionary discipline (40.2%) for subjective offenses (e.g., insubordination and disorderly conduct) outnumbered all other offenses during the course of this single school year.

Table 8. Subjective Offenses Resulting in Exclusionary Punishments, 2012–2013 School Year.

School Unit	Total Number of Subjective Offenses	Offenses Categorized as Insubordination	Offenses Categorized as Disorderly Conduct	Total Percentage of Infractions (%)	Total Percentage of Exclusionary Infractions (%)
Riva Ridge School District	4,204	2,036	2,168	34.2	40.2
Hemlock High School	268	102	166	27.8	37.8
Liberty High School	369	294	75	26.2	30.2
Simba Elementary	527	302	225	53.4	59.9
Boomer Elementary	418	131	287	54.5	58.5

Overall, the results of this study indicate that exclusionary discipline based on subjective interpretations was a constant reaction to the violations of the code of conduct that was taking place. This is a pattern of reaction that was preventing students from being engaged in the learning environment on a regular basis. The results also show that only a very few of all disciplinary actions taken by the school authorities in these school units were for violent offenses.

Creation of the School-to-Prison Pipeline or Perpetuation of the Same by Another Name

It has been said that where there is smoke, there is fire. This study is an important precursor for the continued investigation into the increasing use of exclusionary discipline in schools. This study depicts a set of schools that demonstrated an overreliance on exclusionary discipline, especially for students who were considered to be insubordinate or disorderly in the classroom. The Riva Ridge School district, the largest entity in this study, had 12,279 referrals to school administration by teachers or other school leaders for violations to the school's code of conduct during the course of a single school year with 85% of these referrals resulting in students being removed from the classroom environment, unable to benefit from the instruction taking place. If the presumed goal of school discipline is to create an environment that is both safe and educationally beneficial for well-behaved students then one could argue that this pattern of discipline might be appropriate, but the consensus of previous studies shows that exclusionary discipline does not achieve these goals. Exclusionary discipline has been associated with a number of negative student outcomes, including harm to the ability of the penalized students to learn, increased likelihood of contact with the juvenile justice system, and decreased academic proficiency as a whole.

A significant aspect in making schools safer for students, as predicated by the GFSA, has been accomplished by banning weapons in schools. In this study, it is clear that the possession or use of a weapon in schools was taken seriously and was dealt with properly; however, the overall number of incidents is quite less. Less than .4% of the total incidents that were recorded in this study involved a weapon of any sort and only a very few were for the actual use of a weapon in the schools. This is an important aspect of the study to be aware of; only a very few incidents related to weapons took place during the 2012–2013 school year.

However, a concerning finding in this study is that the school units in this study were quite willing to remove students for behavior construed as insubordinate or disorderly. As seen in the data above, these schools have an arbitrary and loosely defined criterion for insubordination and disorderly conduct, and its subsequent exclusionary punishment, and in many instances eventual incarceration in juvenile and adult institutions. The impact of these exclusions, as seen from other studies, has serious consequences for students both academically and psychologically.

DISCUSSION

The traditional purpose of school discipline was to address problematic behaviors by students in the classroom and provide a safe environment for other students to succeed free of distractions. The current disciplinary protocols in schools across the United States move far beyond traditional patterns of discipline and move headlong into the process of marching misbehaving students out from the classroom and into the criminal justice system in an institutional fashion. The school-to-prison pipeline is a concerning problem facing the youth in US schools. The drift of the zero tolerance drug laws into the realm of education discipline began in the 1990s (Wallace, Goodkind, Wallace, & Bachman, 2008) when a large number of US schools, reacting to the federal GFSA of 1994, began implementing "get tough" policies. Schools across the United States began to implement zero tolerance discipline policies to address not only violent offenses but also a wide array of other behaviors that threatened the order and safety of schools. Dupper (2010) argues that the expansion of zero tolerance school discipline policies is dependent on fear and seeks to pressure students to develop a sense of respect for their teachers. The problem is that this respect is built upon the bedrock of fear and not mutual trust. All of these elements create, as Goffman would refer to, a total institution and one that minors a prison-like environment, especially in schools with large discipline issues.

The belief, during the expansion of the use of zero tolerance discipline policies, was that by acting tough and forcing the dominant national form of punitive measures upon the school setting, classrooms would become orderly and learning would ensue. The expansion of zero tolerance discipline policies can be seen as a form of toughening up schools and as an attempt to ensure that the general public feels that the local schools are safe places of learning (Noguera, 1995). Zero tolerance policies in school discipline have resulted in the treatment of both minor and major disciplinary problems with the same severity (Skiba & Peterson, 1999).

The end result for students is that the institutionalization of zero tolerance school discipline protocols have resulted in a system of discipline that is punitive in nature and does not produce positive changes in student behavior. The introduction and broad overuse of zero tolerance policies has established the cognitive sense that order and control within the school building, despite the negative impacts it may produce, is more important than the learning opportunities that may exist. Thus, the existing system of school discipline has and will continue to be a factor in the creation of the school-to-prison pipeline that relegates large numbers of youth in the penal system rather than the academic system.

Policy Recommendations

This chapter has raised important questions about the purpose of school discipline and the impact of overreliance on the punitive actions of school disciplinarians for students who are subject to punishment for misbehavior in the classroom. As has been highlighted, the evolution of school discipline has morphed into systems that have little respect for the actual violations to the school's code of conduct by the students and has led to a system of punishment that increases the likelihood that students will leave the educational system and find themselves in the clutches of the greater penal system that exists in the society.

The school-to-prison pipeline is a tangible outgrowth of the zero tolerance policies that are reflective of society's overall desire to detain and punish rather than rehabilitate. The overall increase in the suspensions and expulsions for students is a clear concern for schools today. It is critical to comprehend that the disciplinary system that is in place in many schools across the United States has little regard for the future actions of the students and is more concerned about the immediate response to perceived misbehavior in the classroom. As has been highlighted earlier in this chapter, schools are quick to punish, yet reticent to reflect on the impact of the system in place.

As a result of this systemic mismatch between the student population and the members of the school administration and teaching corps, there are a few important methods in which schools can revise their existing discipline policies to provide opportunities for disciplined youths to learn and achieve in the classroom. The first of these methods is to eliminate the immediate removal of students from classrooms for subjective behavioral violations. Second, schools should look to implement policies that are culturally responsive to students and the backgrounds from which the students reach the classroom. Together, these are two (although not exhaustive) methods by which school systems can evolve from a system that is an authoritarian dichotomy of villain and victim to a more collaborative engagement of a team determined to provide a learning environment that is responsive to the shared goals of the school and the students.

First, the elimination of suspensions and expulsions for behaviors that are considered to be subjective in nature (insubordination and disorderly conduct) is a vital step in improving the relationship between the teacher and student. Due to the discretion that school leaders (teachers, disciplinary officials, and principals) have in the identification and treatment of subjective offenses to the school's code of conduct, there is a large window in which school officials have to punish students for behaviors that may be completely acceptable outside the classroom. It is this varying interpretation of disorderliness and insubordination that results in large numbers of students being subjected to punishments that do not fit the actual crime. In an attempt to establish order in the classroom, teachers and school officials are criminalizing student misbehavior. It is imperative that school systems begin to establish more concrete notions of acceptable and unacceptable behavior. With clarity and understanding of what is actual insubordination or tangible disorderly conduct, students have the opportunity to better comprehend what behaviors will lead to acceptable forms of discipline as opposed to a spectrum of potential actions that could lead to a referral based on the whims of a school official. One way to accomplish this feat would be to introduce a form of culturally responsive program that would lead to greater awareness of student culture.

Due to the fact that culture is a malleable understanding depending on location and population, a critical limiting factor in the existing disciplinary cycle is the overall lack of cultural awareness by both parties in the educational setting. One way to overcome this disconnected environment is to establish a set of teams within the school setting, including parents, students, and school officials, to investigate cultural norms that are present in the educational setting. In the process of establishing these teams, schools can locally set norms and expectations that are more in line with the cultures present in the school. This can lead to more culturally responsive disciplinary interventions and have the opportunity to produce significant cultural awareness that may be lacking in the existing hierarchal system. Although complex and time-consuming, the introduction of a discipline system that encourages cultural awareness and cultural self-awareness has the potential to transform the existing school-to-prison system (and to some extent the total institution that is a school) into a reflective and equitable environment that seeks not to eliminate the problem, but a system that honors and legitimizes the cultural background from which students reach the school.

Disciplinary actions should not be a form of social engineering (Boggs & Dunbar, 2015) within the school; disciplinary actions should take into account the action of the student, the impact on the learning environment, and (most importantly) the root cause of the misbehavior. The disciplinary system should not look forward to mold the student into the model student but should provide the framework to identify causative factors of misbehavior and lead to improved future behavior that is in concert with the expectations of the students, the school, the local stakeholders in education, and the wider community.

Several organizations have begun to understand the gravity of the disciplinary crisis that disproportionately impacts Black and brown students for behavior in school that today has them pushed through a "school to a prison pipeline." Incidents that were once handled by school personnel are today referred to the criminal justice system. Schools in large cities, have adopted to establish their own police departments and have gone as far as to adopt language in their code of conduct packets that mirrors language from a police blotter (i.e., aggravated assault, disorderly conduct for running or excessive noise, forgery, etc. and the lists go on and on). Phrases like "the building is on lockdown" are frequently used to emulate expressions that in the past were more typically used in jail/prison situations. One might argue that school records concerned with academic progress may not be as detailed/extensive as code of conduct reports. This is all done under the auspices of making schools safe, although there is no clear evidence that presence of police in school or excessive suspensions and expulsions have made schools any safer. In fact, studies indicate that violent crimes in schools have deceased. So what do we do?

Steps can be taken to address and potentially reduce the number of suspensions/expulsions of students and thus decrease the number of students who find themselves involved in the criminal justice system. Alternatives to police citations and misdemeanor charges for minor offenses have been employed to address student behavior in school. In school suspensions, a positive behavior approach, changing the role of police in school so that their presence is proactive in the support of children, rather than being reactive by walking them out of school in handcuffs are all steps needed to dismantle the school-to-prison pipeline.

NOTE

1. Riva Ridge and all other school names are pseudonyms designed to protect the identity of the schools included in this research.

REFERENCES

Arcia, E. (2006). Achievement and enrollment status of suspended students: Outcomes in a large, multicultural school district. *Education and Urban Society*, *38*(3), 359–369.

Bock, S. J., Tapscott, K. E., & Savner, J. L. (1998). Suspension and expulsion: Effective management for students? *Intervention in School and Clinic*, *34*(1), 50–52.

Boggs, B. J., & Dunbar Jr., C. (2015). An interpretive history of urban education and leadership in age of perceived racial invisibility. In M. Khalifa, N. W. Arnold, A. F. Osanloo, & C. M. Grant (Eds.), *Handbook of urban educational leadership*. New York, NY: Rowman & Littlefield.

Brownstein, R. (2010). Pushed out. *The Education Digest*, March, pp. 23–27.

Dunbar Jr., C. (2015). *For naught: How zero-tolerance policy and school police practices imperil our students' future*. Retrieved from http://www.aclumich.org/blog/2015-01-27/harsh-discipline-pushes-students-out%E2%80%94-fails-make-schools-safer

Dupper, D. R. (2010). *A new model of school discipline: Engaging students and preventing behavioral problems*. New York, NY: Oxford University Press.

Fowler, D. (2011). School discipline feeds the "pipeline to prison". *Phi Delta Kappan, 93*(2), 14–19.

Frank, J. (2002). *The paradox of aging in assisted living*. Westport, CT: Bergin & Garvey.

Goffman, E. (1961). *Asylums: Essays on the social situation of mental patients and other inmates*. Garden City, NY: Anchor Books.

Goffman, E. (1971). Characteristics of a total institution. In A. Goldstein & J. Goldstein (Eds.), *Crime, law and society*. New York, NY: The Free Press.

Gregory, A., Skiba, R. J., & Noguera, P. A. (2010). The achievement gap and the discipline gap: Two sides of the same coin? *Educational Researcher, 39*(1), 59–68.

Hirschfield, P. J. (2008). Preparing for prison? The criminalization of school discipline in the USA. *Theoretical Criminology, 12*(1), 79–101.

Kang-Brown, J., Trone, J., Fratello, J., & Daftary-Kapur, T. (2013). *A generation later: What we've learned about zero tolerance in schools*. Retrieved from https://storage.googleapis.com/vera-web-assets/downloads/Publications/a-generation-later-what-weve-learned-about-zero-tolerance-in-schools/legacy_downloads/zero-tolerance-in-schools-policy-brief.pdf.

Losen, D. J. (2013). Discipline policies, successful schools, racial justice, and the law. *Family Court Review, 51*(3), 388–400.

Losen, D. J., & Skiba, R. J. (2010). *Suspended education: Urban middle schools in crises*. Retrieved from https://www.splcenter.org/20100901/suspended-education-urban-middle-schools-crisis.

Monahan, K. C., VenDerhei, S., Bechtold, J., & Cauffman, E. (2014). From the school yard to the squad car: School discipline, truancy, and arrest. *Journal of Youth Adolescence, 43*, 1110–1122.

Noguera, P. A. (1995). Preventing and producing violence: A critical analysis of responses to school violence. *Harvard Educational Review, 65*(2), 189–212.

Raffele Mendez, L. M. (2003). Predictors of suspension and negative school outcomes: A longitudinal investigation. *New Directions for Youth Development, 2003*(99), 17–33.

Raffele Mendez, L. M., & Knoff, H. M. (2003). Who gets suspended from school and why: A demographic analysis of schools and disciplinary infractions in a large school district. *Education and Treatment of Children, 26*(1), 30–51.

Skiba, R., & Peterson, R. (1999). The dark side of zero tolerance: Can punishment lead to safe schools. *Phi Delta Kappan, 80*(5), 372–376.

Skiba, R., & Sprague, J. (2008). Safety without suspensions. *Educational Leadership, 66*(1), 38–43.

Smith, M. L. (2015). A generation at risk: The ties between zero tolerance policies and the school-to-prison pipeline. *McNair Scholars Research Journal, 8*(1), 125–141.

United States Department of Justice, & United States Department of Education. (2014). *Notice of language assistance dear colleague letter on the nondiscriminatory administration of school discipline*. Washington, DC.

Wallace Jr., J. M., Goodkind, S., Wallace, C. M., & Bachman, J. G. (2008). Racial, ethnic, and gender differences in school discipline among U.S. high school students: 1991–2005. *Negro Education Review, 59*(1–2), 47–62.

CHAPTER 5

PATHOLOGIZING THE WHITE "UNTEACHABLE": SOUTH LONDON'S WORKING-CLASS BOYS' EXPERIENCES WITH SCHOOLING AND DISCIPLINE

Garth Stahl

ABSTRACT

In terms of education attainment in the United Kingdom, the white working class remains the lowest performing ethnic group, and their academic underperformance has ominous implications for their long-term life chances. This chapter investigates how white working-class boys experience pathologization and deficit discourses in their schooling as they negotiate the discipline structures in three educational sites in South London (two state comprehensive schools and one Pupil Referral Unit). Drawing upon empirical data from an in-depth sociological study of 23 white working-class boys (Stahl, 2015), this chapter makes theoretical connections between how pathologization – both within the school and wider society – contributes to how these young men become constructed with *and* through *deficit discourses contributing significantly toward low academic achievement. Where whiteness often equates to power and*

The School to Prison Pipeline: The Role of Culture and Discipline in School
Advances in Race and Ethnicity in Education, Volume 4, 91–112

ISSN: 2051-2317/doi:10.1108/S2051-231720160000004006

entitlement, in the schooling contexts of this study whiteness was often socially constructed as undesirable and equated with low aspirations, stagnation, and antieducational stances.

Keywords: White working class; discipline; school practices; masculinity; educational inequality

The term "prison pipeline" refers to the institutional practice of funneling school students, who are often from disadvantaged backgrounds, into the criminal justice system. The pipeline metaphor, for education reform activists, is premised on the notion that schools in urban areas are failing to break the cycle of poverty and criminality. Schooling practices, which either lack sensitivity (e.g., zero tolerance policies, surveillance and policing, and authoritative control) or are institutionally racist, contribute heavily to how certain populations experience schooling. In schools, particular populations are often subjected to deficit discourses of educators who may construct their pedagogical practice around a perceived shortfall in a student's ability to learn due to their membership in a distinct social or cultural group (Candlin & Crichton, 2011, p. 4). The school-to-prison pipeline, as a recent area of American scholarship, has largely focused on African American and Latino boys from low-income backgrounds (McGrew, 2008; Winn & Behizadeh, 2011). Recent American scholarship on the school-to-prison pipeline has largely focused on African American and Latino boys from low-income backgrounds. We know very little of how deficit and pathologization discourses operate outside the United States and how these discourses contribute to the marginalization of certain populations of students. This chapter draws upon a small qualitative study of a specific ethnic group, the white working class, which is of national concern in the United Kingdom due to poor academic outcomes and high levels of criminality (Strand, 2014). Through the study of 23 white British working-class boys at three different schools in South London (two state schools and one Pupil Referral Unit (PRU)) between 2009 and 2011 (Stahl, 2015), I analyze how the white working-class boys are exposed to various degrees of pathologization, which contribute to educational practices that heighten their disengagement from formal education. Furthermore, I analyze how such school-based practices propel these young men to embrace a certain authentic working-class masculine identity, running the risk of their association with criminality.

The white working-class boys in this study construct their identities within a larger field of white working-class disengagement with education in the United Kingdom (Evans, 2006; Gillborn & Kirton, 2000), where academic attainment remains highly polarized according to class for the white British population (Cassen & Kingdon, 2007). Research indicates that in Britain today "it is possible to combine socio-economic classification of the household with the children's overall developmental score at the age of 22 months to accurately predict educational qualifications at the age of 26 years" (Evans, 2006, p. 3). In terms of attaining educational qualifications, the white working class remains the lowest performing ethnic group in the United Kingdom (Strand, 2014), and their academic underperformance has ominous implications for their long-term life chances. Demie and Lewis (2010), researching in South London, document how the white working class is often associated with low parental aspirations, low literacy levels, feelings of marginalization, and a lack of community engagement, which together shape their experiences with education. As evidenced by the Parliamentary hearing on the "Underperformance of White Working Class Children" in February 2014 (Select Committee on Education, 2014), the phenomenon continues to be a subject of concern and controversial debate. White working-class underachievement was also noted widely in the Office for Standards in Education, Children's Services and Skills annual report for the 2012–2013 academic year (OFSTED, 2014), where low expectations were linked to "stubbornly low outcomes that show little sign of improvement" (p. 1). What this report fails to mention, as a main contributing factor to the "stubbornly low outcomes" of the white working class, is their experiences in navigating schools, which are poorly managed and, as a result, can often be quite painful environments (Stahl, 2015). In such conditions white working-class identities, as learners, become constructed *with* and *through* deficit discourses that contribute significantly toward low academic achievement.

The pathologization of the white working class in wider society is well documented in academic work (Reay, 2009; Skeggs, 2004, 2005; Tyler & Bennett, 2010) and even in more populist texts (Jones, 2012). Existing research on white working-class pathologization in schooling is positioned within debates regarding masculinity in schooling (Stahl, 2015), critical race theory concerning whiteness (Gillborn & Kirton, 2000; Phoenix, 1997; Preston, 2009), working-class disadvantage (Reay, 2009), and media representations (Tyler & Bennett, 2010). Schooling is heavily structured through beliefs concerning gender, race, and class; furthermore, such beliefs can often guide the strategies that school administration and leadership employ to manage the daily lives of students. Theoretical frameworks that are intersectional (Crenshaw, 1991) account for the interaction between gender, race, and other categories of difference within social practices, institutional arrangements, and cultural ideologies and have the capacity to deepen the analysis of boys' social and learner identities (cf. Nelson, Stahl, & Wallace, 2015). This chapter highlights how white working-class boys are thrice marginalized in terms of race, class, and gendered performances within a specific context. For the purposes of this chapter, the meanings and boundaries of white working class, as an ethnic group, are defined as a category of people who identify with each other based on common ancestral, social, and cultural experiences informed by multigenerational class and race history within one nation. This case study, focused on the white working class in South London, is an area which has experienced large influxes of nonwhite immigrants. Bonnett (1998) argues that nonwhite immigration has provided a catalyst for European heritage working-class Britons to "take up" whiteness from the available repertoire of colonial and hierarchical terms where whiteness becomes significant to "their own sense of self, nation and community" (p. 316) and where such identities are symbolically reproduced (p. 318).

As in the United States, the United Kingdom incarcerates many of those living in poverty, and this phenomenon is intermeshed with both class disadvantage and educational inequality. In considering how experiences with schooling contribute to the school-to-prison pipeline, I theorize the identity formation of 23 young men in contemporary London as constituted through multiple, overlapping forms of pathologization, inside and outside of schooling, as they pursue spaces to construct a respectable working-class masculinity. In constructing their identities as learners, the white working-class boys in the study have schooling experiences shaped by low expectations from educators, deficit discourses, and institutional racism. Furthermore, school-based edu-entertainment reality shows, comedic programming, and the standard news cycle capitalize on a societal fascination with social class and poor behavior in education settings. These forms of media contribute significantly to how the white working class in this study is pathologized in school environments. Outside the school, the participants contend with racial profiling and some form quite fraught relationships with the local police, which contribute to the risk of either engagement or association with criminal activity. Theorizing the role schools play in constructing students as prison-ready requires attention to pathologizing discourses as not inseparable entities but mutually constituting. Each discourse interacts to reify a continual pathologization of working-class boys as problematic and "unteachable" (Archer, Hollingworth, & Mendick, 2010, p. 89), thereby contributing negatively to their educational achievement. This chapter will first portray how masculinities are defined in relation to educational inequality before defining for the reader the difficulties in discussing a respectable working-class masculinity in the United Kingdom today. I then discuss how whiteness will be theorized with reference to scholarship on pathologization of the white working class in wider society and how this influences how educators perceive this group as learners. The final section of the chapter draws on empirical data in an attempt to capture the difficulties associated with being a white working-class boy in this schooling environment in this specific part of South London.

EDUCATIONAL INEQUALITY AND MASCULINITIES IN SCHOOLING

In terms of education, the working classes in the United Kingdom have historically attended schools that have been underfunded and poorly resourced (McCulloch, 1998). As a result, "for a majority of the working classes education has remained something to be got through rather than go into" (Reay, 2001, p. 335). The education system in the United Kingdom, in which pupils' performance has an extraordinarily strong positive association with social class, has a state sector mired by persistent issues such as a lack of progress and innovation, deficit thinking concerning students' ability, a fetish for continual change, inadequate teacher training, etc. (MacBeath, 2009). One persistent issue that plagues the state education sector is the poor behavior of students, with a union survey finding that 69% of teachers reported experiencing disruptive behavior weekly or more frequently (Neill, 2001), although the true breadth and depth of this particular issue remains difficult to document (cf. Haydn, 2014). In contemporary schooling, working-class youth experience highly pressurized educational contexts where "tropes of *excellence* and *standards* pepper policy documents and the speeches of education ministers, and a culture of 'rigorous' surveillance and testing prevails" (Francis, 2006, p. 190, emphasis in original). The potency of a high stakes testing, standard-driven approach in shaping the identities of working-class students should not be underestimated.

Historically rebellious antischool and antisocial masculinities have often been portrayed through celebratory accounts of working-class strength and defiance (cf. Willis, 1977; Humphries, 1981) with little attention paid to how the schools' ideological structures or what Carter (2012) refers to as "soft structures," contribute to the formation of a certain working-class masculine identity. However, in contemporary research on boys and schooling, education institutions are no longer treated like a black box. It has been widely theorized that schools are – intentionally or unintentionally – active players in the construction of masculinity where boys' academic performance and behaviors are influenced by the way they construct and express their masculine identities in relation to the school structure (Connell, 1989; Mac an Ghaill, 1994; Martino & Pallotta-Chiarolli, 2003).

Past scholarship has theorized the rebellious, undisciplined "lad" (Willis, 1977) focusing heavily on gender, while future research must embrace intersectional analysis in order to move scholarship on boys and schooling forward (Nelson et al., 2015). The research presented in this chapter considers how white working-class males are potential victims of a school-to-prison pipeline through their negative experiences with schooling, the police, and wider media depictions of the white working class in schools. To understand the experiences of these vulnerable young men, it is important to consider school cultures as a "cacophony of classed, gendered and raced voices" (Reay, 2010, p. 281) where students negotiate both with their learner and social identities.

THE PATHOLOGIZATION OF THE WHITE WORKING CLASS

Theorizing Whiteness

For Preston (2009, p. 5) whiteness is not a homogeneous category; it is "contested, determined and re-classified over time as part of an ongoing process of white racialization." Whiteness is constantly in formation and not all groups benefit from it equally. There exists what Garner (2012) calls a "moral economy of whiteness" where there are "grades of whiteness" (p. 446), where whiteness is always imbued with "clear distinctions of class, gender, nation, religion and status" (Garner, 2012, p. 448). In their scholarship on white British working class, Gilroy (2004) and Bonnett (1998) historicize disadvantage and show how white working-class identities are formed in opposition to migrants. Social and cultural geographers, such as Nayak (2009, p. 3), have addressed how the English working class has been perceived both as "white" and "not-white" – shifting in and out of whiteness – depending on historical and contemporary contexts and cultural and social discourses. Clearly, beyond the United Kingdom, there exists a long history of white pathologization (e.g., Irish, Jews, Italians, and Eastern Europeans). Recent scholarship has argued that Anglo-whiteness, as an ethnic construct, remains largely an unmarked aspect of identity, "invisible" yet dominant, although it is highly classed and performed (Phoenix, 1997). In her analysis of recent white Eastern European migrants to the United Kingdom, Moore (2013) shows how whiteness becomes a performative act whereby whiteness is continually made and remade, "all the while remaining invisible to white people, eluding scrutiny and detection through their apparent normalcy" (p. 5), while within different "shades" of white, other points of distinction such as "language, physical appearance, perceived 'traits' or 'qualities'" (p. 6) rise to the surface as racialized boundaries are constructed.

White Working-Class Pathologization in Society

In the United Kingdom, there exists a long history "in which the working-class have been (through representation) continually demonized, pathologized, and held responsible for social problems" and where "most representations of working-class people contribute to devaluing and delegitimizing their already meagre capitals, putting further blocks on tradability, denying any conversion into symbolic capital" (Skeggs, 2002, p. 76). Whiteness, just like any other ethnicity, is performative and deeply shaped by class and cultural practices (Moore, 2013). Lacking in cultural resources to form a respectable identity, white Britons from low-income backgrounds are frequently associated in popular discourses with the pejorative term "chav," which can reference the whole of the white working class or segments of the underclass (Preston, 2009, p. 35). Typically, chavs are associated with juvenile delinquency and criminality where this label involves a group of young men and women (usually white), prone to antisocial behavior and clad predominantly in cheap sports apparel and clunky gold jewelry.

As a specific subsection of the white working class, the image of the chav has often been portrayed through media outlets as embodying dishonesty, hypersexuality, laziness, fecundity, rudeness, recklessness, ostentatious consumption practices (Skeggs, 2004; Hayward & Yar, 2006), and criminality.

Chavs are not only "represented, but also shaped by disparate discourses of familial disorder and dysfunction" (Skeggs, 2004, p. 87). This heightened attention to chavs is linked to a style of urban poverty, the "visual in the politics of the street" (e.g., hoodie culture), where clothing is frequently adapted to guard against urban surveillance and control (Hayward & Yar, 2006, p. 23) and which simultaneously contributes heavily to police profiling, especially in the part of South London where this case study was conducted.

Having a direct bearing on how the white working class is constructed in the South London schools of this study, chav pathologization is furthered by a morose pop culture fascination in UK society with the interrelationship between social class, education, and behavior. This is evidenced in the popularity of recent television edu-entertainment documentaries such as Channel 4's "Educating Essex," as well as the BBC3's documentary series "Tough Young Teachers," which followed extremely "posh" *Teach First* educators (who are the UK equivalent of *Teach for America* recruits) into challenging schooling environments. Within these shows the "chav student" is associated with antieducational stances through characters such as Vicky Pollard from "Little Britain" (2003–2006) and Lauren Cooper from "The Catherine Tate Show" (2004–2009). Antieducational stances manifest through brash and rude behavior (Jones, 2012) where white working-class boys are depicted as lazy or feral (Stahl, 2015). It is well documented in US educational research that integral to the sustainability of deficit discourses are media portrayals that contribute to perceptions of youth as violent and dangerous (Rapping, 2003; Meiners, 2007). Dorfman and Schiraldi (2001) theorize that American teachers who watch the news and see young people of color constantly represented as violent criminals, internalize this image. In the United Kingdom, a similar style of news exists, which represent the white working class as "rough" and dangerous.

Pathologization through Schooling Practices

In her analysis of "race" in America, Michelle Fine (1997, p. 58) writes: "[s]chools and work … do not merely manage race; they create and enforce racial meanings." As the pathologization of the chav manifests in school contexts, it contributes heavily to the formation of certain students being considered "unteachable." Whiteness in relation to power and entitlement is well documented in society; however, in these South London schools, whiteness is often socially constructed as undesirable and equated with laddish behavior, stagnation, and a lack of ambition (Stahl, 2015). Demie and

Lewis' (2010) research in South London shows how the white working class, as an ethnic group, has specific barriers to educational attainment such as lack of community and school engagement, weaknesses in literacy, low levels of parental engagement, and lack of school-based targeted support. Equally disadvantaged and in need of special support as groups from other ethnic backgrounds, the white working class consistently do not have access to special programs aimed at raising their achievement (Gillborn & Kirton, 2000) and thus are constructed as "new race victims" (Keddie, 2013, p. 3). White working-class families, who often experience high levels of cultural and material deprivation (Charlesworth, 2000), are often blamed for their "failure" to act responsibly in regards to their own education (Reay, 2009) but such discussions conceal massive structural inequalities and barriers.

Gillborn and Kirton (2000, p. 281) show quite poignantly how white working-class boys were aware of both their class and ethnic disadvantages through discussions, which focused on their ineligibility to receive the same level of help as the English as an additional language students, despite having the same literacy proficiencies which have been shown to contribute heavily to the school-to-prison pipeline. Winn and Behizadeh (2011, p. 149) write "Students who do not speak what is often referred to as standard English, or the language of tests and textbooks, often encounter curricula and teachers that devalue their primary language"; however, in the case of white working-class students, this neglect often appears invisible (Gillborn & Kirton, 2000). The "invisibility" (Moore, 2013, pp. 5–6) of whiteness becomes a key problem when considering targeted support where, arguably, whiteness has the capacity to undermine the "right to learn" (Darling-Hammond, 1997).

THE STUDY

The current study was conducted in three school sites in South London, between 2009 and 2011, with 23 white working-class boys, aged 14–16, who were studying for their final two years of compulsory schooling in order to complete their General Certificate of Secondary Education (GCSE) qualification (Stahl, 2015). Using a qualitative research designed to document the aspirations of boys longitudinally, the project drew on observation, semistructured interviews, focus groups, and visual methods, such as photoelicitation. It has been noted that working-class males may be reluctant to speak in a standard question–answer format (McDowell, 2003), and the use of visual methods with the boys responding to pictures of their neighborhood and different types of masculinities opened up space that was more informal and allowed for a coconstruction of knowledge. In understanding how the boys were pathologized, I used discourse analysis to investigate how white working-class learners were constructed in their educational sites. All the names of the participants are pseudonyms. The study, although not an ethnography, drew on school-based ethnographic methods where classrooms, staff rooms, leadership meetings, and detentions were all observed. The school sites were located in one of the five boroughs London Challenge considered to be "the areas of most challenge" (Brighouse, 2007 p. 77) with an unemployment rate well above the average for London and England. In terms of discipline and school cultures, the education institutions in this study were very reactive environments with few proactive and positive strategies in place, creating occasionally taxing working atmospheres for both educators and students. Despite the best efforts of some educators, the school cultures in this study were largely shaped by deficient teaching and learning models, pernicious complacency, and a bigotry of low expectations. Deficit models contribute to a poor classroom climate and widespread behavior issues in UK schools (cf. Haydn, 2014) and, within these South London schools, led to the construction of many white working-class boys as "unteachable" (Archer et al., 2010, p. 89).

To understand the experiences of white working-class boys in these environments and how they are positioned for potential criminality, it is essential to understand how ability was constructed through the ideological structures of the school, the "soft structures" (Carter, 2012) or, more specifically, how ability becomes fixed to student's identities. According to Gillborn and Youdell (2000):

> the view of "ability" that currently dominates policy and practice is especially dangerous. The assumption that "ability" is a fixed, generalized and measurable potential paves the way for the operationalization of deeply racist and class-biased stereotypes. (p. 15)

The notion of ability – ascribed in staffroom discourses through frequent references, observed in the research, to white working-class students as "thick," "feral," or "f***** up" – significantly influences how relationships between students and educators are formed. Labels such as these serve to validate a system which contributes to the construction of daily practices that prevent certain children from the opportunity to learn. As classist and racist language becomes intermeshed with the school's soft structures, my participants are often depicted through deficit discourses as lacking in capacity and motivation for challenging work and, consequently, they are only given lessons which appear to be within the perceived lower capabilities.

PATHOLOGIZING THE WHITE "UNTEACHABLE"

According to Comber and Kamler (2007, p. 293), deficit discourses are dangerous and harmful belief systems that "blame certain groups in society as lacking and responsible for their lack ... the poor, the wilful, the disabled, the non-English speaking, the slow, the bottom 10%." Experiencing pathologization in both schooling and wider society, the white working-class boys in this study have limited spaces where they can access and validate identities which are respectable. I now analyze my fieldwork experiences across the three sites, showing how the white working-class boy was often rendered uncontrollable and rude with a high potential for criminal activity. This was reinforced through comparisons with other ethnic groups and references to edu-entertainment and comedy programs. Finally, I draw on my experiences researching the boys at the PRU and discuss how these boys became "prison-ready" through negative experiences with their schooling and also through their relationship with the local police.

From my fieldwork of observing classroom, staffroom, and leadership meetings, it was clear that, for many administrators and educators, their characterization of white working-class males was negative. Educators referred to white working-class boys as "lazy," "rude," "chavvy," and "dysfunctional" with allusions made to certain soap opera renderings (e.g., BBC1's Waterloo Road) and comedy shows (e.g., Little Britain). In their US study of how the media shapes teachers' perceptions of student ability, Winn and Behizadeh (2011) cite a

> vicious cycle that can develop where teachers expect students of color to misbehave and, consequently, focus on order in the classroom rather than academic rigor, discipline students of color more severely, and, in short, deny students the academic tools they need to be successful. (p. 153)

The media representations contribute to the lowering of expectations for their students, both academically and in terms of their behavior. In the "moral economy of whiteness" (Garner, 2012) where there are "grades of whiteness, as well as between whiteness and non-whiteness" (p. 446), the boundary lines are drawn around class. The perceptions of class, represented in the soft structures of the school, become dominant in the identity formation of these young men in the study. Their teachers, who are mostly white, classify the boys' disengagement as apathy and laziness. The attitude of educators regarding the white working class was that they simply needed to "try harder," "concentrate hard enough," "apply themselves to the work," or "care about their studies" (Field notes, April 2010). When the boys were asked how they thought their teachers saw them, many drew attention to negative labeling, saying the teachers thought they were annoying. One participant, Luke, said, "I'm able but I'm lazy, that's what I think they think."

Contributing to their identity construction, many highlighted gender as playing a significant role whereby they considered girls to be more docile, and being loud or brash was part of being male. Tom claimed, "Yea, I think boys usually stand up more than girls in like classes – and are more usually louder and all that." According to Alan, "Girls are like – they laugh amongst themselves. But boys are like loud and stuff." In his research on white working-class identity in Essex, UK schools, Preston (2009) illustrates what occurs when the dominant social constructions of whiteness influenced the behavior of a group of boys, and vice versa, the boys:

> took pleasure in language, humour, play and what the male students referred to as "larging it." By playing with, parodying and inflating their ascribed identity, the students may have achieved a partial demystification of the irrelevance of the qualification to their working lives. They were using the nature of "Essex-ness" with all of its negative (and positive) connotations in a reflexive manner. Indeed, it may be considered that there is considerable strength in this identity and in "recapturing" certain working class, white identities for cultural work … (p. 55)

Picower (2009, p. 201) documents a rhetoric in US schools which asserts that "people of color should be able to pick themselves up by their straps" or else they are "lazy and victims of their circumstances"; this contributes to fueling deficit thinking in relation to African American and other minority students. In the United Kingdom, as the media both represents and parodies the chav as innately "unteachable," it is important to consider how the "chav caricature implies poverty is the result of personal choices and moral deficiencies-laziness" (Ginsburgh, 2012, para. 2). Terry, a white working-class boy who was a consistent underperformer in a mainstream school setting, felt he lacked good relationships with his teachers:

> Terry: Well most teacher I know think I don't do what I'm told, I don't do my work … but it don't bother me.
>
> Garth: How do you want teachers to see you?
>
> Terry: Like teachers who don't teach me and when they put comments in like they – why do they need to get involved? Like if I do my lessons my teachers are the only ones that tell me what to do, 'cause they ain't my teachers so …

Terry here refers to his reputation around the school where teachers who did not teach him were, in his eyes, aware of his learner behavior and felt they could comment openly to him. His awareness of his reputation contributes heavily to how he engages with the teachers he comes in contact with and his identity as a learner. While this occurred with other students in the school, it seemed to be more apparent with boys, specifically white working-class boys.

In contrast to the pathologization of other ethnic groups, the educators in these schools openly described the white working-class boys in a medley of racist, classist, and misandrist language, but these deficit discourses were not seen as problematic, arguably due to the whiteness of these boys. In my conversations with one teacher, it was clear that the image she had of Ben was that he must have come from "generations of unemployment" which was, in fact, untrue (Field notes, April 4, 2010). It was disconcerting that the teacher equated the student's misbehavior as generational, as "worklessness passed culturally from parent to child," where idleness becomes a fixed and faulty disposition (Macdonald, Shildrick, & Furlong, 2013, p. 203). As Toshalis (2012) notes, teachers consistently deflect blame for student academic deficiencies away from themselves, where students become constructed as:

> culturally deprived, academically unmotivated, or cognitively/behaviorally challenged … these deficit discourses … [define] students as sub-standard, a practice that not only highlights but often reproduces the students' marginalized status by legitimating the institutional structures that track them into arenas where expectations and resources are diminished. (p. 12)

Clearly, such a pejorative culture fosters neither growth nor success but, rather, sets out to prove an outcome that has already been predetermined, with educators, administrations, and students continually repeating a cycle of failure, complacency, and disadvantage. Building on an extensive body of US scholarship regarding the effect of low expectations and racial stereotyping in education systems, Nussbaum and Steele (2007) contend that African American disengagement and "disidentification" with academic work is the result of school-based racist and bigoted practices. According to Nussbaum and Steele, African American students experience a "stereotype threat," whereby they experience negative stereotyping concerning their innate academic ability. My own fieldwork in South London indicates that white working-class boys can be the target of negative stereotyping by educators:

> Mrs. Brown comes into the staff room flustered and sits down next to me and a few other teachers. A teacher asks her if she is all right. She says she isn't and she's just had an argument with Tommy who was disrupting her class. She describes him as "thinking he's 'hot shit'" when – in her eyes – he will "just end up a benefit-thieving chav." Brown goes on to make further negative comments concerning his parents who she would have seen last week for parent's evening. (Field Notes, May 8, 2010)

While I was witness to the misbehavior of white working-class boys, the words of Mrs. Brown, which were said in frustration, highlight a certain mindset around expectations. Students are likely to intentionally disengage from schoolwork rather than engage in a struggle and confirm educators' low expectations. Stereotype threat is directly linked to negative societal stereotyping of intelligence and competence where students "being at risk of confirming, as self-characteristic, a negative stereotype about one's group," come to fulfill "the racial stereotype about their intellectual ability" (Steele & Aronson, 1995, p. 797). As a result, low expectations for both behavior and academic achievement became normative, whereby these young men, "raised on a steady diet of dumbed-down reductive basic curriculum turn out as we could have predicted: uninterested in reading and writing, resistant to, or woefully unprepared for, the intellectual work of the higher grades" (Brown, 1991, p. 223). It has been argued that disengagement and "disidentification" with academic work are the results of bigotry in schools (Nussbaum & Steele, 2007).

Within sociological work on working-class disaffection, there is often an emphasis on schools imposing middle-class values, as there is little doubt about the education system rewards, and even valorizes, middle-class capital rather than working-class capital (Bourdieu & Passeron, 1977). In her study of "hidden" curriculums in Australian schools, Rahman (2013, p. 663) links the participation and performance of students of culturally or linguistically diverse backgrounds to their ability to incorporate middle-class values and thus, for all intents and purposes, assimilate into the middle-class contexts. Success in school is "not simply a matter of academic ability but assumes a reservoir of expertise necessary to understand and play the system" (MacBeath, 2009, p. 82). Or, as Rahman (2013) argues, there exist sets of "unwritten rules, regulations, standards and expectations that form part of the learning process" (p. 660). Within this part of South London, it was the Nigerian immigrants that espoused middle-class values and embodied an "ideal" learner identity (studious, hard-working, etc.). I observed many classrooms where the behavior of Nigerian students was held up as an exemplar to motivate white working-class students to "pull their socks up" and "get on with their work":

> During a routine test preparation for their GCSEs, Michael got off track and was making funny faces at his peers. The teacher, Mr. Wood, stopped the lesson and told Michael he needed to act like Bintu and Alma, the two female Nigerian students sitting near the front of the class taking copious notes. Mr. Wood said to Michael, "Someday they will probably be your boss as a university education counts more than a couple of GCSEs and they have what it takes." (Field Notes, June 10, 2010)

In this case study, the Nigerian immigrants' engagement with norms which were conducive to academic success, juxtaposed against white working-class nonengagement, became an access point for the structuring of deficit discourses. As deficit discourses become embedded, the boys felt devalued and enacted certain behaviors, which gained them validation from their peers but which transgressed the norms of the school, as seen in Preston's research where "larging it" becomes a process of "recapturing" a certain working-class white identity (p. 55).

The Pupil Referral Unit and Interaction with the Police

As part of the wider research project, I focused on five white British working-class boys in a South London PRU, which is an alternative coeducational provision for students who have been expelled from mainstream schooling. The white working-class boys attending the PRU had experienced the institutional practices of educational exclusion, separated out due to problematic behavior whereby the Local Education Authority had decided, often without any input from either the boys, their parents, or the school officials, that mainstream schooling was not working for these students. While the majority of the United Kingdom has not seen metal detectors, locker searches, or a specialist police force in their schooling, the presence of police and continued surveillance within the PRU was much stronger than the mainstream school sites, with frequent mobile phone and contraband searches. McGrew (2008) has argued that youth in poor urban districts are actually "education's prisoners." He documents overpolicing and zero tolerance policies, which enable school security and campus police to punish students for the smallest infractions.

The PRU, as an educational site, faced many daily challenges. Students, of which there was a small cohort of approximately 15 students in year 11, only attended the unit three days a week to complete work for their GCSEs and the remaining two days a week, they attended vocational placement training. The teachers were faced with the task of teaching the entire GCSE courses within the confines of three days a week and were further burdened by nonattendance. As a formal qualification, the GCSE is not designed to be taught in this way, and the chances of gaining these qualifications were, therefore, systemically rendered as minimal. Despite a colorful layout and engaging décor, the physical setting was claustrophobic, which made it challenging for students to concentrate and difficult for teachers to handle high-level behavior problems when they occurred. Pupil conduct was often problematic and when one student "kicked off," it would spread quickly among the other students until exclusions were enacted. The transitory nature of the students made it difficult to maintain a good institutional ethos. In order to entice the students to attend, lunch was provided and they were not required to wear uniforms, in contrast to conventional standards in UK schooling. However, this informality arguably had a counterproductive effect as the students, dressed in "trackies" and "hoodies," found it difficult to turn off the culture of the street and the identity performances ingrained within that culture.

Winn and Behizadeh (2011) argue that zero tolerance policies "create a police state in urban public schools and detract from focused work on education and literacy," where so-called "urban pedagogies" are more concerned with discipline and control than intellectual rigor. Urban pedagogies were in full operation in the PRU where there was a much more authoritative teaching style than in standard classrooms, often in response to boys being openly defiant and hot tempered. In his study of the school-to-prison pipeline in the United States, McGrew (2008, p. 162) notes that in our "current historical period society is generally compassionate towards the children of privilege, who enjoy extended periods of adolescence, and are valued and forgiven," whereas children of poverty face various levels of racially charged pathologization. While there are differences between the United States – as an "incarceration nation" – and other Westernized contexts, Winn and Behizadeh (2011) note that US practices around juvenile justice systems in the United Kingdom and Canada have become increasingly Americanized by focusing on youth who are labeled "at risk" of committing crime. In my conversations with students attending the PRU, each had their own complex relationship with the police; however, every participant I interviewed saw the police as corrupt and undependable:

> No, man. I just don't even like the police – they walk past and go … I don't even, I don't even look them in the face …. (Calum)

In describing how race plays out for the South London streets, Alfie and Tom describe, in a focus group, a sensitivity around race which, they felt, made it more likely that they would be arrested if a physical attack was to occur:

> Tom: I don't reckon [the police] do a good enough job – like say I got into a fight with a black person –
>
> Alfie: – it would be a racist attack.
>
> Tom: If a white person, if a group of white people jumped a black person that would be … even if it wasn't … even if they were like … they went up to the first person they

> see, they would see it as a racist attack. But if a group of black people jumped a white person ... but if a group of black people jumped a white person that would just be labelled as like a gang.
>
> Alfie: When like my mate, yea, him and his cousin ... well his cousin's having a fight with some Muslim kid and then some other Muslim kid come and my mate jumped in and then his mate jumped in and he got arrested for a racial attack.
>
> Tom: Yeah, the government is scared to touch anyone who is not English. Like you see all these terrorists and all that at war. But they can't touch all these people in case they get a bad name for themselves.

Making links to racial profiling, many participants referenced how the police were more likely to ignore crime than actively engage in stopping it, and several participants expressed a paranoia of being framed for crimes they did not commit, where police may, "try to get me nicked or something" (Terry). Liam, a student who started out as part of the study in a mainstream school site, but then was referred to the PRU, describes a recent encounter with the police:

> Liam: Well, I was unlucky. I got arrested for stuff I didn't do.
>
> Garth: OK, what did they arrest you for?
>
> Liam: Well, apparently I was trying to steal a bike when I never. Then someone broke a window on a big building site and then – we matched the descriptions of the kids doing it so we got arrested.
>
> Garth: So did this happen recently?
>
> Liam: No, quite a while ago.
>
> Garth: So how old were you then?
>
> Liam: Probably about a year ago – like [age] 13.

In analyzing Liam's social and learner identity, he was a very conflicted individual. Scared of his own temper, he was a very quiet and disengaged student who did not have good relationships with his teachers, whom he saw as uncaring and apathetic. In considering the prison pipeline metaphor, when schools are unpleasant places, individuals often search for spaces where they feel valued such as the street which, in low-income neighborhoods, contributes to a high risk of associating with some form of criminal activity. Despite being small for his age, Liam tended to overcompensate on the street, picking fights with other boys in an effort to perform a "tough" working-class masculinity that, on the streets of South London, carried a currency as authentic and respectable.

The most significant aspect of the boys' interaction with the police was the frequent use of "stop and search procedures" which, as a form of racial and class-based profiling, has faced widespread criticism for targeting working class or urban poor populations. Dressed in tracksuits, South London youth – and the boys in this study – often adopt cultural signifiers associated with chav style. Looking "rough" can be an important part of masculine identity construction in South London, but the adoption of the chav style, which many of the boys in the PRU did engage with, made the likelihood of engaging with "stop and search" more likely.

> Greg: Because whenever I'm out with my friends – once a week we probably get stopped and searched. There's about ten of us and we go to the youth club. And when we come out of the youth club it's like nine o'clock so we'll either go to Patterson Park until half nine, until we have to go in. And police would just drive past and stop and search us. 'Cause they think we're up to no good.

As part of the CCTV surveillance culture in the United Kingdom, it is important to note that these stop and search procedures were equally as abundant within the PRU as they were outside on the street, contributing to the paranoia the boys articulated. Greg, who had no police record, has captured the surveillance techniques used by South London police whereby he is being profiled due to where he lives. Upon entering the PRU, the boys had to turn in their phones and were padded down for weapons; thus, the educators replicated the stop and search behavior of the police.

IMPLICATIONS

Prevailing social arrangements and patterns of culture within schools remain largely socially oppressive for the working class in the United Kingdom. In the case of white working-class students, this neglect often appears invisible (Gillborn & Kirton, 2000). Garner (2012) reminds us that whiteness "is a position of relative privilege, albeit highly uneven, contingent and situational" (p. 446). Within this case study, whiteness was interwoven with deficit discourses and the practices of teachers in powerful ways which contributed to failing to break the cycle of poverty and potential criminality. According to Winn and Behizadeh (2011, p. 163) "Disrupting and dismantling the school-to-prison pipeline requires research and action challenging the connections between schools and prisons and illuminating the school practices that halt the movement of students to prisons." Dismantling the prison pipeline involves educators contending with their own deficit discourses. Solomona, Portelli, Daniel, and Campbell (2005, p. 149) assert that if educators are not forced to evaluate how their personal attitudes, social positioning, and racial ascription inform their interactions with students, the teaching profession will continue to poorly service students from disadvantaged backgrounds. A few educators I encountered in this study recognized the classist and racist language evidence when discussing white working-class disengagement and behavior. Thus, I argue, that my research supports a consideration that the normative practices embedded in the "soft structures" contribute heavily to the school-to-prison pipeline. Furthermore, given how raising white working-class aspiration is very much on the government radar in the United Kingdom (Select Committee on Education, 2014), it is interesting to note that none of the institutions which participated in the study had any strategy in place for the raising of aspirations, although many had quite robust behavior management systems in place.

CONCLUSION

With the research presented here, we see the tangled relationship "between school structures and practises, students' biographical identities, and educational inequalities" (Youdell, 2004, p. 409). We also see how constituting a respectable working-class masculinity often works in conflict with the practices of formal schooling, leading to ongoing pathologization. In considering the school-to-prison pipeline, we must remember the rejection of schooling for many of these working-class boys is a (gendered and classed) performance – for the most part they are excluding themselves from educational spaces which have already excluded them.

This chapter has critically explored how "whiteness and class are articulated together in educational settings" (Preston, 2009, p. 13) and are informed by the performance of traditional masculinities. While "white working class educational underachievement is far more complex than either any cultural deficit analysis or failing school thesis allows" (Reay, 2009, p. 23), this chapter sought to develop one angle in the white working-class disaffection literature, specifically how the pathologization of white working class is normalized within three South London schools. The white identity of my participants contributed to how they were constructed as "unteachable" in these institutions.

REFERENCES

Archer, L., Hollingworth, S., & Mendick, H. (2010). *Urban youth and schooling: The experiences and identities of educationally 'at risk' young people*. Berkshire: Open University Press.

Bonnett, A. (1998). How the British working class became white: The symbolic (re)formation of racialized capitalism. *Journal of Historical Sociology*, *11*(3), 317–340.

Bourdieu, P., & Passeron, J. C. (1977). *Reproduction in education, society and culture*. London: Sage.

Brighouse, T. (2007). The London challenge – A personal view. In T. Brighouse & L. Fullick (Eds.), *Education in a global city: Essays from London* (pp. 71–94). London: Institute of Education.

Brown, R. (1991). Policy and rationalization of schools. In E. H. Hiebert (Ed.), *Literacy for a diverse society: Perspective, practices, and policies* (pp. 217–227). New York, NY: Teachers College Press.

Candlin, C. N., & Crichton, J. (2011). Introduction. In C. N. Candlin & J. Crichton (Eds.), *Discourses of deficit* (pp. 1–22). London: Palgrave MacMillan.

Carter, P. (2012). *Stubborn roots: Race, culture, and inequality in U.S. and South African schools*. Oxford: Oxford University Press.

Cassen, R. D., & Kingdon, G. (2007). *Tackling low educational achievement*. York: Joseph Rowntree Foundation.

Charlesworth, S. J. (2000). *The phenomenology of working class experience*. Cambridge: University Press.

Comber, B., & Kamler, B. (2007). Getting out of deficit: Pedagogies of reconnection. *Teaching Education*, *15*(3), 293–310.

Connell, R. W. (1989). Cool guys, swots and wimps: The interplay of masculinity and education. *Oxford Review of Education*, *15*(3), 291–303.

Crenshaw, K. (1991). Review mapping the margins: Intersectionality, identity politics, and violence against women of color. *Stanford Law Review*, *43*(6), 1241–1299.

Darling-Hammond, L. (1997). *The right to learn: A blueprint for creating schools that work*. San Francisco, CA: Jossey-Bass.

Demie, F., & Lewis, K. (2010). White working class achievement: An ethnographic study of barriers to learning in schools. *Educational Studies*, *33*(2), 1–20.

Dorfman, L., & Schiraldi, V. (2001). *Off balance: Youth, race & crime in the news*. Retrieved from http://www.buildingblocksforyouth.org/media/media.html

Evans, G. (2006). *Educational failure and working class white children in Britain*. Basingstoke: Palgrave Macmillan.

Fine, M. (1997). Witnessing whiteness. In M. Fine, L. Weis, L. C. Powell, & L. M. Wong (Eds.), *Off white: Readings on race, power, and society* (pp. 57–66). New York, NY: Routledge.

Francis, B. (2006). Heroes or zeroes? The discursive positioning of 'underachieving boys' in English neo-liberal education policy. *Journal of Education Policy*, *21*(2), 187–200.

Garner, S. (2012). A moral economy of whiteness: Behaviours, belonging and Britishness. *Ethnicities*, *12*(4), 445–464.

Gillborn, D., & Kirton, A. (2000). White heat: Racism, under-achievement, and white working-class boys. *Inclusion and Special Educational Needs*, *4*(4), 271–288.

Gillborn, D., & Youdell, D. (2000). *Rationing education: Policy, practice, reform and equity.* Buckingham: Open University Press.

Gilroy, P. (2004). *Melancholia and multiculture.* Retrieved from https://www.opendemocracy.net/arts-multiculturalism/article_2035.jsp

Ginsburgh, N. (2012). 'Chavs', class and representation. *International Socialism, 136,* 111–130.

Haydn, T. (2014). To what extent is behaviour a problem in English schools? Exploring the scale and prevalence of deficits in classroom climate. *Review of Education, 2*(1), 1–34.

Hayward, K., & Yar, M. (2006). The 'chav' phenomenon: Consumption, media and the construction of a new underclass. *Crime Media Culture, 2*(1), 9–28.

Humphries, S. (1981). *Hooligans or rebels? An oral history of working-class childhood and youth 1889–1939.* Oxford: Basil Blackwell.

Jones, O. (2012). *Chavs: The demonization of the working class.* London: Verso.

Keddie, A. (2013). 'There isn't kind of a White History Month or anything like that for them': Equity, schooling and the problematics of group identity politics. *International Journal of Inclusive Education, 18*(8), 809–822.

Mac an Ghaill, M. (1994). *The making of men: Masculinities, sexualities and schooling.* Buckingham: Open University Press.

MacBeath, J. (2009). Border crossings. *Improving Schools, 12*(1), 81–92.

Macdonald, R., Shildrick, T., & Furlong, A. (2013). In search of 'intergenerational cultures of worklessness': Hunting the Yeti and shooting zombies. *Critical Social Policy, 34*(2), 199–219.

Martino, W., & Pallotta-Chiarolli, M. (2003). *So what's a boy?* Maidenhead: Open University Press.

McCulloch, G. (1998). *Failing the ordinary child?: The theory and practice of working-class secondary education.* Buckingham: Open University Press.

McDowell, L. (2003). *Redundant masculinities?: Employment change and white working class youth.* Malden, MA: Blackwell.

McGrew, K. (2008). *Education's prisoners: Schooling, the political economy, and the prison industrial complex.* New York, NY: Peter Lang.

Meiners, E. R. (2007). *Right to be hostile: Schools, prisons, and the making of public enemies.* New York, NY: Routledge.

Moore, H. (2013). Shades of whiteness? English villagers, Eastern European migrants, and the intersection of race and class in rural England. *Critical Race and Whiteness Studies, 9*(1), 1–19.

Nayak, A. (2009). Beyond the pale: Chavs, youth, and social class. In K. P. Sveinsson (Ed.), *Who cares about the white working class?* (pp. 28–35). London: Runnymede Perspectives.

Neill, S. (2001). Unacceptable pupil behaviour: A survey analysed for the National Union of Teachers. University of Warwick, Institute of Education, Warwick. Retrieved from https://www.teachers.org.uk/files/active/0/Violrep2.pdf

Nelson, J. D., Stahl, G., & Wallace, D. (2015). Race, class, and gender in boys' education: Repositioning intersectionality theory. *Culture, Society & Masculinities, 7*(2), 171–187.

Nussbaum, A. D., & Steele, C. M. (2007). Situational disengagement and persistence in the face of adversity. *Journal of Experimental Social Psychology, 43*(1), 127–134.

OFSTED. (2014). Early years annual report 2012/13. Office for Standards in Education, Children's Services and Skills, Manchester. Retrieved from www.ofsted.gov.uk/earlyyearsannualreport1213

Phoenix, A. (1997). 'I'm white! So what?' The construction of whiteness for young Londoners. In M. Fine, L. Weis, L. C. Powell, & L. M. Wong (Eds.), *Off white: Readings on race, power, and society* (pp. 187–197). New York, NY: Routledge.

Picower, B. (2009). The unexamined whiteness of teaching: How white teachers maintain and enact dominant racial ideologies. *Race Ethnicity and Education, 12*(2), 197–215.

Preston, J. (2009). *Whiteness and class in education*. Dordrecht: Springer.

Rahman, K. (2013). Belonging and learning to belong in school: The implications of the hidden curriculum for indigenous students. *Discourse: Studies in the Cultural Politics of Education, 34*(5), 660–672.

Rapping, E. (2003). *Law and justice as seen on TV*. New York, NY: New York University Press.

Reay, D. (2001). Finding or losing yourself? Working-class relationships to education. *Journal of Education Policy, 16*(4), 333–346.

Reay, D. (2009). Making sense of white working class educational underachievement. In K. P. Sveinsson (Ed.), *Who cares about the white working class?* (pp. 22–28). London: Runnymede Perspectives.

Reay, D. (2010). Identity-making in schools and classrooms. In M. Wetherall & C. Talpade Mohanty (Eds.), *The Sage handbook of identities* (pp. 277–294). Los Angeles, CA: Sage.

Select Committee on Education. (2014). *Underachievement in education by white working class children: 1st report*. Session 2013–2014. UK Parliament, House of Commons, London.

Skeggs, B. (2002). *Formations of class and gender*. Nottingham: Sage.

Skeggs, B. (2004). *Class, self, culture*. London: Routledge.

Skeggs, B. (2005). The making of class and gender through visualizing moral subject formation. *Sociology, 39*(5), 965–982.

Solomona, R. P., Portelli, J. P., Daniel, B., & Campbell, A. (2005). The discourse of denial: How white teacher candidates construct race, racism and 'white privilege'. *Race Ethnicity and Education, 8*(2), 147–169.

Stahl, G. (2015). *Aspiration, identity and neoliberalism: Educating white working-class boys*. London: Routledge.

Steele, C. M., & Aronson, J. (1995). Stereotype threat and the intellectual test performance of African Americans. *Journal of Personality and Social Psychology, 69*(5), 797–811.

Strand, S. (2014). Ethnicity, gender, social class, and achievement gaps at age 16: Intersectionality and 'getting it' for the white working class. *Research Papers in Education, 29*(2), 131–171.

Toshalis, E. (2012). The rhetoric of care: Preservice teacher discourses that depoliticize, deflect, and deceive. *Urban Review, 44*, 1–35.

Tyler, I., & Bennett, B. (2010). 'Celebrity chav': Fame, femininity and social class. *European Journal of Cultural Studies, 13*(3): 375–393.

Willis, P. (1977). *Learning to labor: How working class kids get working class jobs*. New York, NY: Columbia University Press.

Winn, M. T., & Behizadeh, N. (2011). The right to be literate: Literacy, education and the school-to-prison pipeline. *Review of Research in Education, 35*, 147–173.

Youdell, D. (2004). Engineering school markets, constituting schools and subjectivating students: The bureaucratic, institutional and classroom dimensions of educational triage. *Journal of Education Policy, 19*(4), 407–431.

CHAPTER 6

"WHAT ARE WE RESTORING?" BLACK TEACHERS ON RESTORATIVE DISCIPLINE

Hilary Lustick

ABSTRACT

School leaders seeking to implement restorative justice discipline practices in diverse urban schools have a series of subtle and crucial decisions to make that are omitted in the literature on alternatives to suspension. The current chapter examines one group of Black teachers from a larger study of schools using restorative practices. In interviews and observations, these teachers demonstrated Du Bois's theory of Double Consciousness; they recognized both the institutional dynamics of the school's discipline policy and the ways in which enactment of that policy ultimately replicated traditional racial inequality. They repeatedly challenged restorative theory and practices in terms of their relevance to students whose everyday reality involved police violence, community violence, and impoverished living conditions. While praising its potential as a foundation for communication and trust building, they perceived its implementation as a way to restore obedience for the student and restore order in the school. While stemming from one group of teachers in one school setting, my findings beg important questions

The School to Prison Pipeline: The Role of Culture and Discipline in School
Advances in Race and Ethnicity in Education, Volume 4, 113–134

ISSN: 2051-2317/doi:10.1108/S2051-231720160000004007

for school leaders, researchers, and policymakers concerned with school discipline reform.

Keywords: School discipline; restorative justice; culturally responsive education

> This, then, is the end of his striving: to be a co-worker in the kingdom of culture.
>
> Du Bois, *The Souls of Black Folk*

School leaders seeking to implement restorative justice discipline practices in diverse urban schools have a series of subtle and crucial decisions to make that are omitted in the literature on alternatives to suspension. My ethnographic research on three New York City public schools suggests that racial and cultural dynamics complicate how students and teachers experience restorative practices. Taken from this larger study, this chapter focuses on the experiences of a group of Black teachers from one of these schools. These teachers repeatedly challenged restorative theories and practices in terms of their relevance to students whose everyday reality involved police violence, community violence, and impoverished living conditions. They supported the theory of restorative justice but felt that, in practice, it did not promote authentic trust and relationship building among staff and students, and restore order in the school. Instead, they felt, it was used to restore obedience for the student and restore order in the school. My findings beg important questions for school leaders, researchers, and policymakers concerned with school discipline reform.

While this study was underway, the New York City mayor's office reformed the School Discipline Code in an effort to reduce citywide suspension rates (New York City Department of Education, 2015a, 2015b). In contrast with the logic of zero tolerance policies, which for decades had required principals to suspend students for violent and other extreme misbehavior, this new policy required principals to seek superintendent permission before granting a principal-level suspension. Schools were explicitly encouraged to apply restorative practices in lieu of suspension. However, schools were still heavily laden with the artifacts of zero tolerance logic. Most visibly, the New York Police Department officials remained employed as safety agents, and routine morning searches (including the use of metal detectors) were left in place. The school this study focuses on, which I call Riveredge, evinced the tensions between zero tolerance logic and restorative practices.

Under the new policy, the principal, Cody,[1] knew the district would frown upon frequent requests for suspension. Yet, safety agents and other principals in the building were more accustomed to zero tolerance logic; that is, the belief that certain extreme misbehaviors are best met with suspension or expulsion. The tenets of restorative philosophy frequently conflicted with the need to maintain trust among building-level administrators, all of whom were more likely to suspend students rather than seek a restorative alternative. Rather than wholly succumb to or eschew zero tolerance logic, Cody was strategic; he was more likely to suspend students when a disciplinary incident involved other schools in the building, but allowed restorative practices for incidents involving students and staff at Riveredge. Colocation, therefore, added an extra layer of complexity to the already-highly political implementation of a restorative discipline program.

Cody conceptualized this fine balance as a matter of pleasing multiple stakeholders: his fellow principals, the New York City Department of Education, his faculty, and his students. He did not seem to recognize that, in trying to maintain any sort of balance between zero tolerance logic and restorative theory, he was undermining the larger project many faculty and staff espoused as primary goals of restorative practice: to dismantle structural racism within the school. Riveredge had a deep commitment to education as liberation, as described in its core school values and curriculum. Faculty, particularly Black faculty, connected this curriculum to discipline policy. However, Cody and other administrators did not share this structural analysis of school discipline policy. There was thus, as Du Bois (1987) would describe it, a Double Consciousness on the part of Black faculty, who consistently perceived the hypocritical nature of Riveredge's discipline procedures, but found themselves having to condone and even reinforce these same procedures in order to maintain their good standing as staff. As evinced in my findings, their ability to earn youth trust and help youth understand the nature of structural racism in the school actually made them indispensable to the administration, because they were able to help maintain the order and legitimacy of Riveredge's erratic and paradoxical discipline practice.

CONCEPTUAL FRAMEWORK: DISCIPLINE REFORM AS RESISTANCE TO "DOUBLE CONSCIOUSNESS"

Du Bois (1987) coined the term "double consciousness" to describe how Black Americans engage in professional and public American society, despite feeling the constant psychological stress of White prejudice and discrimination. He defined the Black American experience as "always looking at one's self through the eyes of others, of measuring one's soul by the tape of a world that looks on in amused contempt and pity" (Du Bois, 1987, p. 3). Prejudice, specifically against the Black race in the United States, was a force of discouragement that Du Bois argued was more durable and formidable than slavery. Prejudice outlived slavery as a means of preventing Blacks from succeeding. Blacks would not get rid of the harmful effects of dual consciousness until they could cast off the constraints of constant prejudice and judgment.

Prejudice prevents the "Negro," a term by which Du Bois connoted not only the individual Black American but also Blacks as a cultural and political collective, from becoming "co-workers in the kingdom of culture" (Du Bois, 1987, p. 2). Caught in a constant battle between how he sees himself and how others see him, the doubly conscious individual loses the opportunity for "self-development," and the organization cannot create a fully inclusive culture.

Strong teacher–student and teacher–teacher relationships are a means of resistance, as they provide an opportunity for Double Consciousness to recede and for individuals to bond over shared hopes, dreams, and goals. Valenzuela (1999) emphasized the power of teacher–student relationships for not only improving student achievement but also supporting Mexican American students' identity development. Bryk and Schneider (2004) operationalized "relational trust" as "a combination of mutual respect, personal regard, and trust among teachers, parents, and administrators" (Gregory & Ripski, 2008). Gregory and Ripski (2008) extended these findings to school discipline, documenting that students are less likely to behave disruptively in the classroom of a teacher whom they trust. Interestingly, they found this correlation to be higher for Black students than for any other group – in other words, Black student behavior was more strongly tied to students' trust in their teacher than any other racial group.

I frame my study with the presumption that racism exists in schools and must be directly resisted in order for it not to mediate the impact of discipline reform. This frame is supported by persistent data suggesting racial disproportionality persists even when principals implement restorative practices. The following two sections demonstrate, respectively, how racial prejudice has impacted discipline reform, and how restorative practices are – in theory – a means of interrupting racial prejudice through relational trust building.

RACE, RESTORATION, AND THE DISCIPLINE DEBATE

For nearly two decades, research has called for alternatives to *zero tolerance policies*, uniform compulsory suspension, and expulsion for certain extreme misbehaviors, that correlate with alienation from school and demonstrate little success in preventing future misbehavior (American Psychological Association, 2008). These policies became popular in the wake of an early 1990s "moral panic" (Herr & Anderson, 2010) around school violence, as well as the 1994 Gun Free School Safety Act passed under the Clinton Administration, after which suspension and expulsion rates spiked for students of all races (Kafka, 2011). Rates increased most dramatically for students of color, particularly for African American students and mostly for subjectively determined misdemeanors such as "insubordination" (Skiba, 2013).

Research has demonstrated that nonpunitive approaches to conflict, such as restorative conferences and positive behavioral interventions and supports, correlate with a drop in suspension rates (Chin, Rowdy, Jimerson, & Rime, 2012; Christle, Nelson, & Jolivette, 2004; Hamilton, 2008; Osher, Bear, Sprague, & Doyle, 2010). Based on this research, in early 2014, the United States Federal Departments of Education and Justice jointly launched the Supportive School Discipline Initiative, which pushes schools to promote a "safe and supportive" learning environment (US Department of Education, 2014). The Department of Justice threatens to investigate any school suspected of disproportionality in school discipline and has already made good on this threat in three different cities (Lustick & Dumas, 2014). New York's new restrictions on principal-level suspensions are an example of how districts are responding to the federal-level push for stronger school culture and fewer suspensions.

One puzzling finding is that restorative practices actually *replicate* racial disproportionality in traditional school discipline (Vincent, Tobin, Hawken, & Frank, 2012). This may be due to the fact that practices held in the context of racial prejudice are likely to disproportionately disadvantage minority youth in high-needs schools (Gregory, Skiba, & Noguera, 2010). Yet, the way current policy is framed, schools are held accountable for reducing racial disproportionality in discipline, while levels of relational trust and racial prejudice – integral as they may be to improving school culture – go virtually undiscussed.

RESTORATIVE PRACTICES: THEORY AND TERMINOLOGY

Restorative practices (Amstutz & Mullet, 2005) vary from mediations to structured circles, but they stem from the criminal justice model of *restorative justice* (Zehr, 2002). Their goal is to build trust and accountability through daily or weekly proactive practices, such as *community-building circles*. When conflict occurs among students or between staff and students, *restorative conferences* are employed to repair the harm done to those involved. These practices are documented to reduce the need for suspension (Chin et al., 2012; Hamilton, 2008) and are often heralded as a means of reducing racial disproportionality in school discipline. For example, Knight and Wadhwa (2014) examine how a small group of teachers within a larger comprehensive high school used restorative practices to help students view their struggles in school in the context of larger systems of oppression they faced in society.

From how these practices are described, it is clear that they capture the political imagination in a way that almost preempts the need for critical examination. In their critiques of zero tolerance policies, Gonzalez (2012) and Browne-Dianis (2011) call for restorative practices as a means of avoiding suspension and improving school-based relationships. The research question for the larger study, as well as for the smaller one, is why do restorative practices replicate the same rates of racial disproportionality when suspensions are used? This chapter hones in on the underlying mechanisms of prejudice and power that play a role in replication of inequality in discipline.

DATA AND METHODS

Site Selection

The data for this chapter is part of a larger multisite ethnography of restorative practice implementation. The current chapter focuses on one of the three schools in this larger study. Riveredge is a 9–12th grade school located on the third floor of a multischool urban building, where the four other schools are also high schools. It enrolled 206 students in the 2014–2015 school year, including 3.2% Asian, 38.5% Black, 47.4% Hispanic, and 9.3% White students (New York City Department of Education, 2015a, 2015b). Approximately 50% of teaching staff identified as White and 50% as Black or

African American. According to its website and founding members of the staff,[2] the school's mission is to provide a more peaceful and open environment for students than what staff saw as the "typical" urban public school, and this involves resolving conflict through discussion rather than suspension.

Of my three school sites, I chose Riveredge for this study because of its paradoxical relationship with restorative practices. Veteran staff talked about restorative philosophy as a political as well as disciplinary tool, and the administration was committed to implementing it consistently across the school. Meanwhile, there was dissent among teachers about how it was being implemented, and there were ways in which it also jeopardized the school's reputation in the eyes of other building staff and the neighborhood. While there were elements of these same tensions at my other two school sites, the staff at Riveredge displayed a unique transparency in sharing them with me. Additionally, the Black educators I interviewed displayed Double Consciousness: a complex analysis of the role race played in complicating what they could also see as a rational, formalized restorative practice implementation.

The Role of Restorative Practices at Riveredge

Since the founding principal left five years ago, the school's academic performance has declined and so has its cultural health; one teacher reported that hallway fights were breaking out on a daily basis. Cody, who had become the school leader a year and a half ago, had introduced the language of restorative practices to staff and students as a way of simultaneously addressing school safety and culture. He was committed to increasing staff and student use of restorative conference to resolve persistent behavioral issues. He also increased the use of community-building circles to enhance the culture of the school, with more teachers being expected to lead community-building circles in advisory at least once per week. Interviews with Cody and two other administrators – all of whom are White – revealed a commitment to restorative practices that mirror the literature. They described restorative practices as a means of not only reducing the overall suspension rates but also supporting racially and socioeconomically marginalized populations in particular.

Data Collection and Analysis

In addition to observing restorative practices and interviewing the students and staff who participated in them, I also attended school events and staff meetings relevant to school discipline. The data for this study came from observations at a staff retreat and follow-up interviews with several Black teachers who participated. The purpose of this retreat was for staff to share their perspectives on restorative practices. The administration facilitated a debate between the philosophies of "restorative discipline" and "traditional" (i.e., punitive) discipline.[3] In the large group conversation, a number of Black veteran educators – all of similar ages, in their 30s and 40s – deemed "restorative" and "traditional" as false dichotomy. They felt this dichotomy obscured the ways in which the school could still be oppressive toward its most vulnerable student populations despite using restorative practices.

Seeking to better understand their critique, I sat with a group of these educators during the small-group discussion. I then interviewed four of them individually in the coming week: Raymond, who had taught English at the school for eight years; Sylvie, who taught American History; Ruth, a social worker and founding staff member; and Theresa, who had taught for four years elsewhere but was, as of this year, Riveredge's first restorative coordinator. All were educated in urban public schools and described themselves as coming from similar cultural and socioeconomic backgrounds to those of their students. More detailed information on these participants is shown in Table 1.

For the larger study, I transcribed all interviews myself. Interviews and fieldnotes were coded using the en vivo method of coding (Saldana, 2009), which strives to honor participant voices by using their words to capture the themes and concepts that arose from the data. I constructed a codebook, whose codes largely clustered around five main themes, one of which was the findings outlined in this chapter. I triangulated interview data with my observations and other interviews at the school.

Table 1. Participant Information.

Alias	Role	Subject	Years Teaching	Location of Childhood/k-12 Education
Raymond	Teacher	English	8	New York
Sylvie	Teacher	History	10	Chicago
Ruth	Counselor	Social Work	8	New York
Theresa	Restorative Coordinator	Restorative practices	7	New York

The current chapter outlines this finding in the context of one school site: Riveredge. The stark contrasts between these interview data and my other data evidence the unique perspective these Black staff at Riveredge had into the lives of students and the way race, class, and culture were handled in discipline.

"WHAT ARE WE RESTORING?" BLACK TEACHERS' DOUBLY CONSCIOUS PERCEPTIONS OF RESTORATIVE PRACTICES

The educators I interviewed view restorative practices as a set of performances and rhetorical phrases that thinly veil what they saw as a fundamentally punitive philosophy of authority coming from the administration. Consistent with Du Bois's Double Consciousness theory, these Black educators were acutely aware of the paradox between the restorative ideals espoused by Riveredge administration and the way discipline policy served in the interest of maintaining order in the school and building. Not only were my research participants, as staff, implicated in these policies – they were indispensable to them. Their ability to understand and communicate the trappings of structural racism to their students was part of why the school depended on them; they were able to provide some legitimacy to an otherwise illegitimate implementation of restorative policy.

This overall finding – that Black staff were conscious of both the relational qualities and institutionally oppressive realities of Riveredge's restorative discipline policies – surfaced in three main ways. First, staff noted that while restorative processes were used to reintegrate a student following a suspension, suspension was also used to restore order and signal to students that the administration had the law on their side. In this way, Cody's authority – and, by extension, the legitimacy of restorative practices – was bolstered by the presence of zero tolerance policies, even though Cody seemed to have discretion over whether to opt in to those policies. Staff recognized how restorative practices actually discounted students' home environments and experiences, particularly in regards to handling conflict. Thirdly, they recognized how the administration's valuation of democracy and progressive education actually obscured racial tensions that interfered with proper trust building among staff and between staff and students. The next sections contrast these conscious perceptions with other data, underscoring the divergence of these staff's insights from those of their colleagues.

Perception #1: Participants Were Conscious That Suspension Restores Order (Rather Than Positive School Climate)

Although the administration maintained an overt commitment to restorative practices, and while the administration labels suspension as a component of the restorative process, my participants perceived that suspension was instead a function of residual zero tolerance logic. Perceived disorder, especially that which called negative attention to the school among other principals in the building, was addressed mainly through suspension, in order to preserve Riveredge's reputation among other principals in the building. The building itself was physically guarded by school safety officers, who scanned student identification cards in order to let them into the building, and from whom students often experience harsh treatment reminiscent of how many of them are treated by police in their neighborhoods. This section compares the administration's perception of the role of restorative practices with the perceptions of the Black educators whom I interviewed.

Cody, the school's principal, explained his position within a building where other principals do not necessarily share their restorative discipline philosophy. In this context, he said, he needed to keep "student safety #1," as well as maintain the school's reputation in the building as an orderly environment. From my observations, this need for order took precedence over the need for taking staff and student experiences into account. In relating an incident of one senior male student "trespassing" between floors, Cody was keenly aware of what he called "optics" – how he and the other principals see each other, to the security officers who work building-wide, to the surrounding community and parents, and to the city. He knew most of the other principals in the building were not amenable to the restorative approach, and this largely determined how he chose to proceed in his interactions with a particular student and parent. For example, in building-wide meetings where I observed him, Cody called aggressively for a more relational approach among principals and school safety agents than zero tolerance policies traditionally allow. Yet in addressing behavioral incidents that involved other schools, he felt if he did not tow the traditional, punitive line, student behavior would spiral further out of control and the school's reputation would sustain damage.

Theresa, the restorative coordinator, acknowledged that in Cody's shoes, she too would feel tension between restorative ideals and the need to maintain the confidence of other principals in the building. However, she felt a sense of urgency to address this tension because she saw and heard about how it impacts students. She gave the example of Elijah, a student who was suspended days before his graduation for speaking disrespectfully to a staff person who he, Elijah, felt had disrespected him first.

> He told me some stories about being locked up, or fights he's had on the bus, and just, like so that would be an example of [me] just giving that kid an open space to have that conversation, to curse, to yell, just going there and being like "damn, that's rough." (December 4, 2015)

Theresa recalled that processing these past experiences only made Elijah angrier, and he nearly left the room to attack the teacher who had violated him. Theresa stood in front of the doorway, blocking him (although not physically, as he is significantly taller and larger). She was able to talk him down because, she said, she had made him feel heard and he was therefore willing to listen to her in return. Theresa calls this "going with a student to a dark place, so I can bring you [the student] out." She sees it as a key step to building trust with students and she does not often see other staff take. Instead, they see an outburst like Elijah's as a threat to security and thus worthy of suspension. She felt Cody focusing on how he had broken a rule rather than on the pressures (within and beyond the school) that might have led to his behavior. By giving voice to the larger issues Elijah was facing, Theresa was able to earn his trust and influence his behavior.

Because Cody was not allied with her on this more critical level, the organizational implications of Theresa's work were that she kept Elijah in line with the school's orders and traditionally oppressive discipline structures. She tried to share her concerns with Cody in a daily informal meeting where the two touched base on the day's events. In this meeting, and others like it, I saw both the lens Cody was bringing to look at these students, and the one with which Theresa was countering him. Essentially, Cody saw Elijah's case as one of a student's refusal to abide school rules and expectations. Theresa saw a misunderstood young man who was not responding to school authority because it reminded him too much of the negative interactions with authority outside of school, namely the police. Below is an excerpt from my fieldnotes, documenting a meeting between Cody and Theresa.

> Theresa: I can see [Elijah's] struggling in general – when people tell him what to do, all his anger comes up, like with the cops – he just kept saying, 'Even when I'm right, I'm wrong.'
>
> Cody: But at the same time there are some things he's doing that are seriously violating, like trespassing [into other schools]. (Fieldnotes, November 12, 2014)

Here, Theresa was trying to make a connection between how Elijah was treated on the street and his behavior at school. She was connecting what is happening in the school to the outside world and, in so doing, hoping to teach Elijah something about that world, his current place in it, and what other choices he has for resistance besides physically attacking his principal. Ruth, a social worker, and Sylvie, a teacher, reported similar conversations with students in similar positions. Cody brought the conversation back to safety and order – the typical mentality from which punitive discipline traditionally arises. His position not only insisted on Elijah's deference to an adult who has disrespected him, but it also insisted on Theresa's compliance. It reinforced the institutional reality in which she and Elijah were ensconced, regardless of how deep, trusting, and critical their conversations may have been. She realized that her success with Elijah – even the success of teaching him to think more critically about his environment – served the interest of restoring order in the school.

Perception #2: Participants Were Conscious That Restorative Practices Discount Students' Reality

Black educators I encountered at Riveredge were keen to the suffering of their students, often because it triggered their own educational trauma. In other words, they were in touch with students' reality because it was, in the past and present, a reality they shared. Raymond, an English teacher and product of the New York City Public Schools, spoke proudly and at length about his curriculum planning and clearly felt pride in the ways students had found to connect his their struggles with great works of Black American literature. When I asked him to talk about restorative justice in terms of discipline, however, he was much less certain. He aired, both in our interview and the full-staff discussion, deep ambivalence and suspicion.

> I felt a little bit unsure about the constant thing [in the staff retreat] about making us label restorative and traditional, creating that dichotomy … folks of color and teachers of color are often told how to teach … I do believe in restorative justice … I wasn't sure if I should … align ourselves with a word. (Fieldnotes, March 24, 2015)

Raymond expressed conflicted feelings about restorative school discipline in theory as well as at his school. On the one hand, he recognized the term as a signal of respecting students' rights. On the other hand, he felt instinctively wary of the way this term was being pushed on him by a White administration and the city. He believed in the practices, in theory, but felt that the labels were going to take attention away from helping individual students and teachers discuss their conflicts freely. He sensed that using a term without clear definition of what it means could result in cosigning an agreement to change his relationships with his students or relinquish his professional authority and identity as a Black teacher of predominantly Black and brown students.

Sylvie, an African American history teacher, felt troubled by restorative practices not only in her work but also in her own psyche as well. Sylvie grew up like many of her current students – poor, a resident of the projects, and exposed to drugs and violence from an early age. Without turning a blind eye to the constant dangers that surrounded her, she also recalls a strong network of family and neighbors who made her feel proud of where she came from. Still, Sylvie internalized a societal message that her home life was inferior and that she needed to succeed in school in order to escape. She earned a scholarship to a top boarding school but, she says, deep down, she always felt "worthless," both because of where she came from and from the subtle and not-so-subtle racist treatment she experienced from teachers and students at her new school. She now saw her teaching career as an opportunity to "give kids what I never had" – a strong education in Black history, alongside a relationship with a strong Black role model who does not devalue them because of where they come from.

What Sylvia described as "educational trauma" is the motivating factor behind her commitment to teaching at a school committed to equity. It rendered her painfully sensitive to the subtle ways in which restorative practices are foisted on her and her Black colleagues without enough critical discussion about what restorative discipline means for their students. For example, she detected an enormously degrading aspect of the restorative process when administered to students who experience violence as a part of their everyday environment. "We need," she said, "to be very aware of that and we need to not like spring it on them, like oh, this is what we do, we need to not invalidate our children's experiences .... It's the same idea, I think, of taking a child's language and building on it, not getting rid of everything and giving them another one and being like, what's the problem. The problem here's you got rid of that child's identity." The phrase "other people's children" evokes Delpit's (2000) famous call for educating African American children in ways consistent with how their parents instruct them at home. Sylvie implied that restorative discipline, in trying to "save" students from their violent communities, risks inadvertently shaming them as she feels she was shamed.

A school social worker, Ruth, echoed Delpit's critique. She recognized that for some students, "talking things out" is a way of "distracting" from the real conflict and can be irritating enough to provoke physical violence.

> Like in my family you didn't talk … about your feelings. You … hear the kids saying, well I don't talk, I pop. Well okay. That's a culture that, if you're busy talking, then you're not really fighting … you have to know how to exist in that when it's getting triggered in this culture, In the school. (Fieldnotes, April 20, 2015)

Ruth emphasized that she was "generalizing;" she realized not all of her students – and actually, very few of them – are hardened gangsters. Instead, she paralleled Dance's (2002) analysis of urban youth culture, arguing that the young people in her study exhibited a gangster or "hard" persona as an initial defense, at least until trust and relationships were established. Restorative practices were, for Ruth and her students, suspicious because they seem to disregard students' legitimate means of addressing conflict in their own environments. Like Sylvie, Ruth instead advocated a *code switching* framework, for telling students that there are simply different ways of resolving conflict in different settings just as there are different ways of speaking in different settings, and that such *code-switching* is a reality their students need to learn in order to gain access to what Delpit called "spaces and discourses of power" (Delpit, 1980, p.280). Ruth feared that the insistence on restorative practices, and their framing as a more appropriate and mature way to handle conflict, alienated the school's most vulnerable students, and that the current administration seems ironically more focused on implementing a certain type of practice than helping its students process their own conflicts in a useful, relevant way.

Drawing on her mental health expertise, Ruth suspected that students' attitudes toward conflict were often shaped not only by what they've been exposed to but also by the effects of early trauma. She wished that community-building circles could serve as a place for students to access their personal traumas and learn how they are related to societal injustices. This, she insisted, is the kind of "restorative justice" students needed – that which surfaces and repairs trauma. To provide it, obviously, advisors would require a great deal of training in social–emotional learning. Having worked with these advisors for many years, she felt many are uncomfortable with these heavily political and psychological topics, even if they were in theory aligned with the school's values. For now, she provided it to interested teachers on an individual basis. She had also proposed to the administration that school counselors attend community-building circles and follow-up with any student who exhibits signs of trauma or emotional distress, since as of right now, that distress often leads to subsequent conflict or fights. Her proposal had not yet been taken up by the administration by the end of my data collection. She did not seem optimistic that they would be; instead, she seemed resolved to coaching as many teachers as were willing to let her into their advisories.

Perception #3: Participants Were Conscious of How Restorative Practices Mask Relational Distrust and Racial Prejudice

Ruth, Sylvie, Theresa, and Raymond all concluded their interviews with almost synonymous recommendations for how to effectively reform school discipline. They praised the administration for facilitating a dialogue about discipline that allowed for diverse perspectives to surface. However, they recognized that while *diverse opinions* were often recognized and celebrated, there was a dearth of attention given to issues of racial prejudice and its impact on restorative practices. They believed this had important consequences for the effectiveness of restorative practice itself since many student–staff relationships lacked the fundamental level of trust that would allow them to "restore" or authentically grow through talking out their conflicts. It also placed significant stress on the educators I interviewed. They saw it as their duty to build trust with students and avail themselves as sounding boards, but their reputation for doing so earned many of them extra responsibilities in facilitating restorative practices.[4]

Theresa, the restorative coordinator, described the mechanisms that made restorative practices mere performances, in the Foucauldian (1975) sense of the word; students sensed they were expected to receive and respond to discipline in a certain way to avoid the isolation and alienation of suspension. They "played along" with the restorative conference by agreeing to change their behavior, even though they personally did not feel that the real underlying conflict – which typically involved some kind of perceived prejudice and lack of trust – went unaddressed.

As the restorative practice coordinator, Theresa was tasked with facilitating restorative conferences among teachers and students. The types of issues these conferences addressed were ones that could, at teacher's discretion or at a different school, have earned a student a suspension, particularly if repeated; for example, classroom disruption; students who disrespected teachers; chronic absence; and lateness. The purpose of these conferences was to connect the student's behavior with one of the core values of the school and motivate the student to choose a more productive path to get his or her needs met. Despite this presumably supportive frame, however, students were often hesitant to attend a conference unless assured that an adult they trusted would be facilitating. "They trust me," Theresa explained, "they don't trust the process."

I observed the restorative conference of one student named Carson, who Jeff had repeatedly caught skipping class to play on the computer. At the beginning of his conference, Carson seemed to put up what Dance (2002) might call a "hard" front, speaking in a low voice and asking, repeatedly and in different ways, if he was in trouble. At the end of the conference, he was smiling and playing an active role in designing a schedule that would accommodate his school responsibilities. Smiling and humbly owning his avoidant behavior, he was genuinely open to feedback about how his chronic absence was affecting his grades and grateful for the opportunity to create a workplan for himself moving forward. In the final "go-around" of the conference, he remarked, "I'm glad I came. I thought Jeff [the administrator who had called him to the conference] was just trying to bother me."

I followed up with Carson after this conference for his impressions of how it went; in that meeting and our formal interview a few weeks later, he consistently expressed the same gratitude and enthusiasm for the restorative process. "Basically," he said, "I was not on what I was supposed to be doing, and that was affecting my work, staying in the hallway, him [Jeff, the administrator] thinking I'm not working at my desk … but recently I quit the job and I've been more … I've been able to put school first." Jeff's impressions of this meeting were similar to mine; he had observed what he called a "fair amount of posturing" from Carson until Carson realized he was not in trouble and that this process was about helping him. He said Carson's attendance had improved since the conference and credited the conference for this as well as the school's ongoing restorative community-building efforts.

Theresa, the restorative coordinator who facilitated Carson's conference, had a surprisingly different perspective to share. Not only had he thought he was in trouble or that Jeff might be trying to "bother" him, but in private conversations with Theresa, he had flat-out balked at the idea of coming to the conference at all until she convinced him it was not to get him in trouble and that she would be there. In fact, while Jeff was at the conference and had initiated it, most of the direct feedback about Carson's work ethic came from Theresa. Perhaps without her brokering the interactions between him and Jeff, he would not even have attended.

> His original response was f*** that, I'm not going, I got things to do, like literally, I quote … so that's why I wanted to facilitate his [conference]. If you don't trust the person running the process, you can't trust the process. (Fieldnotes, December 4, 2014)

How could Theresa's impression of Carson be so starkly different from mine and Jeff's? And hadn't Carson himself expressed gratitude and a stronger commitment to his studies in not one but two private interviews with me? I remarked how "maturely" Carson seemed to carry himself, and she responded with a look of wary bemusement. Clearly, she suspected Carson had performed for me as well as for his conference.

Because students trust people before processes, Theresa feels she has to leverage her own relationships to cajole students into participating in restorative practices. This in itself is a struggle; getting them to authentically participate is all but impossible. The restorative practices she arranges, then, were largely performances; students walked away having engaged in the requisite act of reconciliation but without any greater sense of trust or accountability toward the teacher with whom they'd been in conflict. Theresa, too, saw her work as a performance, carrying out the restorative practices even if she felt that her students' fundamental need for trust was going ignored.

As a result of her close relationship with students, Theresa was privy to the types of what Peirce (1970) called *microaggressions* – subtle and often unconscious acts of racial discrimination – that make it difficult for students to trust staff, in or out of the restorative conference. She explained that the number one impediment to building authentic restorative practice at the school was reluctance at the staff level to discuss issues of race. At the same time, there was an overt schoolwide commitment to social justice and activism. As a result, Theresa noticed, teachers would make racialized comments or jokes about students to which students would take offense, but these incidents would go unprocessed. She relayed one example in which a teacher quipped that a student did not seem like "the type" to play the game Taboo, a popular word guessing game, with family over Thanksgiving.

> I guess they [the teacher] were trying to be funny, but I guess because we haven't developed that trust to the place where we need to, the place where that student immediately took it to was, you're being racist. And I get it. I get it from both sides. (Fieldnotes, December 4, 2014)

Theresa described a pattern similar to the one Ruth witnessed in students whose trauma was triggered by a community-building circle. Not knowing their teachers well enough to understand their good intentions, and not trusting them enough to ask, these students bottled their anger and ultimately exploded at these teachers or others. Their angry behavior was then addressed either through suspension, restorative practice, or a combination of the two, framed in the restorative conference as a matter of the *student* needing to adhere to the school's core values while the adult's provocation went unnamed. A cycle of racism, distrust, and misbehavior persisted below the radar of restorative conferences, rendering the conferences themselves as mere performances of reconciliation and reflection.

What students experienced as "racist" was not necessarily as overt as a comment, however. Ironically, conversations intended to address institutionalized racism in society exacerbated students distrust. Theresa recalled students who came to her office during advisory, seeking refuge from conversations in circle about the Brown and Garner verdicts[5] that were supposed to empower and encourage them.

> Kids are pissed off and can't verbalize why, but I finally pull it out of them, and they say "I'm not sitting [in that restorative circle], I've been mistreated by the system, I've been ignored by the system, and now you want me to sit in a room within this system and be vulnerable and tell you how I feel about this?" (Fieldnotes, December 4, 2014)

Theresa suggested that, although staff may like to think otherwise, students viewed Riveredge as a part of the same "system" that had disempowered them in the past, not just the school system but perhaps other public systems as well. Students perceived a school that treated them as society did, refused to honor their voices and then expected them to act differently than they have in the past. Conflicts that occurred could be restored to the extent that students will not physically break the school rules, but they could not and do not restore harm to students or their trust in their staff. They replicate, rather than repair, many of the societal harms and traumas these students have experienced.

Rather than a space to facilitate relational trust among students and staff, restorative practices at Riveredge became a space in which Blacks were encouraged to act as others wanted them too – in other words, it reinforced Double Consciousness, which in turn prevented the relational trust necessary to create a strong web of communication among staff and students. Without this fundamental trust, there was nothing to "restore" when conflict occurred. As Du Bois articulated, this prevented students' self-development as well as the development of a cohesive school culture to which Black staff and students could authentically contribute.

DISCUSSION: THE DOUBLE CONSCIOUSNESS OF THE RESTORATIVE PUBLIC SCHOOL

These data suggest a deep disconnect between administrators' perceptions of restorative practices (as a means of balancing justice with order) with the Black educators' perception (as a means of maintaining order in the guise of justice). In order to maintain this façade, the teachers themselves could only be successful in restorative practices if they *performed* as restorative facilitators, encouraging honest and open dialogue among teachers and students. In reality, they did a great deal of work behind the scenes to get their students to attend and engage in restorative practices – including comforting, supporting, and empathizing with students' struggles against bias and systemic racism.

The educators I interviewed operated on two levels of consciousness, reminiscent of the "double consciousness" (Du Bois, 1903, p.10) conundrum that Du Bois famously described. On the surface, they facilitated restorative practices as a way to build community and repair harm. They could talk about racism as Raymond did, in the context of fighting injustice and promoting the school's values. Behind this facade, Black practitioners and students maintained the trust necessary to hold these conferences – often through explicit discussion of the bias they witnessed. This dynamic is reminiscent of other racialized institutions, including slavery, in which Blacks were able to discuss resistance only within the spaces not directly accessible to their White overseers. Here, those conversations were taking place in preparation for school disciplinary conferences that were presumably meant to promote authentic communication and equity.

Yet, it is too simplistic to suggest that the administration merely embodied the structure and authority of traditional discipline or White supremacy, that they controlled both teachers and students by ostensibly promoting equality among students while ultimately preventing true vulnerability and growth among staff. The truth was much more complicated, as administrators – and many of the staff – considered themselves to be activists who taught in the name of social justice and spoke critically of what it meant to work with racially and socioeconomically marginalized youth. Cody and the other two administrators I interviewed readily volunteered that there are racial tensions among the staff that impede progress in many areas, including restorative practices. Yet when Black staff tried to call for critical dialogue around race – like Theresa did in defense of Elijah, or like Raymond did in the staff retreat – the administration treated their perspectives as evidence of the school's diversity rather than a call to action.

Thus, Double Consciousness describes not only the professional orientations of the Black teachers but also that of their White administrators and of the school as an institution, as the school struggled to both perform as a safe and orderly environment by societal standards while maintaining its founding staff's ideological commitments to humanity and democracy.

The tension of this Double Consciousness was perhaps most starkly embodied in the current school leader, Cody, who had to navigate not only the competing pressures he perceives within his school but also the pressures he faces among other principals in the building and in the larger school system.

IMPLICATIONS: BUILDING SOMETHING TO RESTORE

These Black educators' perceptions are not only distinct from those of their colleagues but they also help to explain the quantitative evidence that restorative practices replicate traditional patterns of racial disproportionality in school discipline. We can imagine that for many districts, the pressure to reduce suspension rates will result in such thin changes as Ruth and Theresa described, with students and trusted staff working together to grin and bear their way through conferences that they know will not address the real root of their conflict. School discipline reform should not merely count suspensions and restorative conferences but should examine how and to what extent community-building circles support relationships, build trust, and address bias. Unlike suspension rates or number of restorative conferences, this type of form may not be possible to measure quantitatively.

Popular restorative practice implementation strategies, such as that of the International Institute for Restorative Practices J. Baille (Personal communication, January 13, 2013), require school staff to engage in restorative community-building circles for a full year before attempting them with students, and Palmer (2013) has tracked the success of districts in one Midwest state who followed a similar process for reducing racial bias among their public school teachers. Perhaps school leaders could implement restorative practices with a more critical eye toward cultural responsiveness and antibias work. In this work, staff of color who have themselves experienced educational trauma, who build trusting relationships with youth and are privy to their lives in a way other staff are not, are valuable coworkers in this process – but they must be, as Du Bois said, coworkers.

Federal- and district-level policy needs to focus more on practices that build trust and create space for collaboration within the school. Conflict and misbehavior should be framed as breaches of this trust. Restorative practices are heralded as an alternative to exclusion, but what should instead be emphasized is their ability to contain and support full inclusion of diverse school communities. If only the reparative aspects of restorative practices – that is, mediations and reconciliations – receive attention, restorative practices will merely reinforce prejudice and institutional order. Practices will, in fact, be a means of replicating inequality rather than interrupting it or creating the opportunity to, for staff, to build trust and disrupt prejudice.

NOTES

1. All names are pseudonyms.
2. I avoid quoting the school's website directly in order to protect anonymity.
3. These were the definitions administrators gave and seemed to presume staff understood; however, in interviews with both Black and White staff, there was considerable disagreement and confusion.
4. This phenomenon, which I called "relationship brokering" actually appeared in all three school sites.
5. This refers to Michael Brown, a Black teenager fatally shot by police in Ferguson, Missouri, and the pardoning of a New York City police officer accused of strangling a Black man named Eric Garner.

REFERENCES

American Psychological Association. (2008). *Are zero tolerance policies effective in schools?* Retrieved from http://www.apa.org/pubs/info/reports/zero-tolerance.pdf

Amstutz, L. S., & Mullet, J. H. (2005). *The little book of restorative discipline for schools*. Intercourse, PA: Good Books.

Browne-Dianis, J. (2011). Stepping back from zero tolerance. *Educational Leadership*, *69*(1), 24–28.

Bryk, A. S., & Schneider, B. (2004). *Trust in schools: A core resource for improvement*. New York, NY: Russell Sage Foundation.

Chin, J. K., Rowdy, E., Jimerson, S. R., & Rime, J. (2012). Alternatives to suspensions: Rationale and recommendations. *Journal of School Violence*, *11*, 156–173.

Christle, C., Nelson, C. M., & Jolivette, K. (2004). School characteristics related to the use of suspension. *Education and Treatment of Children*, *27*(4), 509–526.

Dance, L. J. (2002). *Tough fronts: The impact of street culture on schooling*. New York, NY: Routledge.

Delpit, L. (1988). The silenced dialogue: Power and pedagogy in educating other people's children. *Harvard Educational Review*, *58*(3), 280.

Du Bois, W. E. B. (1987). Strivings of the Negro People. *Atlantic Monthly*, August. Retrieved from http://www.theatlantic.com/magazine/archive/1897/08/strivings-of-the-negro-people/305446/

Du Bois, W. E. B. (1903). *The souls of black folk*. New York, NY: W.W. Norton & Company.

Foucault, M. (1975). *Discipline and punish*. New York, NY: Vintage Books.

Gonzalez, T. (2012). Keeping kids in schools: restorative justice, punitive discipline, and the schools to prison pipeline. *Journal of Law & Education*, *41*(2), 281–334.

Gregory, A., & Ripski, M. B. (2008). Adolescent trust. *School Psychology Review*, *37*(3), 337–353.

Gregory, A., Skiba, R. J., & Noguera, P. A. (2010). The achievement gap and the discipline gap: Two sides of the same coin? *Educational Researcher*, *39*(1), 59–68.

Hamilton, M. V. (2008). *Restorative justice: Reconceptualizing school disciplinary theory and practice*. Available from ProQuest Dissertations and Theses Database (UMI No. 2008. 3303484).

Herr, K., & Anderson, G. (2010). Violent youth or violent schools? A critical incident analysis of symbolic violence. *International Journal of Leadership in Education*, *6*(4), 415–434.

Kafka, J. (2011). *The history of "zero tolerance" in American public schooling*. New York, NY: Macmillan.

Knight, D., & Wadhwa, A. (2014). Expanding opportunity through critical restorative justice. *Studies in Education*, *11*(1), 11–33.

Lustick, H., & Dumas, M. (2014). Not whether but how: A critical analysis of the supportive school discipline initiative. Paper presented at University Council for Educational Administration Convention, Washington, DC.

New York City Department of Education. (2015a). City announces school climate reforms. Retrieved from http://schools.nyc.gov/Offices/mediarelations/NewsandSpeeches/2014-2015/City+Announces+School+Climate+Reforms.htm

New York City Department of Education. (2015b). NYC Data. Retrieved from http://schools.nyc.gov/Accountability/data/default.htm

Osher, D., Bear, G. G., Sprague, J., & Doyle, W. (2010). How can we improve school discipline? *Educational Researcher*, *39*(48), 48–58.

Palmer, E. L. (2013). *Talking about race: Overcoming fear in the process of change*. Doctoral Dissertation. Retrieved from ProQuest, UMI Dissertations Publishing (3589125).

Skiba, R. J. (2013). *The equity project*. Culturally responsive discipline. Powerpoint presentation. Retrieved from http://www.cssponline.org/wp-content/uploads/2010/09/CR_DisciplineCSSP20102.pdf

United States Department of Education Website. (2014, April 15). www.ed.gov

Valenzuela, A. (1999). *Subtractive schooling: U.S. Mexican youth and the politics of caring*. New York, NY: State University of New York Press.

Vincent, C., Tobin, T. J., Hawken, L. S., & Frank, J. L. (2012). Discipline referrals and access to secondary level support in elementary and middle schools: Patterns across African-American, Hispanic-American, and White students. *Education and Treatment of Children*, *35*(3), 431–458.

Zehr, H. (2002). *The little book of restorative justice*. Intercourse, PA: Good Books.

CHAPTER 7

CAN PBIS BUILD JUSTICE RATHER THAN MERELY RESTORE ORDER?

Joshua Bornstein

ABSTRACT

In a multicase qualitative study, inclusive school leaders attempted to move their schools from the excessive use of suspension; they employed positive behavioral intervention and support (PBIS) as an alternative they thought would be therapeutic rather than punitive. However, the PBIS system traded a disciplinary system of control for a medicalized system of restoring order. Unwanted behavior came to be defined as evidence of possible behavioral disability. Hence, the PBIS system exchanged one deficit identity of "disorderly" student for another of "disordered" student, subsuming other considerations of race, class, and gender identity. Following the study's findings, this chapter proposes more liberatory practices for PBIS that interrupt dominant culture discourses of normal behavior and power, and hold promise for establishing justice, rather than simply reinstating order.

Keywords: PBIS; deficit identity; ableism; critical disability studies

Disrupting the school-to-prison pipeline will be significantly influenced by the way that school leaders encourage their schools to adopt new practices and systems for dealing with unwanted behavior and even to reconceptualize

The School to Prison Pipeline: The Role of Culture and Discipline in School
Advances in Race and Ethnicity in Education, Volume 4, 135–167

ISSN: 2051-2317/doi:10.1108/S2051-231720160000004008

the issue. Ideally, we want to build justice in our schools, rather than simply restore order. We know from research that a hallmark of such inclusive efforts must be stopping the excessive use of school push-out and suspension to deal with unwanted behavior (Kim, Losen, & Hewitt, 2010; Skiba et al., 2003). If we conceive of the project as a social justice effort to build inclusive schools, then we know from the literature that successful leaders envision a place for all students with respect to race, class, disability, sexual orientation, gender identity, and language fluency (Marshall & Oliva, 2006; Ross & Berger, 2009; Shields, 2010; Theoharis, 2009; Vilbert & Portelli, 2000). Positive behavioral interventions and support (PBIS) has been indicated as one of the hopeful possible systems to disrupt excessive suspension (Netzel & Eber, 2003; Vincent & Tobin, 2010).

However, a recent study of inclusive school leaders in five diverse school districts (Bornstein, 2014) indicates that PBIS has its own pitfalls. Although the five school districts varied by size, race, and economics, two dynamics were consistent. First as they implemented PBIS, they fundamentally used it to restore disruptive students to compliance. Thus, PBIS became another mechanism for enforcing order. Second, when intervention efforts failed to achieve compliance, the educators involved with PBIS came to treat the students as potentially having emotional behavioral disorder, even if they lacked the clinical authority to make a diagnosis themselves. Consequently, students who were formerly regarded as disorderly increasingly came to be regarded as disordered.

These outcomes were the ramifications of structural imperatives of PBIS, not simply the results of misguided attempts by a select group of individuals. Qualitative research can illuminate the complexity and contradictions of systems like PBIS as they are lived (Bogdan & Biklen, 2007) as opposed to how they are intended to work in theory. Indeed, programs rarely work as logically and beneficently as intended.

With that caveat in mind, this chapter summarizes the earlier study (Bornstein, 2014) as a cautionary tale to leaders who choose PBIS as the alternative to excessive and disproportionate discipline. In his final book, *Where Do We Go from Here: Chaos or Community?* King (1968, 2010) argued for the likely necessity of social welfare programs as a measure of progress in the Civil Rights Movement, "but not for use as supplicants" he cautioned: "We require programs to hold up to our followers which mirror their aspirations" (King, 1968, 2010, p. 145). Likewise, we can acknowledge that social justice for students requires significant programmatic change to disrupt the school-to-prison pipeline, and that PBIS may be an attractive option. However, it would be hard to imagine that students would prefer to be regarded as possibly having an emotional or behavioral disorder rather than delinquent. Students aspire to belong to a community that embraces them, rather than holds them at arms' length.

Truly dismantling the school-to-prison pipeline requires leaders who will build schools with core ethics, policies, and practices that build King's beloved community. Thus, the study presented here may be read as an admonition about making too facile a move from one system of disciplinary control to another medicalized one. Best practices are offered that may well enhance the promise of PBIS and have a better chance of establishing justice in our schools, rather than merely reimposing order.

CONCEPTUAL FRAMEWORK

This study attempted to understand the actions of leaders by examining power as it was encoded in policy, implemented in systems, and enacted in decision-making practices. As such, it relied on Foucauldian discourse analysis (Baker & Heyning, 2004; Hall, 2001; Jones & Ball, 1995) to unpack the interplay of knowledge and power. In particular, this discourse analysis helped to identify how schools constructed deficit identities for students who showed unwanted behavior and who may thus have been regarded as emotionally disabled (Harwood, 2006) and impossible to include (Youdell, 2006). Furthermore, it relied on an emerging area of analysis known as DisCrit Theory (Annamma, Connor, & Ferri, 2013) that applies both critical race theory and disability studies in education to understand the complex interactions of whiteness and ableism in school systems.

Difference Interpreted as Deviance and as Possible Disability

Disability studies is a powerful framework for understanding how difference can be cast as deviance, which can in turn be cast as disability when institutions analyze individuals in putatively scientific systems. Conrad and Schneider (1992) described this dynamic between families, schools, and medical professionals, creating a discourse that regarded energetic children as hyperactive. Informal and formal diagnoses of attention deficit hyperactivity disorder (ADHD) were powerfully framed by the schools' inability to accommodate active learning. This became a switch from "badness to sickness" (Conrad & Schneider, 1992).

Deficit identities are constructed by comparison to what is considered acceptable or normal. Since so much of the PBIS system is about comparing students' behavior to normative behavior standards, it is instructive to take Davis' (2006) point that

> To understand the disabled body, one must return to the concept of the norm, the normal body. So much of writing about disability has focused on the disabled person as the object of study. Just as the study of race has focused on the person of color. But as with recent scholarship on race, which has turned its attention to whiteness, I would like to focus not so much on the construction of disability as on the construction of normalcy. I do this because the "problem" is not the person with disabilities; the problem is the way that normalcy is constructed to create the "problem" of the disabled person. (Davis, 2006, p. 3)

Broderick and Leonardo (2016) extended and complicated this analysis with DisCrit theory by understanding that school's codes of conduct institutionalize White behavioral patterns as the basic definition of acceptable and normal conduct. This analysis build on similar work from Ferri (2012) and Artiles (2007) regarding response to intervention's (RTI) reliance on White norms for acceptable academic performance. With that baseline established, school systems such as child study and intervention teams examine learning styles and behaviors that deviate from the norm. Brantlinger (2006) encapsulated the dynamic elegantly when she described efforts to fix students who measure up as deficient by established school standards. She took on both meanings of the word "fix" (1) to remedy purported deficits and (2) to "determine a place for certain individuals such as through classification or other specialized classroom arrangements" (Brantlinger, 2006, p. viii). Hence, these efforts operate within systems whose goal is to return all students to normalcy and which do so by placing them in some form of classification scheme, such as the PBIS pyramid.

Thomas and Glenny (2000) argued that when schools characterize students as needing emotional and psychological therapy, this can often be a diversion that is fundamentally about the schools' exercise of disciplinary power over students. Qualitative research has borne this out with respect to specific diagnoses such as ADHD (Conrad, 1988, 2006) and conduct disorder (Harwood, 2006), noting that psychopathologizing of students brought them in line as purposefully as did explicit school discipline. Compliance through clinical intervention was thereby more prevalent and preferred to the alternative of creating classrooms and schools that accepted a broad range of student behaviors (Danforth & Smith, 2005; Smith, Danforth, & Nice, 2005).

Two senses of disorder have figured prominently in these discourses that prioritize compliance: disorder-as-organizational-turmoil and disorder-as-illness. In the first sense of disorder, students who routinely, dramatically, or dangerously disrupt class and school, have come to be regarded as too disorderly for school to handle, and thus also legitimately excludable (Fabelo et al., 2011; Losen & Gillespie, 2012; Reid & Knight, 2006; Skiba et al., 2003). These policies and practices associated with this meaning of disorder will be well known to readers of this volume on the school-to-prison pipeline.

The second sense of "disorder" connotes illness or disability, as in Conrad and Schneider's (1992) "medicalization of deviance." The formal diagnosis of emotional behavioral disorder has historically been vastly disproportionately applied to males, students of color, and students who live with poverty (Harry & Klingner, 2006; Hosp & Reschly, 2003; Oswald, Coutinho, & Best, 2002). Furthermore, the diagnosis has been used across the nation to rationalize segregated placements out of general education classrooms and yet further to alternate schools (Fierros & Conroy, 2005). Research with principals indicates that they regarded disruptive behavior as their greatest challenge when building inclusive schools (Avissar, Reiter, & Leyser, 2003; Houser, Bell, Dickens, & Hicks, 2010). Even inclusive principals have been willing to segregate students who were regarded as having diagnoses of emotional and behavioral pathologies (Barnett & Monda-Amaya, 1998; Praisner, 2003). Thus, an examination of the school-to-prison pipeline can also quite legitimately take up medicalized segregation as a twin practice to disciplinary exclusion via suspension.

PBIS as Policy and Practice

The leaders in this study worked within the framework of the Individuals with Disabilities in Education Act (IDEA) (United States Department of Education, 2004), reauthorized in 2004. IDEA established PBIS and RTI as major features of the landscape of inclusion. PBIS intended to replace exclusionary discipline practices such as suspension and expulsion with more therapeutic supports in the classroom and the school when students showed emotions and behaviors that were most troubling in the context of school (Sugai, 2010). RTI intended to do likewise with respect to disabilities that impacted academics (Jimerson, Burns, & VanDerHeyden, 2007). The system was based on a public health triage model for diagnosing the most critical cases and applying appropriate interventions to return a basic stasis to the situation (Merrell & Buchanan, 2006). Importantly, both RTI and PBIS prioritized giving all students access to high-quality instruction for academics and clear expectations for behavior as precursors to any further examination of learning or behavior that may go awry.

The terms RTI and PBIS have sometimes been used interchangeably (Gresham, 2005; Hawken, Vincent, & Schumann, 2008). For example, Gresham (2005) proposed the systematic use of RTI as an alternative means to effectively identify up to 20% of the student population he believed had undiagnosed emotional disabilities. Whether called RTI or PBIS, the essential protocols and assumptions of this public health model remain adroitly similar. The pyramid graphic below typifies the images used to represent the RTI/PBIS pyramid, as for example, at a Fairview board of education meeting. The "Academic" side of the pyramid was conventionally referred as RTI, whereas the "Behavioral" side was known as PBIS (Fig. 1).

PBIS established several significant system-wide practices. First, schools and districts established and promulgated consistent behavioral norms and expectations across all spaces and times (Dunlap, Sailor, Horner, & Sugai, 2009), represented by the base of the pyramid. In the parlance of PBIS, this was the Universal Tier I. Indeed, most schools implement PBIS thoroughly only at Tier I.

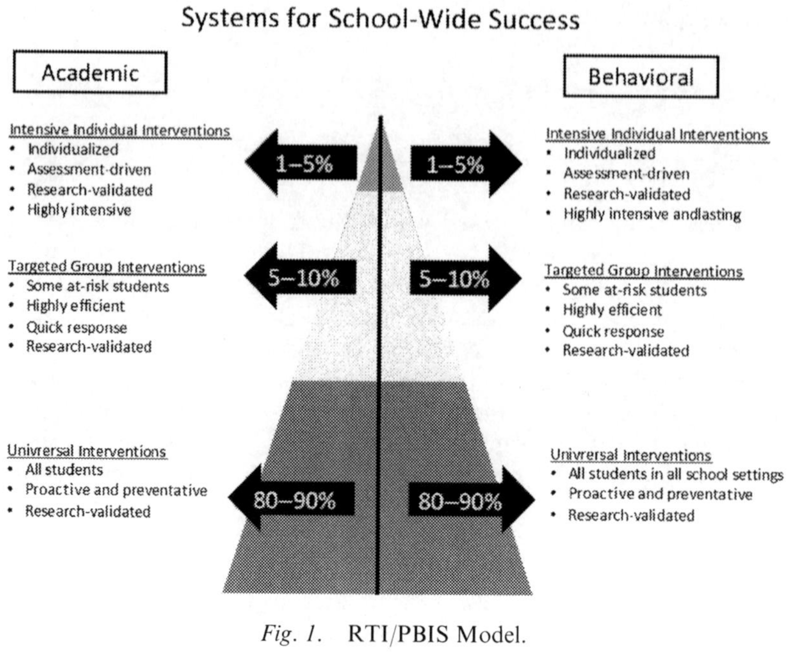

Fig. 1. RTI/PBIS Model.

Nonetheless, the upper tiers of the system have remained important. The upper tiers of the pyramid have represented an escalation of the severity of the labels assigned to the unwanted behavior and the interventions as applied to return the student to baseline expectations. The use of interventions have had two roles: restoring Tier I behavior, and providing data on the student that could be relevant for further analysis and diagnosis. If an intervention at a given tier has restored the student to Tier I behavior, then all was well and good. However, if an intervention has failed in this regard, then this has been taken to indicate that the student had more intense needs, and thus required more intensive interventions (Dunlap et al., 2009). While school personnel themselves have not been diagnosticians, this system became a powerful medicalized discourse, in which unwanted behavior is increasingly seen to originate in an inherent deficit within the student – medicalization of deviance.

Third, PBIS brought with it data collection and analysis as a first level of screening for the entire population of students (Burke et al., 2010). The most prominent data in PBIS – and the most relevant for this chapter – were office discipline referrals (ODRs), used to determine when the level of concern about a student moved from one tier to another (Flannery, Fenning, McGrath Kato, & Bohanon, 2011; McIntosh, Campbell, Carter, & Zumbo, 2009). Some concern has been raised about the validity of using ODRs, in that some researchers believe that early referrals did not necessarily predict a pattern of more referrals to follow (McIntosh, Frank, & Spaulding, 2010). On the opposite end of concern, Bezdek's (2011) study of ODRs revealed the possibility of false negatives, in which students with grave emotional or psychological needs slipped through the cracks of ODR analysis as conducted by PBIS teams.

Herein, some of the confusion between RTI and PBIS has arisen. Some schools may use the PBIS process solely as a Tier I education and universal screening tool to evaluate the entire school (Mass-Galloway, Panyan, Smith, & Wessendorf, 2008), and save RTI for identifying and intervening with individuals of concern (Hawken, Adolphson, MacLeod, & Schumann, 2009; Hawken et al., 2008; Pearce, 2009). Others however, use PBIS for both, ascending the pyramid with more intense identification of an individual's emotional and psychological needs and more intense interventions to match (Eber et al., 2009; Sailor, Dunlap, Sugai, & Horner, 2009; Sugai et al., 2000). Indeed, as the findings below demonstrate, the same confusion existed among leaders in this study. Nevertheless, for the purposes of this chapter in considering PBIS as an alternative to discipline, it is important to identify the basic dynamics of a system that can locate a deficit within the student and avoid other dynamics of institutional power that may be at work.

When school leaders have believed that establishing an orderly school environment requires them to choose between inclusion and exclusion, therapy and discipline, the logics of badness-as-illness and compliance-as-health have been further entangled. The critical lens offered by the present study provides insight into paradoxes that arose in the work of inclusive leaders endeavoring to build schools that worked for all students. For educators who seek to disrupt the school-to-prison pipeline and establish justice in practice, the examples described here may help emphasize how thoroughly we must examine even the reforms put in place with the best intentions.

METHODS

This multicase study was undertaken in five school districts in a Northeastern state. Participating districts and individuals were selected as a criterion sample (Patton, 2002) of inclusive leaders. All five districts and 15 of 18 individual participants had participated in university partnerships or professional development programs on inclusive leadership (Table 1).

Greendale was the largest city in this region. Pleasant Hills and Fairview were adjacent to Greendale, where Fairview operated like an extension of the city itself and Pleasant Hills the middle class suburb. Lakeview was a small rural community an hour from Greendale. Finally, Clearwell was a mix of rural and suburban, adjacent to a different small college city in the region.

The sites' demographic differences as urban, rural, and suburban were a deliberate part of the study's design because of the opportunities for comparing and contrasting practices and policies among them. Since they were all in one state, the districts were also subject to the same governing policies on discipline and special education. Greendale is the largest city in this economically depressed region of the state. The city was identified in the top tier of cities across the nation with the highest concentration of poverty in African American and Latino communities for the period covered by this study (Jargowsky, 2015).

Within each district, I included the superintendent, the director of special education (or central office equivalent), and at least one principal. The participants were positioned both to set a vision for inclusion and to implement it via policy and application, thereby potentially manifesting principles and practices of inclusive leadership (Frattura & Capper, 2007). Superintendents set the tone and policy for the entire district. Directors of Special Education

Table 1. District Demographics.

	Greendale	Clearwell	Fairview	Lakeview	Pleasant Hills
Number of schools	>30	<10	<5	<5	<10
Total enrollment	>20,000	1,000–3,000	1,000–3,000	<1,000	3,000–5,000
Race and ethnicity					
American Indian or Alaska Native	2%	1%	1%	1%	2%
Black or African American	53%	3%	3%	1%	4%
Hispanic or Latino	12%	0%	5%	1%	1%
Asian or native Hawaiian/ other Pacific Islander	6%	1%	1%	1%	2%
Multiracial	0%	0%	4%	0%	1%
White	28%	96%	86%	97%	90%
Additional services					
Limited English proficiency	10%	1%	4%	0%	1%
Students with disabilities (all)	19%	17%	13%	14%	14%
Students with emotional or behavioral disabilities	3%	4%	2%	0%	1%
Free or reduced-price lunch	79%	37%	46%	51%	29%

Note: Data collated from annual State Education Department school district report cards and reports of students receiving special education programs and services (State Education Department, 2010, 2012a, 2012b, 2012c, 2012d, 2012e).

and their equivalents implemented PBIS, especially in terms of establishing an alternative to suspension as per Individuals with Disabilities in Education Act (2004). Principals set the discourse and implemented practices for their schools (Table 2).

Data Collection and Analysis

This study triangulated data from multiple sources and data collection strategies (Denzin, 1978). I conducted individual semistructured interviews (Rubin & Rubin, 2005) ranging from 60 to 90 minutes with the 18 respondents individually from January 2011 to June 2012. Initial interviews helped to establish the discourses that each participant employed and

Table 2. Sites and Participants.

Greendale	Clearwell	Fairview	Lakeview	Pleasant Hills
Superintendent				
Angela Silva	Ruby Trumbull	Lesley Newsome	Bill Boniwell	Carol Ferrara
District office personnel				
Patrick Quinn, Director of Special Education	Denise Galliano, Director of Special Education	Mary Danton, Chair of Committee on Special Education	Claire Carson, Director of Special Education	Alice DeMartino, Director of Special Education
		Rob Nielsen, Director of Admin.		Michelle Vinter, Coordinator of Youth Development
Principal (school, grades)				
Sian Ingraham (Jones, K-8)	Erin Sanders, Asst. Principal (Clearwell Elementary K-5)	David Underwood (Fairview Middle, 4–8)	Vanessa Blanton (Lakeview Elementary, K-5)	Marcia Brumson (Heights Elementary, K-5)
	Grace Lowthian (Warren, K-8)			

identified opportunities for field observation and pertinent district documents. Final member check interviews (Lincoln & Guba, 1985) with all but two participants who had left their posts during the course of the study probed two essential questions on developing theories: (a) "Do I have this correct?" and (b) "What is the story to be told about this?" I also presented the respondents with the interpretive theories about those data points that I had developed during data analysis (Denzin, 1994) and repeated the same questions in order to verify the validity of my data and conclusions.

For 12 months beginning in March 2011, I conducted 19 field observations (Adler & Adler, 1994; Bogdan & Biklen, 2007). Participants indicated that their leadership on relevant matters could be observed in these sessions. The observations included planning and implementation meetings for PBIS, data review sessions on individual students and on aggregate data, staff development sessions, and faculty meetings.

Documents gathered from the field and from websites associated with the districts constituted another data set (Hodder, 1994; Zeeman, Poggenpoel,

Myburgh, & Van, 2002). Participants volunteered artifacts of field observations and documents to me during interviews, such as data recording forms, meeting agendas, and supporting graphics. I also gathered documents from websites of the five districts and of the State Department of Education.

Within a grounded theory approach (Glaser & Strauss, 1967) to the data, I used open and axial coding via NVivo software to yield emerging themes (Richards & Richards, 1994; Welsh, 2002). Critical discourse analysis (Gee, 2012) and Foucauldian discourse analysis (Hall, 2001; Harwood, 2003) of the data helped to establish the discourses of order and medicalization that emerged. Numerous strategies validating my conclusions included data and method triangulation (Denzin, 1978), negative case analysis (Morse et al., 2002), sample adequacy and saturation (Morse, 1991), member check interviews (Lincoln & Guba, 1985), analytic humility (Kincheloe & McLaren, 1994), and noting my subjectivities (Walkerdine, Lucey, & Melody, 2002) via reflective journaling (Rolfe, 2006).

SEEKING INCLUSION VIA COMPLIANCE

Inclusive leaders wanted earnestly to include all students. As they described their efforts and led others through planning inclusive systems and problem-solving sessions, they indicated the belief that the tenets of PBIS offered them the best opportunity to do so. Paradoxically, the systems they embraced built a logic that could ultimately justify excluding students who were regarded as having emotional or behavioral disabilities. The commitment to inclusion while simultaneously rationalizing moments of exclusion was neither hypocritical nor insincere. Indeed, it was painful, as all leaders acknowledged their own struggles when sending a disorderly student to a more restricted, segregated environment.

Pulling apart the logic of that rationalization took several steps. In these findings, I have reviewed first the participants' definitions of inclusion. In particular, they defined the principles of successfully including children whom they regarded as having emotional or behavioral disorders. Second, I have compiled their descriptions of the types of behaviors and emotions they found most challenging to include. Third, I have examined actual instances in which these students were identified. Finally, I have presented an extended scenario from one participant. The scenario is an example of how the discourses surrounding a PBIS approach could exchange one deficit identity of the disobedient student for the disabled one.

Disciplinary Normalcy in Codes of Conduct

Some of the leaders studied called their practice RTI. Some called it PBIS. Some called it both, and some called it neither. Regardless of the label, the leaders used several of the basic tenets of the RTI/PBIS system as described by theorists (Jimerson et al., 2007; Sugai, 2010). Notably, they (1) expected fidelity to standardized school rules and PBIS procedures; (2) used data to identify students in need of assistance, to determine their needs, and then to prescribe ways to meet those needs; (3) applied a graduated continuum of interventions they regarded as research-validated; and (4) regularly assessed students' behavior in the process known as progress monitoring.

The founding point for their work was how to include students who were regarded as disorderly. And the basis for that identity lay in codes of conduct established in each district and school. All school districts followed a state mandate to specify student behavioral expectations (Project Safe Schools Act, 2000). Normal behavior was codified in the "Student Responsibilities" section. All five districts' discipline policies were notably similar in their expectations. Following school rules was first or second on every list, thereby cementing school authority and power in determining what constituted a good or bad student (Table 3).

Every discipline code instituted normative behavior by requiring students to be responsible for an environment "conducive to learning." The students were thus not only responsible for themselves, but also for the

Table 3. Student Responsibility for Learning Environment as per Codes of Conduct.

District	Excerpt from "Student Responsibilities"
Greendale	Contribute to maintaining a safe and orderly school environment that is conducive to learning and to show respect to other persons and to property.
Clearwater	Contribute to maintaining a safe and orderly school environment that is conducive to learning and show respect to other persons and to property.
Fairview	Contribute to the maintenance of an environment that is conducive to learning and to show due respect for other persons' property.
Lakeview	To work to the best of his/her ability in all academic and extracurricular pursuits and strive toward the highest level of achievement possible.
Pleasant Hills	Contribute to the maintenance of an environment that is conducive to learning and to show due respect for other persons' property.
	Be safe, and not interfere with the educational process.

common good. Individual students could be held accountable for disruption of the organization of school. Most codes aligned order and safety with learning. While Fairview did not explicitly call for safety and order, respect for property substituted as an equivalent.

In other sections of the codes of conduct, three districts identified some classroom behaviors presumably conducive to learning. Greendale, Clearwater, and Fairview wanted their students to ask questions when they did not understand what was going on in class or with their assignments. Within the text of the codes of conduct, students were not expected to collaborate, show curiosity, create, or even participate. Indeed, the verb "participate" arose only in the most passive sense in the clauses in which students were expected to behave well when "participating in" or "attending" extracurricular events. Typically, in those instances, the students' good behavior was normalized as acting like "representatives" of the district when they might be on display for other members of the general public. Furthermore, although students were tasked with maintaining an environment conducive to learning, that environment was never actually described. A discourse analysis must examine what is not said along with what is made explicit. The codes of conduct were silent on other behaviors that could enhance environment for learning, such as collaboration and curiosity. This silence contrasted with explicit expectations for respectful and safe behavior created a discourse in which orderly compliance was the basis of normative behavior.

Definitions of Disorderly Behavior: Runners, Biters, and Chair Throwers

Disorderly behavior arose again and again in interviews and observations as the greatest challenge for inclusive leaders and their staffs. Several behaviors emerged from interviews and observations repeatedly as icons of disorder. Running from class, biting, and throwing furniture were shorthand monikers for the most significant challenges of building fully inclusive schools. In the initial interview, I asked each leader about the most difficult challenges to inclusion. Their responses are shown in Table 4. All respondents focused on behavioral challenges.

Unpacking Director Denise Galliano's description proves an instructive example of the discursive strategy that defined students based on disorder. She gave her example within an extended discussion of how she wanted Clearwell to use the diagnostic and prescriptive process of PBIS. She

Table 4. Descriptions of Behavior.

Participant/District	Behavioral Description
Greendale	
Superintendent Silva	"Basic insubordination, talking back. Not so much egregious behaviors. It's mainly students being defiant to teachers."
Director of Special Education Quinn	"We do have a lot of angry kids, and that is where we have got aggression replacement training in some schools."
Principal Ingraham	"I have teachers right now with kids who are extremely violent. They bite a lot."
Principal Lowthian	"She sees demons, threatens suicide when she sees demons approaching. She is interfering with her own education and the education of others."
Clearwell	
Superintendent Turnbull	"Runners are very challenging. The kids who have a 'flee' response to stress are very challenging."
Director of Special Education Galliano	"When their learning is so disrupted or when they are so disruptive to others' learning, when there is a possibility of injury to others or injury to themselves, when they are spending more and more time out of the classroom due to behaviors, which is going to disrupt their learning, when there are constant office referrals."
Assistant Principal Sanders	"We do have students with severe behaviors, as most schools do. Violent."
Fairview	
Superintendent Newsome	"I look at, 'How do we change any behavior that interferes with that child's education or the education of others?'"
Principal Underwood	"The emotionally disturbed kids … they had big breakdowns and meltdowns, a lot of noise."
Director of Administration Nielson	"I think the kinds of behaviors are when a teacher's authority is challenged or when they think that kids might be in danger of getting hurt. I think that those are the kinds of behaviors that are most challenging."
Committee on Special Education Chair Danton	"Explosive. Harmful to self or others. I get involved there, when they rise to that level."
Lakeview	
Superintendent Boniwell	"Disruption in classrooms. We do not get a lot of physical stuff here. It is mostly just disruptive behavior, upset."

Table 4. *(Continued)*

Participant/District	Behavioral Description
Director of Special Education Carson	"He [Superintendent Boniwell] is not going to tolerate kids throwing chairs and hurting other kids."
Principal Blanton	[Regarding a boy who had hidden in the bathroom one week prior to the interview.] "And the next day he was fine. But who knows when that can happen again. That's a real challenge. It makes me really nervous when I can't be in the building. Not that I'm any miracle worker but to let somebody else be responsible for that kinda stuff – and that's a dangerous situation, have him locked in the bathroom and then climbing on top of the walls. So those are challenges."
Pleasant Hills	
Superintendent Ferrara	"Acting out behaviors can be avoiding work I have trouble doing. Also, there's the kid who makes poor choices because experiences and role models have developed that pattern. Choices are impulsivity, rather than making good choices."
Coordinator for Youth Development and Leadership Vinter	"Slapping, biting, hitting other children. There were really truly safety issues. Running out of the classroom."
Principal Brumson	"The bigger challenge still remains for the cafeteria staff and it's really about aides who don't get it. You know, they just see somebody being naughty and needing to make him comply."
Director of Special Education DeMartino	"Defiance and noncompliance."

expected that the schools should identify a student as needing interventions when

> [t]heir learning is so disrupted or when they are so disruptive to others' learning, when there is a possibility of injury to others or injury to themselves, when they are spending more and more time out of the classroom due to behaviors, which is going to disrupt their learning, when there are constant office referrals.

"Disruption" grounded her description. The disruption was to classroom order regarded as necessary for learning. Galliano also signaled that her scope of concern was not simply the child herself, but also peers. Disruption was followed by the threat of injury early in the description and yet bore repeating in a reprise.

As for safety, Galliano reemphasized a duty to protect the student and peers. Furthermore, it was not the act of violence per se, but the potential of violence that she noted. In this phrase, the person who could predict or interpret "the possibility of injury" was unnamed. Tacitly, the listener was to assume this was an educator.

"...spending more and more time out of the classroom" described the establishment of a pattern. This was an important moment in the description. It indicated that single incidents may not warrant concern, but repeated and patterned ones did. Patterning was epistemologically significant. It conveyed the truth of interpreting student behavior as disruptive.

"...constant office referrals" reinforced two hallmarks of this troubling scenario. First, the constancy spoke to patterns. Second, sending a child to the principal's office via a referral was an official action, resulting from adult judgment of something wrong. Thus, the adult's judgment was verified as a way of knowing students as disorderly.

Referrals were more than acts, though. When they were collated, calculated, and tracked, they became data that evidenced disorder. Galliano embedded the example of problematic behavior in a discussion of the data-driven regime of PBIS, even if she did not specifically call it so at this moment. Moreover, her focus on reading the data and searching for causes in the patterns signaled the power of school authorities. In her view, they had a responsibility to maintain order and safety plus a further duty to diagnose the underlying etiology of unwanted behavior and do their best to find a therapeutic cure. Grounding that work in data – as she alluded to the PBIS tenets – demonstrated a positivist discourse that lay at the heart of medicalization.

Running, biting, and chair throwing showed up repeatedly in these descriptions as paradigmatic behaviors and were echoed in most interviews and observations. They were used so frequently that I chose to examine them as symbols of disorder. They held power as explanatory devices in discourses of alterity and mental illness. For example, chairs were ubiquitous classroom objects. How they were arranged in any classroom spoke volumes about the order of that learning space: Were they arranged in rows, indicating decades of stand-and-deliver teaching? Were they arranged around tables, hinting at cooperative learning pedagogies?

Thus, whenever these educators invoked "throwing a chair" in descriptions of student behavior, that language symbolized that the student was misusing the furniture according to the accepted social organization of a classroom. Also, students were to sit on their chairs. References to chairs thus not only spoke to the use of those objects but also to the regulation of student bodies in the classroom. Sitting on chairs was passive, whether done in rows, at collective tables, or in a circle. Throwing was far more active – transgressively active – because sitting was the socially sanctioned use of chairs. Throwing chairs also signaled danger from an irrational threat. A thrown chair could not be caught like a ball in physical education class or at recess – the conventional ways of throwing anything in school. Thus, the phrase "throwing a chair" conveyed two ideas: (1) a student was harming others and (2) a student was irrational. In effect, that icon alluded to disorder in both its meanings: disorder-as-turmoil and disorder-as-pathology.

Applying PBIS Principles

Pleasant Hills, Fairview, and Greendale had been cited by the State Department of Education for suspending too many students with disabilities in recent years. Furthermore, during the same period as this study, Greendale was investigated as one of 20 urban districts that regularly, excessively, and disproportionately suspended students of color and students with disabilities (Losen & Martinez, 2013). Impelled by these accountability measures, the leaders turned to PBIS as their systematic remedy.

In Pleasant Hills, Coordinator Vinter made her case for PBIS by focusing on the power of fidelity when an entire institution was using the same PBIS practices. She compared two schools in the district through the lens of a school nurse who transferred from one to the other. The nurse had moved from the school with the longest history of using PBIS to the newest.

> They've been implementing for 10 years. She went from going to South Street Elementary to Rhodes Elementary. Rhodes was our last elementary on board with PBIS. She called me one day, and she said, "Michelle, there's a marked difference between the behavior of the kids at South Street," which is our lowest socioeconomic, Title I school, "to the kids at Rhodes," just typical kids.
>
> The kids at South Street really embraced the model and understood the expectations and followed the rules better. To me that was just kind of anecdotal testimony that if you implement the model with fidelity, you're going to get positive results. South Street has the fewest discipline problems. I know some of that is based on the principal and the personalities of the teachers, but all in all, I think it's testimony to the fact that teachers really embrace PBIS.

Vinter found the nurse's analysis of such a disjuncture between the two schools compelling. As she described the power of implementing PBIS with fidelity, she was actually talking about social class more than each school's history with PBIS. Vinter decoded what was so shocking to the nurse. She explained parenthetically that South Street was a school of the "lowest socioeconomic" class, as opposed to Rhodes' population of "just typical kids." Title I was a federal support program for schools whose academic performance and socioeconomic status were low. Thus, Vinter intimated that South Street was not only a poor school economically but also academically. In this narrative about South Street, orderly behavior was remarkable not only because it was pervasive, but also because one would expect good behavior more from "typical kids" than from those in a low performing and low socioeconomic class school. Those deficit identities did not fit with normative orderly behavior.

What got the credit for breaking that expectation? Implementing PBIS with fidelity over time was the evident cause in this discourse. And, beyond 10 years of implementation, "embracing" PBIS also epitomized success. Systematic fidelity was more powerful than social class and even more powerful than the "personalities" of the teachers or the leadership of that school in this narrative, although Vinter believed they may have a part in South Street's success as well. The major lesson of this account of two schools was that if fidelity led to success in a significantly deviant school, then it should certainly work in a normal one.

All the schools included in this study had teams that focused on troubling students. Although the precise composition of each team varied, they generally included the building administrator, social worker, psychologist, and academic specialists, such as a reading teacher and a nurse. Items pertaining to disorderly students dominated agendas of these teams. At Jones School in Greendale, Principal Ingraham presided over a weekly meeting of her Student Staff Support Team (SSST). In two hours, the SSST discussed 16 students. All but one were behavioral concerns.

The same pattern was evident in meetings of the Lakeview School Based Intervention Team (SBIT). The team worked through an agenda of 13 students in June 2011. As each child was discussed, emotions and behavior were not always presented first. However, for 12 of 13 students, the discussion turned to emotions and behavior as the presumed roots of the issues at hand.

When Principal Vanessa Blanton reflected on this afterward she was surprised, but believed it may have been due to the calendar. She reasoned that by May and June, teachers had tried all the strategies they knew. Having exhausted their repertoire and energies, teachers came to believe that behavioral or emotional causes were undermining their students' success in class. Checking out that calendar explanation, I attended another SBIT team meeting in October 2011. That meeting was conspicuously similar to the June gathering. Again, behavior became the eventual topic of discussion for all ten children on the agenda.

The SBIT team often employed two deficit discourses of family to explain students' disorderly behavior and unruly emotions. The first deficit discourse described students' homes as chaotic. Parents in jail, the loss of a job, the intermittent presence of pseudo-parental boyfriends or girlfriends of mother or father, prolonged illness, all figured in the SBIT team's analysis of causes for a student's disorderly behavior. Second, the team made comparisons to other family members. Team members explained the current child's behavior by referring to disorderly behavior and emotions of siblings, parents, and other relatives who attended Lakeview schools.

The team also used pathology as an identity marker in itself. This came in several forms. One version was using psychopathological diagnosis as shorthand for student need. Psychiatric diagnostic labels (American Psychiatric Association, Task Force on DSM-IV, 2000) such as Asperger's syndrome, pervasive developmental disorder, and attention deficit disorder mixed with other diagnostic references, such as "selective mutism," and "obsessive compulsive" (which only needs the word "disorder" to itself be a DSM-IV label). A second related strategy was invoking pharmacology as an effective response or intervention, as when the nurse reinforced her claim that a student had attention deficit disorder by commenting that she would be a good candidate for medication. Third, the team entwined pathology ("selective mutism"), bad parenting, and heredity as causes for disorder, noting that the parents allowed the children to "run the house."

Using Data

These team meetings exhibited this kind of anecdotal data analysis. All the included districts identified disorderly students based on what they considered to be sound data. Greendale's Special Education Director Quinn presided over meetings of a broad district team of administrators, teachers, and mental health specialists from the district and the city. He had convened this diverse group to design Greendale's PBIS pyramid because he regarded the planning and implementation of PBIS as "bigger than special ed." The participants in those meetings came back repeatedly to endorsing ODRs and attendance records as data to identify students in need of support beyond Tier I and as trigger data to move a student up subsequent tiers of their PBIS pyramid.

In one pivotal meeting, that endorsement withstood challenges from the Director of Elementary Education and the Parent Advocate who questioned how PBIS would function in a district with a discomfiting legacy of institutional racism. How could ODRs be trusted when "teachers who don't look like our students" wrote petty referrals, according to the Director? Furthermore, behavioral data and analyses had a danger of being used to construct "our kids" as "buck wild and needing mental health services" in the view of the Parent Advocate. After some meandering discussion, a school psychologist asserted that she and other clinical specialists held the keys to solving that dilemma because "good assessment drives strategies." Director Quinn allowed that declaration to stand. His clear message was that Greendale was choosing PBIS data analysis to diagnose students as a way to "deal with race" as the Elementary Director insisted they should.

Although he did not refer to it in this meeting, Quinn regarded Warren School's use of data as a model for the district. During one of my field observations at Warren, Principal Lowthian highlighted for me the school's "war room" that had earned Quinn's approval. The room featured a wall of response to intervention charts for reading achievement facing a wall of PBIS charts for behavior (Fig. 2). A PBIS pyramid on which the teacher had written students' names in the appropriate colored tier represented each class. The room gave Lowthian and colleagues an immediate way to know the school at a glance. They might also zoom in on a particular class or student to see where s/he was placed on the pyramid. The room's nickname drew on military symbolism of course, in which the stakes are high, resources are precious, accurate "target" assessment is necessary, and the overall corrective system intends to work reliably on the population in question. In the context of regarding PBIS as dealing with emotional or behavioral disorder, the analogy was much like symbolism used in the "war on cancer" (Sontag, 1990).

Medicalization Discourse Permeates Data Analysis, Identification, and Intervention

On a staff development day, Assistant Principal Sanders called together the district's social workers, counselors, and an elementary principal for a discussion on how to implement RTI strategies for children whose behaviors were regarded as disorderly. Sanders introduced a data review of ODRs to set the ground for when and how to apply interventions. She brought the group's attention to an accounting that 36 students received 448 referrals last year, and translated that into percentages: "17% of the kids got 61% of the referrals."

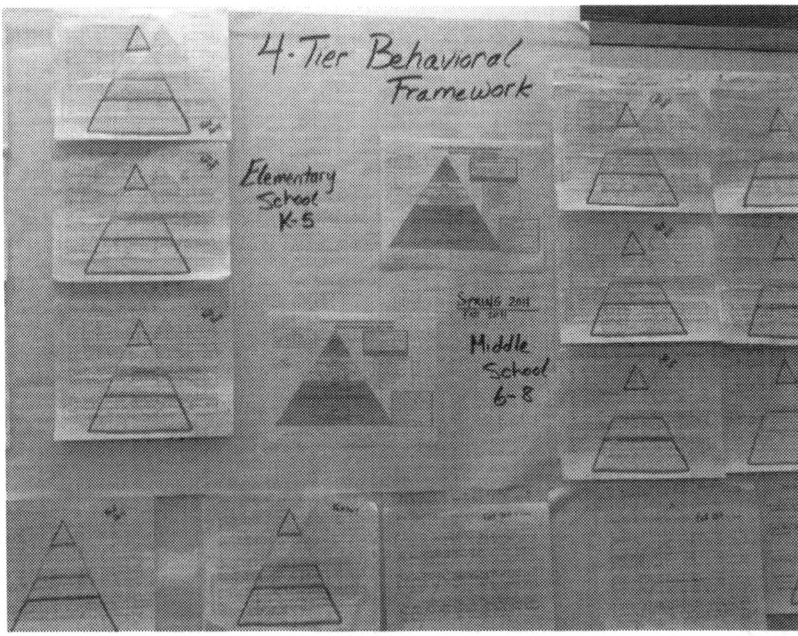

Fig. 2. PBIS Data Wall in the "War Room."

One social worker's reaction was immediate. "They're mine! They're ED!" By this she meant that they were part of her caseload because they had been classified as emotionally disturbed.

From there, the discussion moved to examining the referrals themselves, whether they were consistently entered in the electronic student database called SchoolTool, and what the coded behaviors meant. For example, Sanders noted that she and the principal of her school were continually reinforcing with teachers that they should log referrals in SchoolTool. At the same time, she challenged the usefulness of some codes. "Inappropriate behavior is not always a good descriptor," she said. The social worker reinforced this point, noting that the statistics for "inappropriate language" would have been be a lot higher "if we SchoolTooled every incident."

Sanders responded assertively that students "need to know that we will suspend for threats of 'I will kill you.'" As evidence that this sanction had become more accepted, she noted that suspensions were down for that behavior. Thus she believed students had gotten the message. "We talk about biculturalism, where they know that school is different."

With "biculturalism," Sanders used the discursive strategy of normalizing orderly behavior in this discussion. The "biculturalism" she referred to here picked up a point from an earlier exchange at this meeting in which the turmoil of many Clearwell families was attributed as a root cause for ODRs. Sanders was telling the group that a school culture of order and safety would prevail and would be the basis against which deviance was judged.

This "biculturalism" also harkened back to our initial interview, in which Sanders explained her position as an inclusive leader. Sanders understood her mission as "compassionate," particularly in reference to negotiating the social class discourses of home and school.

> You know, love is. I'm pretty tough on the kids. I grew up working class. I am not from an educated family. My older brother. I moved around a lot, my family, so I identify actually with some of our most severe families here. That's my background. I have my degrees up on the wall because that's a miracle to me. Those are a miracle. If you knew my upbringing, you would know that that's a miracle. The dissertation's a miracle. I identify with those kids. I'm getting emotional. I'm working class, and one of the things I always have to mitigate is middle class discourse, because sometimes our kids need tough love. No one's going to save them. No one saved me.

Sanders preferred to read disorderly behavior as an expression of working class culture, rather than illness. She saw that her school's behavioral expectations were grounded in middle class values, which she believed were likely different from the values of her students' homes. Her heartfelt mission was to help students navigate school's middle class norms for orderly behavior. She tacitly accepted that working class culture was constructed as a deficit by the school – "those kids" with whom she identified were from "some of our most severe families." In essence, she was coaching working class on how to pass as middle class while in school.

During the staff development meeting, this tension between pathology and class emerged again. As the group worked their way through creating Clearwell's set of "tiered interventions," they contrasted two students as examples. In the excerpt below from my observation notes, Sanders and a social worker disagreed about one of the two children.

> Principal: You [Sanders] mentioned children of incarcerated family members, and you're [Social Worker's] mention of kids with more needs is important. Let's look more at that.
>
> Sanders: We could go down the case list [of students getting Tier II support], to see what are the themes of what's going on with them.
>
> Social Worker: We have kids with emotional disabilities, or things going on that are emotional, and kids with bad behavior. Teachers have a hard time distinguishing.

Like S11,[1] crying and carrying on. He has emotional issues now, but not nearly what they were in 2nd grade. That's a bad example. There's no ED with him.

How about S12, who has emotional issues and will always have issues? He is emotionally disturbed. Tomorrow, he will be emotionally disturbed. He will always be emotionally disturbed.

S11 will tell you, "I have different rules at home and school, and sometimes I get mixed up." He hasn't got deep-seated emotional issues.

Sanders: I'd argue with you about S11. I worry about taking him out of this safe context.

Social Worker: [Chuckling] She always argues with me about him!

Sanders: I worry about him. He's been crying and crawling under his desk.

Social Worker: That's what he does at home.

Sanders: [Collecting her papers.] When can we meet again?

The group used the list of children receiving Tier II intervention as a reference point. The RTI/PBIS pyramid thus became the technology for defining students' deviant identities. Regardless of whether the etiology of deviance was coming from a home with an incarcerated family member or "deep-seated emotional issues," the pyramid showed the students to be comparable.

Could schools deal effectively or not with that deviance, and what did that mean for the student's identity? This was the subtext of disagreement between the social worker and Sanders. Indeed, it was the logic at the heart of diagnosing someone's response to intervention. Sanders implicitly concurred with the social worker that there were students like S12 who had a legitimate disability. She attempted to destabilize that category, however, stating that a "safe context" was crucial to this student. Furthermore, she signaled that a student with an emotional disability might legitimately be excluded by being taken out of that safe context.

The social worker asserted that the student's behavior was the "same at home." She acknowledged Sanders' list of disruptive or disorderly behaviors, such as crying and crawling. However, if they were the same at home, the social worker implied that the cause lay within the student, regardless of context. Thereby, she discursively constructed the student as having an emotional disability. Significantly, Sanders dropped her challenge at this point and shifted the agenda to scheduling their next meeting.

In a follow-up interview, Sanders reflected on that exchange. Although the moment had a playful, collegial tone, it underscored some tensions. "I think that's part of, probably, what we're wrestling with as a community. What is the difference between those two concepts of a student?"

Sanders laid out how best to make that distinction. Her description was a powerful statement of the diagnostic discourse of response to intervention.

> I think part of it might be that, for the student who's naughty, there's a possibility that that child could self regulate and relearn behaviors and be shifted in their behaviors. I think, when we start looking at that Tier III level, we're also looking at students who may not have the capacity themselves to regulate, who are subject to … They themselves don't have the skills in them. And I think that's where, with that one student, we go back and forth on, "Can the student regulate, can he not regulate? Will this student ever have a moment where they know what's right and what's wrong?"

For Sanders, a naughty child could learn, change behavior, and could internalize that change to the point of self-regulation. This was posed as normalcy. Within that normalcy, she had earlier signaled that she believed that someone who switches codes between working class behaviors and middle class behaviors is skillful and admirable. Thus, she expected students to have made school's behavioral expectations so thoroughly their own that they could self-discipline (Foucault, 1979) – and even do so nimbly.

From Sanders' perspective, if disruptive students were not naughty-turned-disciplined, then they might never show the capacity to tell right from wrong. Importantly, Sanders posited that tiered interventions would reveal the true pathology in a student. Thus, the technology of the pyramid discursively created the student as having a disability.

CONCLUSIONS AND IMPLICATIONS

Paradoxically, the leaders in this study enacted discourses that pathologized and prioritized control, even as they sought to move away from punishment. To begin with, they rooted their description of ideal behavior in Codes of Conduct that emphasized compliance and order. Second, they used office discipline referrals as the fundamental data to measure students' deviation from that behavioral norm. Third, the protocols of PBIS drove them to interpret that data as evidence of behavioral disability. Such analysis led them to substitute one deficit identity – disordered student – for another – disorderly student. Indeed, it could even lead them to substitute one version of exclusion – medical placement at another facility – for disciplinary suspension.

A growing body of literature challenges the cultural proficiency of a one-size-fits-all PBIS system (Bal, Thorius, & Kozleski, 2012; Fallon, O'Keeffe, & Sugai, 2012; Sugai, O'Keeffe, & Fallon, 2011). In related critiques of RTI, Artiles (2007) and Ferri (2012) dispute the validity of a medicalized approach to students that psychopathologizes them. Annamma, Morrison, and Jackson (2014) draw the two together in examining their connection to the school-to-prison pipeline.

The evidence in this chapter argues that in order to create a system that "mirrors the aspirations" of our students, social justice leaders should not only implement culturally responsive practice but also deconstruct the falsely scientific medicalizing discourses embedded in conventional PBIS practices. They ought not fall prey to a system that swaps one deficit identity for another. Both "bad" students and "disabled" students are marginalized students whom schools make impossible to include (Youdell, 2006).

Nonetheless, I would contend that there are several promising possibilities for culturally responsive and democratic practices that may significantly disrupt the school-to-prison pipeline. The first would be seeking balance in the analysis of PBIS data. As documented here, the upper tiers of PBIS as practiced were fundamentally analyzing deficits. Data-informed leadership could interrupt this practice simply by documenting strengths as thoroughly as documenting deficits. In another balancing data analysis, the lens of data analysis and intervention could be turned back on adults and the school's systems as much as it is trained on students. For example, it is one thing to analyze who is receiving office discipline referrals and disciplinary consequences for student patterns. Better practice would be to profitably disaggregate for race, class, disability, gender, and language proficiency of the students, as suggested in a new wave of literature on culturally responsive PBIS (Bal, Kozleski, Schrader, Rodriguez, & Pelton, 2014; Bal et al., 2012; Jewell, 2012). If in theory, PBIS is supposed to address both student and staff behaviors, it would be equally profitable to turn the same focus on the teachers, administrators, and discipline codes that enact those referrals and consequences. In that way, analysis shifts from the passive voice in which students are the objects of disproportionate discipline to the active voice in which a school and its adults are the subjects. Disaggregating referrals by race, gender, disability, and economic status of the adults would constitute a balanced and culturally responsive data analysis. Likewise, examining codes of conduct for implicit sexism, ableism, racism, and classism would provide a richer and more just understanding of the culture, climate, policies, and practices of a school.

This balanced and culturally responsive data analysis will occur best in a democratic sharing of school power. With all stakeholders involved in analyzing data and setting behavioral expectations, other perspectives come to the table to guide the process, as some districts are doing in the work described by Bal et al. (2014, 2012). Although broader participation is promising, it may not be sufficient, as the Greendale planning meeting illustrates. The literature on effective social justice leadership suggests strongly that democratic participation on implementation must be joined with uncompromising visionary leadership for just and inclusive schools (Capper, Theoharis, & Sebastian, 2006; Larson & Murtadha, 2002; Theoharis, 2007). To that end, leaders would do well to keep the focus on establishing justice rather than restoring order and avoid swapping disciplinary stigmas of "disorderly" students for medicalized stigmas of "disordered" ones. This chapter argues that maintaining a critical eye toward the allegedly scientific discourses of PBIS is one important component in doing so.

Some more early work on culturally responsive PBIS not only speaks of democratizing the process but also grounding the school's expectations in terms that are relevant to the cultures of the students of that school. In one New Mexico school for example, much productive work went into reinterpreting Tier I expectations from a generic PAWS (*P* = Be *P*ositive and *P*olite, *A* = *A*chieve Your Goals, *W* = *W*ork Hard, and *S* = *S*tay *S*afe) to the Diné word *T'aahwiajiiteego*, meaning that an individual is "responsible and accountable for one's own choices" (Jones, Caravaca, Cizek, Horner, & Vincent, 2006). Relevant biographies of Jim Thorpe, Chief Wilma Mankiller and others communicated the core principles in the Tier I lessons promoting those values.

One can imagine local stakeholder groups doing likewise in communities across the country. However, I would argue that the democratic process should go further than defining a locally relevant set of expectations. PBIS systems must use data that reflect those expectations and not default to disciplinary data such as office discipline referrals.

They may have to create such data points. For example, if a school used universal expectations such as mastery, belonging, independence, and generosity such as are found in a promising multicultural behavioral program known as the Circle of Courage (Brendtro, Brokenleg, & Van Bockern, 2002), many more kinds of data would count as identifying acceptable and unacceptable behavior. Likewise, different interventions would be applied, as the PBIS teams tried to encourage either mastery, belonging, independence, or generosity, rather than compliance alone. Developing those new definitions of acceptable behavior, signifying data, and interventions would involve the courageous conversations (Singleton & Linton, 2006) that deconstruct White privilege and culture as they manifest in behavioral data, as they then define more liberatory paradigms.

What these promising alternatives have in common is that they more closely resemble restorative justice paradigms. When disruption occurs in a community, these methods call into question the imbalance of power in that community. Understanding the root expectations of a community and its structures for maintaining them is crucial in establishing justice. Understanding how power comes to be expressed by individuals is likewise at the heart of building justice rather than restoring order. Changing the PBIS conversation in these ways would acknowledge that the structure is a fixed part of the current landscape, as King (1968, 2010) did in identifying the necessity of social welfare programs. Doing so and having the courage to analyze adults and the school culture as a whole I argue would be major contributions to creating school systems that builds justice rather than simply restores order.

Furthermore, restorative justice should be the first option rather than PBIS to disrupting the excessive discipline of the school-to-prison pipeline. Restorative justice fundamentally shifts away from blaming students for the conflicts in which they find themselves, and seeks just resolution rather than stigmatizing deficit labeling. Implementing culturally responsive PBIS can itself be a practice of restorative justice but only if it simultaneously takes on the medicalizing deficit practices and assumptions within conventional PBIS. Challenging the school-to-prison pipeline should be rooted in creating schools that affirm our students' aspirations, not replacing the disciplinary structure of enforcing compliance with another.

NOTE

1. S11 and S12 are the eleventh and twelfth students discussed in the meeting.

REFERENCES

Adler, P. A., & Adler, P. (1994). Observational techniques. In N. K. Denzin & Y. S. Lincoln (Eds.), *Handbook of qualitative research* (pp. 377–392). Thousand Oaks, CA: Sage.

American Psychiatric Association, Task Force on DSM-IV. (2000). *Diagnostic and statistical manual of mental disorders: DSM-IV-TR* (4th ed.). Washington, DC: American Psychiatric Association.

Annamma, S., Morrison, D., & Jackson, D. (2014). Disproportionality fills in the gaps: Connections between achievement, discipline and special education in the school-to-prison pipeline. *Berkeley Review of Education*, *5*(1), 53–87.

Annamma, S. A., Connor, D., & Ferri, B. (2013). Dis/ability critical race studies (DisCrit): Theorizing at the intersections of race and dis/ability. *Race Ethnicity and Education, 16*(1), 1–31.

Artiles, A. J. (2007). Challenges to response to intervention (RTI) models: Equity and cultural considerations. Paper presented at the NCCREST. Retrieved from http://www.nccrest.org/publications/RTI-CoP_9-17RTI24

Avissar, G., Reiter, S., & Leyser, Y. (2003). Principals' views and practices regarding inclusion: The case of Israeli elementary school principals. *European Journal of Special Needs Education, 18*(3), 355–369.

Baker, B. M., & Heyning, K. E. (2004). *Dangerous coagulations? The uses of Foucault in the study of education*. New York, NY: Peter Lang.

Bal, A., Kozleski, E. B., Schrader, E. M., Rodriguez, E. M., & Pelton, S. (2014). Systemic transformation from the ground-up: Using learning lab to design culturally responsive schoolwide positive behavioral supports. *Remedial and Special Education, 35*(6), 327–339.

Bal, A., Thorius, K. K., & Kozleski, E. (2012). Culturally responsive positive behavioral support matters. Paper presented at the American Educational Research Association, Vancouver, BC.

Barnett, C., & Monda-Amaya, L. E. (1998). Principals' knowledge of and attitudes toward inclusion. *Remedial and Special Education, 19*(3), 181–192.

Bezdek, J. M. (2011). *An examination of the validity of Office Disciplinary Referrals (ODR) as a behavioral screener: A descriptive study*. PhD dissertation, University of Kansas, Lawrence, KS.

Bogdan, R., & Biklen, S. K. (2007). *Qualitative research for education: An introduction to theories and methods*. Boston, MA: Pearson A & B.

Bornstein, J. (2014). *Runners, biters, and chair throwers: Discourses of order and medicalization in inclusion*. Doctor of philosophy dissertation, Syracuse University, Syracuse, NY.

Brantlinger, E. A. (2006). *Who benefits from special education?: Remediating (fixing) other' people's children*. Mahwah, NJ: Lawrence Erlbaum Association Inc.

Brendtro, L. K., Brokenleg, M., & Van Bockern, S. (2002). *Reclaiming youth at risk: Our hope for the future* (Rev. ed.). Bloomington, IN: National Educational Service.

Broderick, A. A., & Leonardo, Z. (2016). What a good boy: The deployment and distribution of "goodness" as ideological property in schools. In D. J. Connor, B. A. Ferri, & S. A. Annamma (Eds.), *DisCrit: Disability studies and critical race theory in education* (pp. 55–70). New York, NY: Teachers College Press.

Burke, M. D., Davis, J. L., Lee, Y. H., Hagan-Burke, S., Kwok, O.-M., & Sugai, G. (2010). Universal screening for behavioral risk in elementary schools using SWPBS expectations. *Journal of Emotional and Behavioral Disorders, 20*(1), 38–54.

Capper, C. A., Theoharis, G., & Sebastian, J. (2006). Toward a framework for preparing leaders for social justice. *Journal of Educational Administration, 44*(3), 209.

Conrad, P. (1988, 2006). *Identifying hyperactive children: The medicalization of deviant behavior* (2nd ed.). Burlington, VT: Ashgate.

Conrad, P., & Schneider, J. W. (1992). *Deviance and medicalization: From badness to sickness* (2nd ed.). Philadelphia, PA: Temple University Press.

Danforth, S., & Smith, T. J. (2005). *Engaging troubling students: A constructivist approach*. Thousand Oaks, CA: Corwin Press.

Davis, L. J. (2006). Constructing normalcy: The bell curve, the novel, and the invention of the disabled body in the nineteenth century. In L. J. Davis (Ed.), *The disability studies reader* (2nd ed., pp. 3–16). New York, NY: Routledge.

Denzin, N. K. (1978). *The research act* (2nd ed.). New York, NY: McGraw-Hill.

Denzin, N. K. (1994). The art and politics of interpretation. In N. K. Denzin & Y. S. Lincoln (Eds.), *Handbook of qualitative research* (pp. 500–515). Thousand Oaks, CA: Sage.

Dunlap, G., Sailor, W., Horner, R. H., & Sugai, G. (2009). Overview and history of positive behavior support. In W. Sailor, G. Dunlap, G. Sugai, & R. H. Horner (Eds.), *Handbook of positive behavioral support* (pp. 3–16). New York, NY: Springer.

Eber, L., Hyde, K., Rose, J., Breen, K., McDonald, D., & Lewandowski, H. (2009). Completing the continuum of schoolwide positive behavior support: Wraparound as a tertiary-level intervention. In W. Sailor, G. Dunlap, G. Sugai, & R. H. Horner (Eds.), *Handbook of positive behavioral support* (pp. 671–704). New York, NY: Springer.

Fabelo, T., Thompson, M. D., Plotkin, M., Carmichael, D., Marchbanks III, M. P., & Booth, E. A. (2011). *Breaking schools' rules: A statewide study of how school discipline relates to students' success and juvenile justice involvement.* New York, NY: Council of State Governments Justice Center Public Policy Research Institute.

Fallon, L. M., O'Keeffe, B. V., & Sugai, G. (2012). Consideration of culture and context in school-wide positive behavior support: A review of current literature. *Journal of Positive Behavior Interventions, 14*(4), 209–219.

Ferri, B. A. (2012). Undermining inclusion? A critical reading of response to intervention (RTI). *International Journal of Inclusive Education, 16*, 863–880.

Fierros, E. G., & Conroy, J. W. (2005). Double jeopardy: An exploration of restrictiveness and race in special education. In D. J. Losen & G. Orfield (Eds.), *Racial inequity in special education.* Cambridge, MA: Harvard Education Press.

Flannery, K. B., Fenning, P., McGrath Kato, M., & Bohanon, H. (2011). A descriptive study of office disciplinary referrals in high schools. *Journal of Emotional and Behavioral Disorders, 21*(2), 138–149.

Foucault, M. (1979). *Discipline and punish* (A. Sheridan, Trans.). New York, NY: Pantheon.

Frattura, E. M., & Capper, C. A. (2007). *Leading for social justice: Transforming schools for all learners.* Thousand Oaks, CA: Corwin Press.

Gee, J. P. (Producer). (2012). *Discourse analysis: What makes it critical?* (Essay) Retrieved from http://www.jamespaulgee.com/sites/default/files/pub/CriticalDiscourse.pdf

Glaser, B. G., & Strauss, A. L. (1967). *The discovery of grounded theory: Strategies for qualitative research.* Chicago, IL: Aldine.

Gresham, F. M. (2005). Response to intervention: An alternative means of identifying students as emotionally disturbed. *Education and Treatment of Children, 28*(4), 328–344.

Hall, S. (2001). Foucault: Power, knowledge, and discourse. In M. Wetherell, S. J. Yates, & S. Taylor (Eds.), *Discourse theory and practice: A reader* (pp. 72–81). London: Sage.

Harry, B., & Klingner, J. K. (2006). *Why are so many minority students in special education? Understanding race & disability in schools.* New York, NY: Teachers College Press.

Harwood, V. (2003). Subjugation and disqualification: Critiquing the discourses of psychopathological behaviour used in education. *Melbourne Studies in Education, 44*(1), 45–62.

Harwood, V. (2006). *Diagnosing 'disorderly' children: A critique of behaviour disorder discourses.* London: Routledge.

Hawken, L. S., Adolphson, S. L., MacLeod, K. S., & Schumann, J. (2009). Secondary-tier interventions and supports. In W. Sailor, G. Dunlap, G. Sugai, & R. H. Horner (Eds.), *Handbook of positive behavior supports*. Issues in clinical child psychology (pp. 395–420). Berlin: Springer.

Hawken, L. S., Vincent, C. G., & Schumann, J. (2008). Response to intervention for social behavior: Challenges and opportunities. *Journal of Emotional and Behavioral Disorders, 16*(4), 213–225.

Hodder, I. (1994). The interpretation of documents and material culture. In N. K. Denzin & Y. S. Lincoln (Eds.), *Handbook of qualitative research* (pp. 393–402). Thousand Oaks, CA: Sage.

Hosp, J. L., & Reschly, D. J. (2003). Referral rates for intervention or assessment: A meta-analysis of racial differences. *Journal of Special Education, 37*(2), 67–80.

Houser, M. A., Bell, G. C., Dickens, V., & Hicks, T. (2010). *The relationship between selected leadership behaviors and attitudes toward behavioral and social inclusive practices among middle school principals in North Carolina.* (Faculty Working Papers from the School of Education No. 17). Fayetteville State University. Fayetteville, NC. Retrieved from http://digitalcommons.uncfsu.edu/soe_faculty_wp/17

Individuals with Disabilities in Education Improvement Act, Pub. L. No. 42 U.S.C. §1400 (2004).

Jargowsky, P. A. (2015). *Architecture of segregation: Civil unrest, the concentration of poverty, and public policy*. Retrieved from http://apps.tcf.org/architecture-of-segregation. Accessed on September 23.

Jewell, K. (2012). *Examining proportional representation of ethnic groups within the SWPBIS model.* Doctor of philosophy dissertation. University of Washington, Seattle, WA.

Jimerson, S. R., Burns, M. K., & VanDerHeyden, A. M. (2007). *Handbook of response to intervention: The science and practice of assessment and intervention*. New York, NY: Springer US.

Jones, C., Caravaca, L., Cizek, S., Horner, R. H., & Vincent, C. G. (2006). Culturally responsive schoolwide positive behavior support: A case study in one school with a high proportion of native American students. *Multiple Voices for Ethnically Diverse Exceptional Learners, 9*(1), 108–119.

Jones, D. M., & Ball, S. J. (1995). Michel Foucault and the discourse of education. In P. L. McLaren & J. M. Giarelli (Eds.), *Critical theory and educational research* (pp. 39–51). Albany, NY: State University of New York Press.

Kim, C. Y., Losen, D. J., & Hewitt, D. T. (2010). Challenging suspensions and expulsions. *The school-to-prison pipeline: Structuring legal reform* (pp. 97–111). New York, NY: NYU Press.

Kincheloe, J. L., & McLaren, P. L. (1994). Rethinking critical theory and qualitative research. In N. K. Denzin & Y. S. Lincoln (Eds.), *Handbook of qualitative research* (pp. 138–157). Thousand Oaks, CA: Sage.

King, M. L., Jr. (1968/2010). *Where do we go from here: Chaos or community?* Boston, MA: Beacon.

Larson, C. L., & Murtadha, K. (2002). Leadership for social justice. In J. Murphy (Ed.), *The educational leadership challenge: Redefining leadership for the 21st century* (pp. 134–161). Chicago, IL: University of Chicago.

Lincoln, Y. S., & Guba, E. G. (1985). *Naturalistic Inquiry*. Beverly Hills, CA: Sage.

Losen, D. J., & Gillespie, J. (2012). *Opportunities suspended: The disparate impact of disciplinary exclusion from school*, p. 48. In The Civil Rights Project. University of California, Los Angeles, CA.

Losen, D. J., & Martinez, T. E. (2013). *Out of school and off track: The overuse of suspensions in American middle and high schools*, p. 105. The Center for Civil Rights Remedies, The Civil Rights Project, University of California, Los Angeles, CA.

Marshall, C., & Oliva, M. (2006). *Leadership for social justice: Making revolutions in education*. Boston, MA: Pearson/Allyn and Bacon.

Mass-Galloway, R. L., Panyan, M. V., Smith, C. R., & Wessendorf, S. (2008). Systems change with school-wide positive behavior supports: Iowa's work in progress. *Journal of Positive Behavior Interventions*, *10*(2), 129–135.

McIntosh, K., Campbell, A. L., Carter, D. R., & Zumbo, B. D. (2009). Concurrent validity of office discipline referrals and cut points used in schoolwide positive behavior support. *Behavioral Disorders*, *34*(2), 100–113.

McIntosh, K., Frank, J. L., & Spaulding, S. A. (2010). Establishing research-based trajectories of office discipline referrals for individual students. *School Psychology Review*, *39*(3), 380–394.

Merrell, K. W., & Buchanan, R. (2006). Intervention selection in school-based practice: Using public health models to enhance systems capacity of schools. *School Psychology Review*, *35*(2), 167–180.

Morse, J. M. (1991). Strategies for sampling. In J. M. Morse (Ed.), *Qualitative nursing research: A contemporary dialogue* (Revised ed., pp. 117–131). Newbury Park, CA: Sage.

Morse, J. M., Barrett, M., Mayan, M., Olsen, K., & Spiers, J. (2002). Verification strategies for establishing reliability and validity in qualitative research. *International Journal of Qualitative Methods*, *1*(2), 1–19.

Netzel, D. M., & Eber, L. (2003). Shifting from reactive to proactive discipline in an urban school district: A change of focus through PBIS implementation. *Journal of Positive Behavior Interventions*, *5*, 71–79.

Oswald, D. P., Coutinho, M. J., & Best, A. M. (2002). Community and school predictors of overrepresentation of minority children in special education. In G. Orfield & D. J. Losen (Eds.), *Racial inequality in special education* (pp. 1–14). Cambridge, MA: Harvard Education Press.

Patton, M. Q. (2002). *Qualitative research and evaluation methods* (3rd ed.). Thousand Oaks, CA: Sage.

Pearce, L. R. (2009). Helping children with emotional difficulties: A response to intervention investigation. *The Rural Educator*, *30*(2), 34–46.

Praisner, C. L. (2003). Attitudes of elementary principals toward the inclusion of students with disabilities. *Exceptional children*, *69*(2), 135–145.

Project Safe Schools Act § 2801 (2000).

Reid, D. K., & Knight, M. G. (2006). Disability justifies exclusion of minority students: A critical history grounded in disability studies. *Educational Researcher*, *35*(6), 18–23.

Richards, T. J., & Richards, L. (1994). Using computers in qualitative research. In N. K. Denzin & Y. S. Lincoln (Eds.), *Handbook of qualitative research* (pp. 445–462). Thousand Oaks, CA: Sage.

Rolfe, G. (2006). Validity, trustworthiness and rigour: Quality and the idea of qualitative research. *Journal of advanced nursing*, *53*(3), 304–310.

Ross, J. A., & Berger, M.-J. (2009). Equity and leadership: Research-based strategies for school leaders. *School leadership and management*, *29*(5), 463–476.

Rubin, H. J., & Rubin, I. S. (2005). *Qualitative interviewing: The art of hearing data*. Thousand Oaks, CA: Sage.

Sailor, W., Dunlap, G., Sugai, G., & Horner, R. H. (2009). *Handbook of Positive Behavioral Support*. New York, NY: Springer.

Shields, C. M. (2010). Leadership: Transformative. In P. Peterson, E. Baker, & B. McGraw (Eds.), *International encyclopedia of education* (3rd ed.). Oxford: Elsevier.

Singleton, G. E., & Linton, C. (2006). *Courageous conversations about race: A field guide for achieving equity in schools*. Thousand Oaks, CA: Corwin Press.

Skiba, R., Simmons, A. S., Staudinger, L., Rausch, M., Dow, G., & Feggins, R. (2003). Consistent removal: Contributions of school discipline to the school-to-prison pipeline. Paper presented at the school-to-prison pipeline conference. Harvard Civil Rights Project, Cambridge, MA.

Smith, T. J., Danforth, S., & Nice, S. (2005). Creating a participatory classroom community. *Engaging troubling students: A constructivist approach* (pp. 57–92). Thousand Oaks, CA: Corwin Press.

Sontag, S. (1990). *Illness as metaphor; and, AIDS and its metaphors*. New York, NY: Doubleday.

State Education Department. (2010). *Number of children and youth with disabilities receiving special education programs and services*. Education setting (least restrictive environment). Capital City.

State Education Department. (2012a). *State district report card 2010–11*. Clearwell Central School District, Capital City.

State Education Department. (2012b). *State district report card 2010–11*. Fairview Central School District, Capital City.

State Education Department. (2012c). *State district report card 2010–11*. Greendale City School District, Capital City.

State Education Department. (2012d). *State district report card 2010–11*. Lakeview Central School District, Capital City.

State Education Department. (2012e). *State district report card 2010–11*. Pleasant Hills Central School District, Capital City.

Sugai, G. (2010). School-wide positive behavior support and response to intervention. *RTI Network*. Retrieved from http://www.rtinetwork.org/learn/behavior/schoolwidebehavior

Sugai, G., Horner, R. H., Dunlap, G., Hieneman, M., Lewis, T. J., Nelson, C. M., … Ruef, M. (2000). Applying positive behavior support and functional behavioral assessment in schools. *Journal of Positive Behavior Interventions*, *2*, 131–143.

Sugai, G., O'Keeffe, B. V., & Fallon, L. M. (2011). A contextual consideration of culture and school-wide positive behavior support. *Journal of Positive Behavior Interventions*, *14*(4), 197–208.

Theoharis, G. (2007). Navigating rough waters: A synthesis of the countervailing pressures against leading for social justice. *Journal of School Leadership*, *17*(1), 4–27.

Theoharis, G. (2009). *The school leaders our children deserve: Seven keys to equity, social justice, and school reform*. New York, NY: Teachers College Press.

Thomas, G., & Glenny, G. (2000). Emotional and behavioural difficulties: Bogus needs in a false category. *Discourse: Studies in the Cultural Politics of Education*, *21*(3), 283–298.

Vilbert, A., & Portelli, J. (2000). School leadership and critical practice in an elementary school. *Exceptionality Education Canada, 10*(1–2), 23–36.

Vincent, C. G., & Tobin, T. J. (2010). The relationship between implementation of School-Wide Positive Behavior Support (SWPBS) and disciplinary exclusion of students from various ethnic backgrounds with and without disabilities. *Journal of Emotional and Behavioral Disorders, 19*(4), 217–232.

Walkerdine, V., Lucey, H., & Melody, J. (2002). Subjectivity and qualitative method. In T. May (Ed.), *Qualitative research in action* (pp. 179–196). London: Sage.

Welsh, E. (2002). Dealing with data: Using NVivo in the qualitative data analysis process. *Forum: Qualitative social research, 3*(2).

Youdell, D. (2006). *Impossible bodies, impossible selves; Exclusion and student subjectivities.* London: Springer.

Zeeman, L., Poggenpoel, M., Myburgh, C. P. H., & Van, D. L. (2002). An introduction to a postmodern approach to educational research: Discourse analysis. *Education, 123*(11), 96–102.

CHAPTER 8

A SYSTEMS THEORY ANALYSIS FOR ENDING THE SCHOOL-TO-PRISON PIPELINE: USING DISABILITY RIGHTS LAWS TO KEEP CHILDREN IN SCHOOLS AND OUT OF COURTS, JAILS, AND PRISONS

Andrea Kalvesmaki and Joseph B. Tulman

ABSTRACT

This chapter considers the school-to-prison pipeline (STPP) within the United States as a network of flows and feedback loops that connects the education and delinquency systems. This system is heavily biased to funnel students with disabilities, disproportionately from low-income minority families, away from productive educational outcomes through punitive, exclusionary, and restrictive measures that too often result in incarceration. Congress intended special education and disability rights laws to ameliorate injustice and ensure long-term positive outcomes for all students. Through a systems theory perspective, this chapter outlines key leverage points inherent in disability rights laws, which can and should be activated to interrupt and reverse the STPP. Many provisions

The School to Prison Pipeline: The Role of Culture and Discipline in School
Advances in Race and Ethnicity in Education, Volume 4, 169–194

ISSN: 2051-2317/doi:10.1108/S2051-231720160000004009

within the law are overlooked or inadequately enacted within current educational practices. The authors present problem-solving strategies, rooted in the Individuals with Disabilities Education Act (IDEA) and other disability rights laws, for educators, juvenile justice advocates, and policymakers to use in order to reduce school exclusion and incarceration of vulnerable youth and to provide education opportunity for all students.

Keywords: Discipline disproportionality; students with disabilities; disability rights law; systems theory

If the measure of the greatness of a society lies in how it treats its most vulnerable citizens, the United States is not "measuring up" with regard to its treatment of children. The United States has, by far, the highest juvenile incarceration rate in the world (Zakaria, 2012). In 2006, the United States incarcerated children and youth under the age of 18 at a rate of approximately 300 per 100,000 (Trzcinski & Allen, 2012). In fact, children are incarcerated in the United States at a rate almost five times higher than the next highest country (Mendel, 2011). Much research has targeted public schools as a prime source of referrals for prosecuting children resulting in what is described as a "school-to-prison pipeline" (STPP) feeding US mass incarceration (Aull, 2012; Losen, 2015; Skiba et al., 2003; Teske, 2011; Wald & Losen, 2003).

The STPP metaphor describes a deleterious flow of children from the education system into the delinquency system. It has long been identified that racial and ethnic minority students and students with disabilities are most at risk of entering the school-to-prison pipeline, especially through severe and disparate school disciplinary actions (Aull, 2012; Losen, 2015; Skiba et al., 2003). According to federal data, one out of every four students of color with disabilities was suspended in 2011–2012 (OCR, 2014). In the same year, approximately 12% of K-12 students were identified as having disabilities, and over 58% of the students placed in seclusion or held in solitary confinement within school settings were IDEA eligible.[1] Increasing evidence demonstrates that students of color are often disproportionately identified as having certain disabilities (i.e., emotional disturbance or intellectual disabilities), which are more likely to result in educationally restrictive environments such as self-contained classrooms or result in exclusion from schools (Fenning & Rose, 2007; Losen, 2015; Losen & Orfield, 2002; Skiba, Poloni-Staudinger, Gallini, Simmons, & Feggins-Azziz, 2006).

Some advocates contend, quite sensibly, that to challenge the STPP requires a primary emphasis on schools and shutting down exclusionary school policies (for a substantive treatment on this subject, see Losen, 2015). However, other leverage points exist and must be considered in tandem. In passing the federal special education law and other education and civil rights laws, Congress meant to end the discriminatory exclusion of children of color and children with disabilities from schools. Furthermore, in passing the Americans with Disabilities Act (ADA, 1990), Congress intended to reverse and end the unnecessary institutionalization of people with disabilities. In other words, before the widespread recognition of the "school-to-prison pipeline," federal legislation was already enacted to prevent the unnecessary institutionalization of particularly vulnerable citizens. Nevertheless, increasing numbers of children with disabilities, particularly children of color with disabilities, are excluded from schools and pushed into delinquency courts. How school officials and administrators fashion and implement policies, including school discipline codes, dramatically influences these outcomes (Irby, 2014; Tulman & Weck, 2010). In addition, how states, districts, schools, and even individuals respond to disability rights laws greatly affects the trajectories for many children.

The STPP can be conceived not just as a flowing "pipeline" from schools into the court system but as a system in and of itself which has multiple and complex systemic functions (Fasching-Varner, Martin, Mitchell, & Bennett-Haron, 2014; Lospennato, 2009). This chapter is an effort to show educators and child advocates where, in the law, to find key leverage points that can and will change the systemic paradigm of the STPP in order to interrupt, reverse, and, ultimately, to dismantle the STPP.

Specifically, this chapter identifies and explains, through a systems theory lens, key legal leverage points that Congress built into special education law and reaffirmed in broader disability rights law. Leverage points are intervention points in systems for initiating change and redirection. This chapter first describes systems theory and its use in application to address and ameliorate issues compounding the STPP. Second, this chapter highlights key components of federal special education and disability rights law which are currently underutilized or overlooked, and which can function as leverage points to ensure children as well as schools receive the services needed to produce more positive academic and social outcomes. These include the Individuals with Disabilities Education Act of 2004 (20 U.S.C. §1400 *et seq.*);[2] Title II of the Americans with Disabilities Act of 1990

(42 U.S.C. §12101 *et seq.*), and section 504 of the Rehabilitation Act of 1973 (29 U.S.C.A. §794). State organizing efforts and case law precedent, which rely upon provisions from these laws, illustrate strategies that advocates, educators, judges, and others (including education policymakers) can use to generate balancing or reinforcing feedback loops at the nexus of the education and delinquency systems. Effectively engaging provisions from disability rights laws should restrict the flow of children out of schools, extricate children from the delinquency system, and reestablish those children in school with greater prospects of receiving and benefiting from appropriate general and special education services.

THEORETICAL FRAMEWORK

Systems theory (Laszlo, 1972; Meadows, 1997; Meadows & Wright, 2008; Von Bertalanffy, 1967) provides a distinct framework for identifying and understanding systems and their operational components to examine the STPP. Systems operate based on their philosophical purpose and underlying paradigms. The more complex the system is, the harder it becomes to distinguish systemic components for shifting the system to alternate purposes or to interrupt its function. Systems theory asserts that systems function in a continuously fluid process, defined by interconnected structures of stocks, flows, and feedback loops that shape behaviors. To adapt or change the functional outcome of a system requires an understanding of the overarching structure of systems and the behaviors that occur within systems (Meadows & Wright, 2008). By examining the structures and behaviors of a system, hidden leverage points can be detected and activated in order to shift, change, or deter a system's function.

Key Definitions

This chapter uses key terms to describe various system components of the STPP. *Systems* are traditionally described as a network of interconnected elements that are ordered together to produce an outcome. Systems can be "open" or "closed" depending on their characteristics, with an "open" system generally describing a more organic and fluctuating composition of interconnected operations that include continuously shifting inputs and outputs (Von Bertanlaffy, 1967). Lospennato (2009) indicates that because the STPP transcends the boundaries of education, court, and even social services, the system is both open and unbounded. This implies a system porous in nature, where operational flows may or may not be easily detected. This chapter recognizes the system of the STPP as fed through a series of stocks and flows residing in both the educational and delinquency systems – an open system fluctuating in either direction.

The *stocks* of a system can be conceived of as the location of content for that which flows through a system. This chapter refers to stocks in terms of where children are located within the respective systems. This term seems cold and impersonal, yet in the framework of the STPP, it may adequately capture the depersonalized nature in which children are shuttled in and out of school and court systems.

Finally, this chapter most frequently uses the terminology of *feedback loops* and *leverage points*, to describe where and how to insert and engage law to intervene in the STPP. Structures of stocks and flows within a system produce reinforcing feedback loops, which allow the system to thrive and adapt as needed. Feedback loops are not always easily identifiable, yet are the sources of growth, expansion, and sometimes collapse within a system (Meadows & Wright, 2008). A reinforcing feedback loop is one in which the system fluidly operates, often with little effort. The term *feedback loop* is used to describe where the STPP system may be operating in a vicious cycle across system functions, stocks, and flows (i.e., from the education system into the criminal justice system). Throughout this chapter, the term *leverage point* is specifically used to indicate a particular component of practice or law that can be used to either adjust a current feedback loop in the STPP or introduce a new feedback loop within the system's operation.

Systems Theory in Education

Applying systems theory to education has allowed researchers to address complex topics transcending school, district, and federal concerns within education. Educational systems from the local to the national can be conceived of as loosely coupled, independent, and yet interconnected systems (Weick, 1976). More recently, the concept of "formative feedback systems" has been used to describe the interconnected relationship of people, practices, and organizational structures that allow masses of student data and the practices that produce these student data to be converted into measurable educational outcomes (Halverson, 2010). Nicolescue and

Petrescu (2013) argue that systems theory as applied to educational systems can provide understanding for the multifaceted, complex, and even competing interrelated components of the overall system. Understanding school systems as a "dynamic system with equilibrium properties" (Nicolescue & Petrescu, 2013, p. 586) can allow educational researchers to understand and address complex relationships inherent in providing services to students. The systems framework is also well applied to studying the impacts of high-stakes testing and federal mandates requiring testing compliance on school systems. Nichols and Valenzuela (2013) suggest that while individual schools may function as their own system, education policy enacted at the federal or state level constitute a macrosystem in which the subsystem of the school must function. Specifically, educational disparities, including the increasing rates of disciplinary exclusion and a stagnating achievement gap, can be identified as outcomes of microsystem (within school) reactions to macrosystem requirements such as federal mandates for high-stakes testing (Nichols & Valenzuela, 2013).

A SYSTEMIC "PIPELINE" TOWARD INCARCERATION

Education policy research has yet to fully address the confluence of system factors and network effects present in the STPP. While the STPP has been researched in terms of school discipline, rates of incarceration, and which children are most at risk for entering the STPP, little has addressed the function of the STPP as its own system. Recent critical analyses of the STPP have suggested that, as a system, it is "functioning as intended" (Fasching-Varner et al., 2014, p. 411). The direction of children and youth in key groups (i.e., defined by race and disability) are funneled by default through gatekeeping access to educationally advanced courses and by disproportionately disciplining and excluding children of color and children with disabilities. Through this lens, racial and ethnic disparities in educational achievement gaps and disciplinary actions can actually be interpreted as expected outcomes of the overall system.

Fasching-Varner et al. (2014) call for "educational realism" (p. 420) on the part of educational policy analysts to address the function of policies and practices within the education system. Education policies, however, do not operate in isolation. Just as schools are located within greater communities, networks of policies are interacting and operating at local school as well as broader state and federal levels. Education systems have embedded systems of disciplinary policies and procedures which function as forms of social control at the school, district, and state level (Irby, 2014). Current school discipline policy and practice, student arrests either on or off campus, combined with the lack of coordination between both the education and juvenile justice systems, result in a double punishment of students and a confluence of a greater system which ultimately fails children (Buckingham, 2013). In fact, "the education and court systems mistreat the very children whom society should be trying to educate about the value of justice" (Buckingham, 2013, p. 203). While some juvenile court judges have recognized the STPP as complex system in which feedback loops between schools and court can and should be systemically redirected (Teske, 2011; Teske & Huff, 2010), cross-system functions of the STPP have yet to be adequately addressed.

USING SYSTEMS THEORY TO ADDRESS LEVERAGE POINTS IN THE STPP

Systems theory provides a framework to encapsulate the complex arrangements that operate between the education system and the delinquency system, thereby leading to the STPP. Meadows (1997, 2015; Meadows & Wright, 2008) stipulates that to be effective in producing *more of what you want and less of what you do not want* requires identifying critical leverage points and then using them to change, interrupt, or reverse the flow of products and outputs in the system. The most effective leverage points for intervening in a system's function include intervening in reinforcing feedback loops, controlling information flows, and affecting the rules by which the system functions (Meadows & Wright, 2008).

The STPP system is fed through a series of stocks and flows, including overcrowded and underfunded public schools, as well as a delinquency system and a criminal system burgeoned with long court dockets, crowded courtrooms, and large probation and parole caseloads. Hidden within all systems are leverage points which provide opportunities for monitoring, shifting, regulating, and providing order for a system's function (Meadows, 1997, 2015; Meadows & Wright, 2008). To engage a reinforcing feedback loop as a leverage point, Meadows and Wright (2008) recommend locating the feedback loop and either reducing the gain of the feedback loop in order to curb its growth potential, delaying the process by which the feedback loop can function to reduce its expansion, or triggering an increase response that would force the collapse of the feedback loop and interrupt function.

Rules govern the feedback loops that operate within a system, and it is precisely through uncovering and engaging rules and their parameters that feedback systems can be engaged to interrupt a system. Engaging rules (and the parameters by which the rules of a system can function) forces the altering of the underlying system paradigm (Meadows, 1997, 2015; Meadows & Wright, 2008). For educators and child advocates who work on STPP issues, engaging the rules within disability rights laws provides, as noted above, awareness of and access to leverage points which can be used to interrupt the STPP.

Systemic Pressures

Systemic pressures within both the education and the delinquency systems[3] operate to frustrate and often to thwart compliance with laws to keep children, particularly children with disabilities, in school and out of delinquency and other institutional settings. Urban school districts "face a constellation of barriers" to providing services for all students, through fiscal constraints, highly mobile student and teacher populations, and aging facilities (MacArdy, 2009, p. 879). These schools are often low performing in general and are often ill-prepared or unable to detect students who are eligible for Individuals with Disabilities Education Act (IDEA) services (MacArdy, 2009). The problem of detection is not necessarily satisfied by a child's placement in special education classrooms.

Especially within underfunded schools and districts, qualifying for disability services is not equivalent to addressing the cognitive, emotional, and other academic support needed by these children (Cannon et al., 2013).

Systemic pressures within schools may inadvertently reward pushing students with disabilities into the STPP. For example, school administrators might perceive a benefit in excluding, particularly at times of high-stakes testing, students who are achieving academically at a relatively low level (Nichols & Valenzuela, 2013). Overburdened teachers who refer children with significant behavioral challenges to school administrators may inadvertently trigger exclusionary discipline such as in-school or out-of-school suspension (OSS) (Pane, Rocco, Miller, & Salmon, 2014). School resource officers, trained ostensibly as police officers, may believe that enforcing a safe school environment through court referral is the most appropriate course of action for both the student and the school (Price, 2009).

Teachers and school resource officers are often ill-equipped to engage students with disabilities. These frontline adults may be unaware of the requirements of special education law to refer a student for evaluation and behavioral supports (Fedders & Langberg, 2013). Similarly, delinquency system intake personnel or intake probation officers fail to investigate and detect children who should be receiving intervention or special education services for whom the delinquency system is an inappropriate form of "treatment" (Tulman & Weck, 2010; Tulman, Feinstein, & Kule-Korgood, 2015). Precisely because schools are not equipped with the services (or the fiscal capacity) needed to address mental health, disability, personal safety, or other concerns for students, adults may sometimes maneuver children into the delinquency system in order to ensure availability of direct and immediate, ostensibly supportive intervention (Maschi, Smith Hatcher, Schwalbe, & Rosato, 2008). Treating the delinquency system as a no-reject repository for children for whom other service providers have failed to serve overburdens the delinquency system and is a counterproductive approach.

Leverage Points Already Exist

Congress intentionally designed the law for the purpose of providing necessary services for children *as well as* the needed information and support for schools. Through federal disability rights laws, educators are required to identify and address, as early as possible, disabilities that affect learning. The "child find" provision of the IDEA requires school personnel to identify and to evaluate children with disabilities. The purpose is to ensure that children with disabilities obtain meaningful educational benefit, progress year by year to graduation from high school, enter college, integrate into the work world, and live independently. The law was meant to provide education systems with additional resources necessary to reach these outcomes for students, with these resources coming from both the state and federal governments. Clearly, Congress understood that this additional investment in individualized services for children with disabilities will improve their lives and ultimately will provide systemic dividends by increasing the number of people with disabilities who become taxpayers and productive members of society, thereby decreasing the number dependent on social security disability and Medicaid. In passing the ADA in 1990, similarly,

Congress intended to stop the unnecessary, expensive, and discriminatory institutionalization of people with disabilities. Unfortunately, although these laws have been in place for some time, disability rights advocates have indicated that the leverage points provided in these laws are frequently overlooked and are misunderstood within the educational contexts (Buckingham, 2013; Cannon, Gregory, & Waterstone, 2013; Tulman & Weck, 2010).

USING DISABILITY RIGHTS LAW TO ACTIVATE LEVERAGE POINTS TO INTERRUPT, REVERSE, AND DISMANTLE THE STPP SYSTEM

The US Supreme Court famously ruled, more than a half century ago, in *Brown v. Board of Education* (1954), that racial segregation in public schools violated the constitutional right to equal protection. That precedent fueled two landmark federal district court rulings, *Pennsylvania Association for Retarded Children (PARC) v. Commonwealth* (1972) *and Mills v. Board of Ed. of the District of Columbia* (1972), finding that the segregation and exclusion of public school students with disabilities also violated equal protection. Spurred by those two cases and based also on its own findings that school officials across the country had been segregating and excluding millions of children with disabilities, Congress, four decades ago, passed federal legislation to ensure that children with disabilities would have access to a free appropriate public education (FAPE) through initial legislation, which would later become the IDEA (IDEA, 2004).[4]

Congress was particularly concerned that educators had been misusing school discipline rules and exclusionary sanctions against children with disabilities. For that reason explicitly, Congress designed and passed protections to end these abusive practices.[5] In interpreting the disciplinary protections in the federal special education law, the US Supreme Court emphasized, in *Honig v. Doe* (1988), that "Congress very much meant to strip schools of the unilateral authority they had traditionally employed to exclude disabled students, particularly emotionally disturbed students, from school" (p. 323). Even when the IDEA allows for the removal from the current educational placement of a child with a disability because of disciplinary infractions, the child must still receive a free appropriate public education.[6]

The IDEA includes provisions aimed at ensuring that children with disabilities are not removed for disciplinary reasons more than their nondisabled peers, and that school personnel not exclude children of color with disabilities at rates that are significantly disproportionate.[7] For example, each state must include in its plan for implementing the IDEA (as a condition for receiving federal funding) arrangements for measuring and reporting rates of school exclusion disaggregated by race and ethnicity in order "to determine if significant discrepancies are occurring in the rate of long-term suspensions and expulsions of children with disabilities."[8] When disparities in exclusion based on disability, race, and ethnicity are detected, districts are required to change policies, procedures, and practices affecting individualized education programs, behavioral interventions and supports, and procedural safeguards in order to ensure compliance with the law and a provision of high-quality educational services for all students.[9]

In addition to the IDEA, Congress has passed other broad disability rights laws, most notably, Section 504 and the ADA, to prohibit discrimination against people with disabilities and to require reasonable accommodations for people with disabilities, including children with disabilities in public schools. Congress meant for Section 504 and the ADA also to end discriminatory segregation of people with disabilities and unnecessary (and therefore discriminatory) institutionalization of people with disabilities (*Olmstead v. L.C.*, 1999).[10] Clearly, the law of the land, which has been crafted, illuminated, and reinforced at the highest levels of government, commands that officials and administrators not discriminate in public schools based on race and disability.

INSTITUTIONAL DISTANCE FROM THE LAW

In response to changes in law mandating inclusion of individuals with disabilities, the United States has lurched forward over the past three or four decades in closing institutions that housed people with mental illness and institutions that housed people with developmental disabilities. Since 1970, however, the United States has increased the use of jails and prison facilities on a massive scale, multiplying incarceration for adults from 150 per 100,000 to 760 per 100,000 (Zakaria, 2012). This dramatic increase in incarceration rates, often dubbed "mass incarceration," is widely recognized as based on radically elevated and accelerated rates of incarceration of people of color, principally African Americans (Alexander, 2010; Forman, 2012). Less easily identifiable is the degree to which the increase in incarceration rates represents a rise in the institutionalization of people with disabilities. A survey of youth correctional facilities investigating the percent of children estimated to be eligible for IDEA provisions in 2005 indicated a wide range of incarcerated children (from 30% to 70% depending on the state) were estimated to be eligible for special education services (Quinn, Rutherford, Leone, Osher, & Poirier, 2005). The estimates, while self-reported by youth correctional facilities, indicated that juvenile facilities housed more than four times the percent of children in need of special education services than were provided for in schools in that same year (Quinn et al., 2005). In addition, research predicting rates of school exclusion for children who are diagnosed with emotional or behavioral disorders indicated that key diagnoses predict multiple disciplinary actions that result in school exclusion (Bowman-Perrott et al., 2011). Diagnoses, such as ADHD and emotional disturbance, are often overlooked by school administrators for academic intervention services in school environments, and instead, these children may be referred for delinquency prosecution for relatively minor behavioral infractions notwithstanding an awareness of the child's diagnosis and that the presenting behavior is a manifestation of the disability (Bowman-Perrott et al., 2011; Rivkin, 2009). Furthermore, a review of data from the National Child Traumatic Stress Network-Core Data Set (NCTSN-CDS) indicates that, on average, approximately 70% of incarcerated youth meet the criteria for an observable mental health disorder (Dierkhising et al., 2013). The high rate of incarceration of children and adults with disabilities flies in the face of the legal requirements to integrate people with disabilities, the progress in closing mental hospitals and similar institutions, and case law that underscores these legal requirements (*Olmstead v. L.C.*, 1999).

While legal requirements within the IDEA, ADA, and Section 504, as well as within states' delinquency statutes, should operate as leverage points to create feedback loops at the nexus of the educational and delinquency systems, the expanding STPP evidences precisely the opposite outcome. The IDEA, for example, provides key leverage points for enhanced educational outcomes by increasing the information flows to parents of students with disabilities and ensuring that students are provided with FAPE. Unfortunately, school districts and state education systems often have to be prodded into engaging many of the provisions of the IDEA (Buckingham, 2013). In some cases, educators need clearer understanding of these provisions in order to intervene early to create better outcomes for both students and schools.

THE IMPORTANCE OF "CHILD FIND" AND PARENTAL ENFORCEMENT OF THE IDEA

The IDEA provides key leverage points for enhanced educational outcomes by mandating access to information for parents of students with disabilities, by ensuring that parents are involved in all decision-making, and by empowering parents to enforce their IDEA rights. The IDEA creates, through the "child find" provision,[11] an affirmative obligation for public school personnel to identify children with disabilities who may require special education services. A parent has a right, with no charge to the parent, to evaluations of the child in every area of suspected disability,[12] a right to a comprehensive reevaluation at least every three years,[13] and a right to an independent educational evaluation, again at no charge to the parent, if the parent disagrees with an evaluation performed by the public school evaluator.[14] A parent has a right to examine educational records regarding the child[15] and a right to detailed, prior written notice if school personnel propose or refuse to make a change regarding the identification, evaluation, educational placement of the child, or the provision of a FAPE to the child.[16]

Congress envisioned the parent as an important member of the individualized education program (IEP) team that makes decisions about the child's evaluation, eligibility, and services.[17] Of equal importance, Congress empowered the parent to enforce the law. The parent has a right to an administrative hearing, with an impartial hearing officer, if the parent disagrees with any aspect of the identification, evaluation, or educational placement of the child or believes the child is not receiving a FAPE.[18] The federal regulations also ensure that the parent has, as an alternative approach for enforcement, access to a state investigation process of any complaint regarding the special education system and IDEA services for the child.[19] After exhausting administrative remedies, an aggrieved parent can file a lawsuit in court.[20] To ensure that the parent is aware of these rights, Congress required school representatives to provide the parent with a written list of procedural safeguards, including, of course, the right to enforce the law through an administrative hearing or lawsuit.[21] The Supreme Court has emphasized that "the importance Congress attached to these procedural protections cannot be gainsaid … Congress placed every bit as much emphasis upon compliance with procedures … as it did upon the measurement of the resulting IEP against a substantive standard" (*Board of Educ. v. Rowley*, 1982). To further empower parents, Congress subsequently amended the law to authorize courts to award attorneys' fees to parents who prevail against the school system.[22]

USING DISABILITY RIGHTS LAW TO INTERRUPT AND REVERSE THE STPP

Notwithstanding these multiple efforts to empower parents to enforce their rights, considering the high and disparate rates of disciplinary exclusion and overrepresentation among incarcerated youth, the rate of special education hearing requests across the country is remarkably low, at approximately 2.6 due process requests per 1,000 special education students (Tulman et al., 2015). The national rate of due process hearing requests is even lower when one omits data from three jurisdictions, the District of Columbia (DC), New York City, and Puerto Rico. Those three jurisdictions accounted for 53% of all due process filings (and 85% of all fully litigated hearings) during the 2012–2013 school year (Tulman et al., 2015). Without these three jurisdictions, the national annual rate of due process filings has been 1.3 per 1,000, and the rate of rulings from administrative hearings[23] drops from 39 to 6.6 per 100,000 special education students. In addition, longitudinal evidence indicates that compliance with the "child find" requirement and assertions of parent rights are more likely to occur when a child is from a White, middle-income family (Bowman-Perrott et al., 2011). By contrast, special education advocacy within the three outlier jurisdictions has been available at relatively higher rates for minority, low-income families (Tulman et al., 2015).

For three or four years in the early to mid-2000s, DC, a jurisdiction with about 11,700 special education students, accounted for roughly half of the special education hearings in the country (Tulman & Schofield, 2015).[24] Indeed, parents also won at a much higher rate in DC than anywhere else (Tulman et al., 2015). The phenomenal and unique rate of parental empowerment in DC was largely a product of an intentional effort spearheaded by faculty members in the Juvenile and Special Education Law Clinic of the public law school (then, the DC School of Law; now, the U.D.C. David A. Clarke School of Law), starting in 1990, to train and mobilize court-appointed attorneys (i.e., attorneys who represent children in delinquency matters and who represent parents and children in child welfare matters) to enforce the special education rights of their clients (Tulman & Schofield, 2015). The organizers of the training and mobilizing effort intentionally used the leverage point in the law that provides the right to attorneys' fees for parents who prevail in a special education case, in order to create a reinforcing feedback loop. This effort provided a win-win situation for low-income minority families in Washington, DC and for the court-appointed attorneys. Court-appointed attorneys in delinquency and child welfare matters typically have unmanageably large caseloads. By enforcing the special education rights of court-appointed clients, and then by prevailing against the education agency in special education hearings, a lawyer can earn attorneys' fees from the government. Thus, the attorney can afford to maintain a manageable caseload and have the resources to effectively serve clients. The lawyer can then enforce the parent's rights to special education services, help to stabilize the child in school, and, in many cases, insulate the child from punitive and counterproductive responses in the delinquency system (Aull, 2012; Teske & Huff, 2010; Tulman & Schofield, 2015). In many respects, obtaining appropriate special education services prevents, preempts, or negates the need (or the perception of need) for processing children through the delinquency system (Aull, 2012; Cannon et al., 2013). Through this effort, court-appointed delinquency and neglect attorneys are incentivized to use special education representation to advance their clients' interests. School representatives are incentivized to settle parents' meritorious special education claims, and school officials are incentivized to provide appropriate special education services.

This training and mobilizing strategy (also known as a case-aggregation strategy) created a multiplier effect, which resulted in the unprecedented rise of special education enforcement in DC. Moreover, this massive enforcement effort targeted the needs and rights of children from low-income and otherwise marginalized families, the children who predominantly populate the STPP. Coincident with this massive increase in special education enforcement, DC replaced three large juvenile detention and long-term incarceration facilities (with a total of more than 500 beds) with two small facilities (with a total of 148 beds). Similarly, the rate of delinquency prosecutions dropped by over two-thirds (Tulman & Schofield, 2015).[25]

Another unique facet of the DC special education advocacy training and mobilization effort was the remarkable support of the judges presiding over delinquency and neglect cases. Recognizing the value of the special education advocacy, DC judges institutionalized a system for appointing and paying special education attorneys for low-income parents in the context of delinquency and neglect cases (Tulman & Schofield, 2015). DC is currently the only jurisdiction where judges are actively appointing and paying special education lawyers to represent students referred to the court system.

Clayton County, Georgia (GA) provides another example of the willingness of judges to recognize the importance and the value of enforcing the education rights of children who have been relegated unnecessarily and perhaps illegally to the delinquency system. In Clayton County, the number of children referred from schools to the court for delinquency and status offense matters increased 1,248% from the implementation of zero tolerance policies in the schools since the 1990s (Teske & Huff, 2010). Using the authority of the court, the presiding delinquency judge (Hon. Steven Teske) convened the system stakeholders to develop and to implement two protocols in 2004 to reverse the wholesale referral of children from schools into the court. One protocol required alternatives to court referrals. The second protocol established a panel to refer children with chronic disciplinary issues in school to an integrated system of care developed through a network of community providers (including mental health and social services). At the time of implementation, the juvenile detention rate in the county was at an all-time high. Through the networked system of community services, schools had an alternative to OSS, and middle school OSS declined in the first year by 8% (Teske, 2011). By the end of the 2009 academic year, the graduation rates for Clayton County had increased by 20% overall (Teske, 2011). The most impressive result, however, was a two-thirds reduction in the volume of court delinquency referrals for children (Teske & Huff, 2010). Through an integrated systems change approach, Clayton County experienced an 86% reduction in secure confinement of children, a substantial reduction in felony referrals and in the referral of children from racial and ethnic minority populations, and a 44% reduction in referrals of children with disabilities (Teske & Huff, 2010). Teske and Huff (2010) advocate for

> an intermediary, preferably a multidisciplinary team, to assist schools with alternatives to suspension and arrest. It's not enough to wait for children with disabilities to come to the [juvenile court] system when, in many circumstances, they shouldn't have been referred in the first place. Effective advocacy eradicates this paradoxical system for our children, especially those with disabilities. Effective advocacy doesn't begin in the courtroom. It begins with leadership in the community advocating for systems change. (p. 15)

The purpose of the delinquency court is not to punish but rather to provide care and rehabilitation. If a child does not require treatment from the delinquency system, an intake probation officer in the delinquency court should recommend against petitioning the case (Teske & Huff, 2010; Tulman & Weck, 2010). Similarly, a prosecutor who determines that the evidence is sufficient to establish guilt beyond a reasonable doubt still should weigh whether protection of the community requires prosecution and, more to the point, whether the child requires services through the court (Tulman & Weck, 2010). Indeed, if the child is, or should be, receiving services through the special education system that address the child's needs, then prosecution is unnecessary and potentially harmful (Teske & Huff, 2010).

Congress has provided other leverage points for containing and reducing the unnecessary and unfair referral of children with disabilities from schools to delinquency courts. Specifically, the IDEA requires that school administrators provide discipline and disability records to appropriate authorities when referring a child for prosecution.[26] This design to transfer information should empower intake probation officers, judges, prosecutors, and defense attorneys to discover on a case-by-case basis the advantages realized at a systemic level in both Washington, DC and Clayton County, GA.

Congress enforced the requirement of providing discipline and disability records in reaction to a remarkable litigation and legislative battle that emanated from a case in Tennessee, *Morgan v. Chris L.* (1994, 1997). For a prolonged period, school personnel ignored the special education needs of Chris L. and the procedural rights of his parents. When Chris L. allegedly committed a minor property offense at school, school administrators referred him for delinquency prosecution (*Morgan v. Chris L.*, 1994; Rivkin, 2009). Attorneys representing Chris L.'s parents demonstrated that school administrators were attempting to circumvent the IDEA and were illegally attempting to change Chris L.'s current educational placement. The hearing officer accordingly ordered the school administrators to withdraw the delinquency petition. Attorneys for the school system appealed and lost in federal district court; appealed and lost in the federal court of appeals; and then unsuccessfully petitioned the US Supreme Court to take the case (*Morgan v. Chris L.*, 1994; Rivkin, 2009).

Prosecutors and state government officials portrayed the outcome as an unjust encroachment on the state authority to prosecute people for crimes. They rallied school system representatives from around the country to push Congress to amend the IDEA to clarify that state and local prosecutors had unfettered discretion to prosecute children, including children with disabilities. As a result of this bruising battle, Congress included language in the IDEA that nothing in that law precludes the prosecution of children with disabilities for crimes (allegedly) committed in school.[27] However, Congress also included the requirement that school administrators provide the child's discipline and disability records to the appropriate authorities. Rivkin's (2009) account of the case indicates:

> *Chris L.* stands as a determined effort by the courts that rendered the string of favorable, non-punitive, disability-centered decisions in the case to breathe life into the meaning of what Congress intended in enacting the IDEA. In the tradition of *Honig v. Doe*, *Chris L.* represents a pragmatic recognition that the juvenile courts are unsuitable forums for handling low-level misbehavior by students. (p. 57)

Many states have provisions in their delinquency statutes that empower and obligate court intake personnel, prior to a decision by the delinquency prosecutor, to investigate the circumstances of a child referred for delinquency prosecution and to recommend whether to proceed with the delinquency case. If the child is not in need of care and rehabilitation, even assuming that the child committed the delinquency offense, then the intake probation officer should recommend against petitioning the case (Teske & Huff, 2010; Tulman & Weck, 2010).

The power of the intake probation officer, under state law, to review records and to recommend against petitioning meshes with the requirement in federal law that school administrators provide discipline and disability records for children referred for prosecution based on alleged delinquent acts at school. This has the potential to preclude the possibility that a child gets the "worst of both worlds," that is, an illegal denial of IDEA services in school and unfettered prosecution for behavior that may be a manifestation of the child's disability or that may have resulted from the failure of school personnel to have provided IDEA services (Teske & Huff, 2010; Tulman & Weck, 2010). The transmittal of special education and disciplinary records of children combines with the investigation authority and gatekeeping function of the delinquency court's intake personnel to create a balancing feedback loop to hold school personnel accountable and extricate children with disabilities from the STPP.

For the meshing of federal and state law to create a reverse flow in the STPP, at least two additional conditions must exist. First, intake probation officers (as well as judges and prosecutors) must understand the purposes and specific applicability of the IDEA and other disability rights laws. Second, defense attorneys also must understand the law and be prepared to file motions to dismiss delinquency cases when school personnel fail to send records and court personnel fail to hold school personnel accountable. In almost every jurisdiction in the country, these two necessary conditions do not currently exist. To make the law work will require training for judges, prosecutors, defense attorneys, and probation officers.

THE "BURLINGTON REMEDY" AS A WAY TO ASSERT THE RIGHT TO TRANSITION SERVICES

Case law from the US Supreme Court interpreting the IDEA can provide a leverage point to enforce the right to transition services and create a reinforcing feedback loop for reversing the STPP. For children aged 16 and older, and for younger children, if appropriate, the special education law requires school personnel to provide transition services. These are services meant to prepare the child for postsecondary education, for independent living, and for integration into the world of work.[28] For a student who is discouraged with and disengaged from school, transition services offer a path back to school and a meaningful alternative to the STPP. Yet, surveys of special education students who have received transition services indicate little satisfaction and an overall underpreparation for postsecondary success (Janiga & Costenbader, 2002). Unfortunately, many IDEA-eligible students never realize their ability to access these services.

Many students with disabilities who are between the ages of 16 and 21, frustrated and embarrassed by failure in school and a lack of meaningful transition opportunities, may drift away from school and seek opportunities outside of education to feel competent, independent, and to be grown-up. School districts across the country are pervasively not compliant with individualized and result-oriented transition services for eligible students with disabilities, and transition services remain a high litigation concern (Katsiyannis, Losinski, & Prince, 2012).

The IDEA authorizes, for a parent of a child with a disability who has not received a free appropriate public education, "such relief as the court determines is appropriate." The Supreme Court, in three cases, has interpreted that power "to award appropriate relief" broadly and upheld the unilateral right of parents to place children, for whom public school personnel are denying FAPE, in private schools and to receive tuition reimbursement from the public school system (*Burlington School Comm. v. Mass. Dept. of Educ.*, 1985; *Florence County School Dist. IV v. Carter*, 1993; *Forest Grove School Dist. v. T.A.*, 2009). After the Supreme Court's ruling in *Carter* and before *Forest Grove*, Congress amended the IDEA to include explicitly this parental right to unilateral placement and tuition reimbursement.[29] The *Burlington* remedy is available to a parent or a majority-age special education student who correctly rejects the portion of an IEP that provides inadequate transition services. Students may then be provided privately sourced transition services.[30]

Payment from the school system for private transition services can be costly. However, through applying the *Burlington* remedy, parents are also able to identify private placements within the local community to provide practical vocational training, job readiness, and employment opportunities for their children. A combination of legal advocacy and community supports can result in children with disabilities from low-income families receiving individualized job coaching from responsible adults in their neighborhoods.

As a potential leverage point, the application of the *Burlington* remedy to secure appropriate, results-oriented transition services addresses a portion of the STPP that is as yet insufficiently studied. Similarly, the prospect of using the *Burlington* remedy as part of a systematic provision of transition services for children with disabilities from low-income neighborhoods could spur community reinvestment and a boon for small businesses that train and then employ young people. Without appropriate and adequate transition services, there is still a high risk that a young person with disabilities will enter the STPP. Specifically, the risk includes the possibility that a young person could learn illicit behaviors in the absence of job opportunities or continued education. Through the *Burlington* remedy, children in underresourced schools and districts have options by which they can secure individualized, legitimate job training in the community.

This example of a leverage point within the IDEA with the potential for activating a virtuous reinforcing feedback loop is provided as a concluding call to action. In passing the special education and other disability rights laws, Congress adopted a paradigm of inclusion and productivity for children with disabilities and outlawed discriminatory school exclusion and unnecessary institutionalization. Nevertheless, for four decades since Congress enacted the special education law, increasing budgets for juvenile jails and prisons and increasing use of exclusionary practices in schools have insidiously undermined the intention of the law to ensure the civil rights of children. Educators, policymakers, judges, prosecutors, defense attorneys, probation officers, parents, and other child advocates can use the *Burlington* remedy as a leverage point to require investments in the future of young people, the ultimate reinforcing feedback loop.

CONCLUSION

By using systems theory to address components of the STPP in operation and to harness the power of disability rights laws to intervene within the STPP system, this chapter broadens the discussion within education policy and law regarding the STPP. The STPP is a metaphorical representation of a much broader system that operates in complicated ways spanning multiple levels of the education and justice systems. Systemic pressures, largely unexamined, derail the intention of the law for equality and for positive educational outcomes for all students. Systems theory provides a framework for understanding that actors from both the education and justice systems operate under systemic pressure to perform duties and may actually be unaware of various systemic components operating in tandem. Through a systems theory lens, power resides in challenging the system function through the system itself. If the STPP is truly "operating as intended" (Fasching-Varner et al., 2014, p. 411), then harnessing existent system operations through multiple leverage points can and will enact much needed change.

This chapter has identified and illustrated some of the leverage points and feedback loops available through special education law that, when used as intended, have the potential to interrupt the STPP. The DC and Clayton County, GA examples provide concrete illustrations of the great effect employing a systems-based strategy can have to challenge and disrupt the system of the STPP. More research is needed to tie systemic components together across local, state, and federal systems and to demonstrate how those components jointly elevate the rates of child incarceration.

This chapter has not addressed systems other than the education and justice systems which may contribute to the increased vulnerability for children of color and children with disabilities to be excluded from educational environments, institutionalized, incarcerated, or otherwise marginalized. These include state welfare systems, foster care systems, and others not described here. Nevertheless, the examples in this chapter demonstrate how to activate leverage points and feedback loops that Congress created which are at the disposal of all who work on behalf of vulnerable children. Through special education law and other disability rights law, Congress has provided mechanisms to ensure that all students receive a free appropriate public education and that their rights are protected. The power of special education law *as it already exists* is that it provides the groundwork to shift the pervasive paradigm from mass incarceration to education for the masses.

NOTES

1. As defined under the Individuals with Disabilities Education Act of 2004.
2. The name of the law in 1975 was the Education for All Handicapped Children Act. After later amendments, the name of the law changed to its current

name, the Individuals with Disabilities Education Act. 20 U.S.C. §1400(a). Because Congress has amended the federal special education law several times since 1975, the citations in the United States Code for some provisions in the law have changed. In order to avoid confusion, citations used in this chapter will be to current statutory citations (2004).

3. Similar pressures exist within related, ostensibly child-caring systems, like the child welfare and Medicaid (e.g., Early Periodic Screening Diagnosis and Treatment) systems. These related systems, however, are beyond the scope of this chapter.

4. FAPE is defined in 20 U.S.C. §1401(9) & §1412(a)(1).

5. Congress included provisions to prevent school administrators from excluding from school children with disabilities even and especially when alleged behavior that may be disruptive in an educational environment may be a manifestation of a child's disability (see 20 U.S.C. §1415(k) (Placement in Alternative Educational Setting) and §1415(j) (Maintenance of Current Educational Placement, the so-called "stay-put" provision; see also 34 C.F.R. §300.530-536; see generally, §1415(a)-(i) (range of procedural protections for parents of children with disabilities to ensure that their children remain in school and receive FAPE). Congress subsequently added a provision to the IDEA to allow school administrators to exclude, for up to 45 days, students with disabilities even if the misconduct was a manifestation of the disability if the behavior involved serious bodily injury, possession of weapons, or possession of illegal drugs. 20 U.S.C. §1415(k)(1)(G).

6. 34 C.F.R. §300.530(b)(2) and 34 C.F.R. §300.530(d).

7. 20 U.S.C. §1418(d). See generally, id., §1400(c)(12)(A) ("Greater efforts are needed to prevent the intensification of problems connected with mislabeling and high dropout rates among minority children with disabilities.").

8. *Id.*, §1412(a)(22)(A)(i)&(ii).

9. 20 U.S.C.§1412(a)(24).

10. In *Olmstead v. L.C.* (1999), the US Supreme Court interpreted the requirement of the Americans with Disabilities Act not to discriminate against people with disabilities by unnecessarily institutionalizing them. The ADA's requirement to place people in the most integrated setting that is reasonable is equivalent to the IDEA's "least restrictive environment" requirement. The US Department of Education recognized that disparate rates of referring children with disabilities for prosecution might violate section 504. "Of course, it would be a violation of Section 504 of the Rehabilitation Act of 1973 if a school were discriminating against children with disabilities in how they were acting under this authority" 64 Fed. Reg. 12631 (March 12, 1999).

11. 20 U.S.C. §1412(a)(3)(A).

12. *Id.*, §1414(a)-(c).

13. *Id.*, §1414(a)(2)(B)(ii).

14. *Id.*, §1415(b)(1); 34 C.F.R. §300.502.

15. 34 C.F.R. §§300.501(a), 300.613-300.621.

16. 20 U.S.C. §1415(b)(3)(A)-(B).

17. *Id.*, §1414(d)(1)(B).

18. *Id.*, §1415(b)(6)(A).

19. 34 C.F.R. §§300.151-300.153.

20. 20 U.S.C. §1415(i)(2)(A).

21. *Id.*, §1415(d); see also id. §1415(h) (right to be accompanied by counsel; to present evidence; to compel witnesses to attend, etc.).

22. *Id.* §1415(i)(3)(B).

23. The filing of a due process complaint can lead to a settlement, a hearing, or the complaining party withdrawing the complaint. As Tulman et al. (2015) detail, few disability cases are fully adjudicated through a hearing.

24. For each year between 2005 and 2010, as the rate of hearings in DC started to decline, approximately 33–13% of special education students in DC were the subject of due process hearings. New York City and Puerto Rico did not reach 3% during that period (Tulman et al., 2015).

25. Data regarding school discipline rates in District of Columbia Public Schools were not analyzed in conjunction with this study; however, the reduced referral of students to the courts is indicative of an educational system change.

26. *Id.*, §1415(k)(6)(B). ("An agency reporting a crime committed by a child with a disability shall ensure that copies of the special education and disciplinary records of the child are transmitted for consideration by the appropriate authorities to whom the agency reports the crime.").

27. *Id.*, §1415(k)(6)(A) ("Nothing in this part shall be construed to prohibit an agency from reporting a crime committed by a child with a disability to appropriate authorities or to prevent State law enforcement and judicial authorities from exercising their responsibilities with regard to the application of Federal and State law to crimes committed by a child with a disability.").

28. The IDEA states that "providing effective transition services to promote successful post-school employment or education is an important measure of accountability for children with disabilities." 20 U.S.C. §1400(c)(14).

29. See *id.*, §1412(a)(10)(C); 34 C.F.R. §300.148(c).

30. See *id*,. §1412(a)(10)(c) and 34 C.F.R. §300.148(c).

REFERENCES

Alexander, M. (2010). *The new Jim Crow: Mass incarceration in the age of colorblindness.* New York, NY: New Press.

Americans with Disabilities Act, Title II, P.L. 101-336. 42 U.S.C. §12101 *et seq.* (1990).

Aull, E. H. (2012). Zero tolerance, frivolous juvenile court referrals, and the school-to-prison pipeline. Using arbitration as a screening-out method to help plug the pipeline. *Ohio State Journal on Dispute Resolution, 27*, 179–206.

Board of Educ. v. Rowley, 458 U.S. 176 (1982).

Bowman-Perrott, L., Benz, M. R., Hsu, H., Kwok, O., Eisterhold, L. A., & Zhang, D. (2011). Patterns and predictors of disciplinary exclusion over time. *Journal of Emotional and Behavioral Disorders, 21*(2), 83–96.

Brown v. Board of Educ., 347 U.S. 483 (1954).

Buckingham, S. (2013). A tale of two systems. How schools and juvenile courts are failing students. *University of Maryland Law Journal of Race, Religion, Gender, and Class, 13*(2), 179–278.

Burlington Sch. Comm. v. Mass. Dept. Ed., 471 U.S. 359 (1985).

Cannon, Y., Gregory, M., & Waterstone, J. (2013). A solution hiding in plain sight: Special education and better outcomes for students with social, emotional, and behavioral challenges. *Fordham Urban Law Journal*, *41*, 403–497.

Dierkhising, C., Ko, S., Woods-Jaeger, B., Briggs, E., Lee, R., & Pynoos, R. (2013). Trauma histories among justice-involved youth: Findings from the National Child Traumatic Stress Network. *European Journal of Psychotraumatology*, *4*, 1–12.

Fasching-Varner, K. J., Martin, L. L., Mitchell, R. W., & Bennett-Haron, K. P. (Ed.). (2014). Beyond school-to-prison pipeline and toward and educational and penal realism. Breaking the pipeline: Understanding, examining, and dismantling the school-to-prison pipeline [Special Issue]. *Equity & Excellence in Education*, *47*(4), 410–429.

Fedders, B., & Langberg, J. (2013). School-based legal services as a tool in dismantling the school-to-prison pipeline and achieving educational equity. *University of Maryland Law Journal of Race, Religion, Gender, and Class*, *13*(2), 212–236.

Fenning, P., & Rose, J. (2007). Overrepresentation of African American students in exclusionary discipline: The role of school policy. *Urban Education*, *42*(6), 536–559.

Florence County School Dist. IV v. Shannon Carter, 510 U.S. 7 (1993).

Forest Grove School Dist. v. T.A., 557 U.S. 230 (2009).

Forman, J. Jr. (2012). Racial critiques of mass incarceration: Beyond the new Jim Crow. *New York University Law Review*, *87*(1), 21–69.

Halverson, R. (2010). School formative feedback systems. *Peabody Journal of Education*, *85*(2), 130–146.

Honig v. Doe, 484 U.S. 305 (1988).

Individuals with Disabilities Education Act, P.L. 108-446. 20 U.S.C. §1400 *et seq*. (2004).

Irby, D. J. (2014). Trouble at school: Understanding school discipline systems as nets of social control. *Equity and Excellence in Education*, *47*(4), 513–530.

Janiga, S. J., & Costenbader, V. (2002). The transition from high school to postsecondary education for students with learning disabilities: A survey of college service coordinators. *Journal of Learning Disabilities*, *35*(5), 462–479.

Katsiyannis, A., Losinski, M., & Prince, A. (2012). Litigation and students with disabilities. *NASSP Bulletin*, *96*(1), 23–43.

Laszlo, E. (1972). *Introduction to systems philosophy: Toward a new paradigm of contemporary thought*. New York, NY: Gordon and Breach.

Losen, D. (Ed.). (2015). *Closing the school discipline gap: Equitable remedies for excessive exclusion*. New York, NY: Teachers College Press.

Losen, D., & Orfield, G. (Eds.). (2002). *Racial inequality in special education*. Cambridge, MA: Harvard Education Press.

Lospennato, R. K. (2009). Multifaceted strategies to stop the school-to-prison pipeline. *Clearinghouse Review*, *42* (11–12), 528–541.

MacArdy, A. L. (2009). Jamie S. V. Milwaukee public schools: Urban challenges cause systemic violations of the IDEA. *Marquette Law Review*, *92*, 857–889.

Maschi, T., Smith Hatcher, S., Schwalbe, C. S., & Rosato, N. S. (2008). Mapping the social service pathways of youth to and through the juvenile justice system: A comprehensive review. *Children and Youth Services Review*, *30*, 1376–1385.

Meadows, D. H. (1997/2015). Places to intervene in a system. *Nonprofit Quarterly*, August 3. Reprinted with permission from *Whole Earth*. Retrieved from http://nonprofitquarterly.org/2015/08/03/places-to-intervene-in-a-system/

Meadows, D. H., & Wright, D. (2008). *Thinking in systems: A primer*. White River Junction, VT: Chelsea Green Pub.

Mendel, R. A. (2011). *No place for kids: The case for reducing juvenile incarceration*. Baltimore, MD: Annie E. Casey Foundation.

Mills v. Board of Educ. of District of Columbia, 348 F.Supp. 866 (D.D.C. 1972).

Morgan, v. Chris L., 927 F.Supp. 267 (E.D. Tenn. 1994), *aff'd*, 106 F.3d 401 (6th Cir. 1997) (unpublished opinion), *cert. denied*, 520 U.S. 1271 (1997).

Nichols, S. L., & Valenzuela, A. (2013). Education policy and youth: Effects of policy on practice. *Theory into Practice*, *52*, 152–159.

Nicolescu, B. N., & Petrescu, T. C. (2013). Dynamical systems theory – A powerful tool in the educational sciences. *Procedia – Social and Behavioral Sciences*, *76*, 581–587.

Olmstead v. L.C., 527 U.S. 581 (1999).

Pane, D. M., Rocco, T. S., Miller, L. D., & Salmon, A. K. (2014). How teachers use power in the classroom to avoid or support exclusionary school discipline practices. *Urban Education*, *49*(3), 297–328.

Pennsylvania Assn. for Retarded Children (PARC) v. Commonwealth of Pennsylvania, 343 F. Supp. 279 (E.D. Pa. 1972).

Price, P. (2009). When is a police officer an officer of the law? The status of police officers in schools. *The Journal of Criminal Law and Criminology*, *99*(2), 541–570.

Quinn, M. M., Rutherford, R. B., Leone, P. E., Osher, D. M., & Poirier, J. M. (2005). Youth with disabilities in juvenile corrections: A national survey. *Exceptional Children*, *71*(3), 339–345.

Rehabilitation Act, Section 504. 29 U.S.C.A. § 794 (1973).

Rivkin, D. H. (2009). Decriminalizing students with disabilities. *New York Law School Law Review*, *54*, 909–952.

Skiba, R. J., Poloni-Staudinger, L., Gallini, S., Simmons, A. B., & Feggins-Azziz, R. (2006). Disparate access: The disproportionality of African American students with disabilities across educational environments. *Exceptional Children*, *72* (4), 411–424.

Skiba, R. J., Simmons, A., Staudinger, L., Rausch, M., Dow, G., & Feggins, R. (2003). Consistent removal: Contributions of school discipline to the school-prison pipeline. Paper presented at the Harvard Civil Rights Conference on the School-to-Prison Pipeline, Cambridge, MA, May 16–17. Retrieved from http://varj.asn.au/resources/documents/consistent%20removal.pdf

Teske, S. C. (2011). A study of zero tolerance policies in schools: A multi-integrated systems approach to improve outcomes for adolescents. *Journal of Child and Adolescent Psychiatric Nursing*, *24*(2), 88–97.

Teske, S. C., & Huff, B. (2010). The paradox of education in America: Integrating systems for children with disabilities. *ABA' Children's Legal Rights Journal*, *12*(3), 12–15.

Trzcinski, E., & Allen, T. (2012). Justice towards youth: Investigating the mismatch between current policy and public opinion. *Children and Youth Services Review*, *34*, 27–34.

Tulman, J. B., Feinstein, A. A., & Kule-Korgood, M. (2015). Are there too many due process cases? An examination of jurisdictions with relatively high rates of special education hearings. *University of the District of Columbia Law Review*, *18*(2), 244–272.

Tulman, J. B., & Schofield, K. A. (2015). Reversing the school-to-prison pipeline: Initial findings from the District of Columbia on the efficacy of training and mobilizing court-appointment lawyers to use special education advocacy on behalf of at-risk youth. *University of the District of Columbia Law Review*, *18*(2), 210–243.

Tulman, J. B., & Weck, D. M. (2010). Shutting off the school-to-prison pipeline for status offenders with education-related disabilities. *New York Law Review*, *54*(4), 875–907.

U.S. Department of Education, Office of Civil Rights (OCR). (2014). Civil rights data collection. Data snapshot: School discipline. U.S. Department of Education, Washington, DC. Retrieved from http://www2.ed.gov/about/offices/list/ocr/docs/crdc-discipline-snapshot.pdf

Von Bertalanffy, L. (1967). General theory of systems: Application to psychology. *Social Science Information*, *6*(6), 125–136.

Wald, J., & Losen, D. J. (Eds.). (2003). *New directions for youth development: Deconstructing the school-to-prison pipeline*. Hoboken, NJ: Wiley.

Weick, K. E. (1976). Educational organizations as loosely coupled systems. *Administrative Science Quarterly*, *21*(1), 1–19.

Zakaria, F. (2012). Incarceration nation. The war on drugs has succeeded only in putting millions of Americans in jail. *Time Magazine*, April 2. Retrieved from http://content.time.com/time/magazine/article/0,9171,2109777,00.html

CHAPTER 9

WHAT WE CAN DO RIGHT NOW: WHAT NEEDS FURTHER RESEARCH?

Felecia M. Briscoe, Nathern S. Okilwa and Muhammad Khalifa

ABSTRACT

This chapter sums up the previous chapters beginning with personal life stories of how school-to-prison pipeline (STPP) disastrously affects the lives of students, most especially African American youth, Chicano youth, working-class students, and those with disabilities. From there we moved to the institutional level where the authors described factors in schools that contribute to the STPP. Also at the institutional level, contributing authors critically examined current approaches in schools, which were designed to help dismantle the STPP. Finally, from policy prospective the contributing authors explained how some existing policies could be used differently to disrupt the STPP. After each summary, we present bullet points suggesting what we (school stakeholders – leaders, faculty, etc., and policy makers) can do right now to disrupt the STPP.

Keywords: School-to-prison pipeline; recommendations; policy; school leaders

The School to Prison Pipeline: The Role of Culture and Discipline in School
Advances in Race and Ethnicity in Education, Volume 4, 195–204

ISSN: 2051-2317/doi:10.1108/S2051-231720160000004010

Through the contributions of the chapter authors, this book has presented a multifaceted understanding of the school-to-prison pipeline (STPP). This problem is both pervasive and ubiquitous in Western society, as indicated by sites, in which the STPP has been studied (from London to Utah). Instead of beginning with abstractions and statistics, we began on a personal level with life stories of how STPP disastrously affects the lives of students, most especially African American youth, Chicano youth, working-class students, and those with disabilities. From there we moved to the institutional level where the authors described factors in schools that contribute to the STPP. However, also at the institutional level the authors also proposed and examined approaches in schools, which are to help dismantle the STPP. Finally, we took a policy prospective where the author explained how some existing policies could be used differently to disrupt the STPP. In this chapter, we draw upon the major points made by each of the contributing authors to summarize what we (school stakeholders – leaders, faculty, etc., and policy makers) can do right now to disrupt the STPP.

WHAT WE CAN DO RIGHT NOW

In this chapter, we begin with what school stakeholders (leaders, faculty, and parents) can do right now at a micro level based on the experiences described in Chapters 2 and 3. For the most part these two chapters describe daily practices and other factors educational stakeholders should seek to ameliorate or change in our schools. Both of these chapters describe how students began to adopt the identity of being a problem as they internalize negative stereotypes that are explicitly and implicitly ascribed to them.

Going from Having Problems to Being a Problem – Irby

In the second chapter, Decoteau J. Irby describes the process by which two young Black men gradually transform from someone with problems to forming an identity of being a problem. Pivotal in this process is a lack of an adult figure that exhibits true caring for the whole child over an extended period of time, especially male adult figures. The disproportionate amount of African American men in prisons contributes to this particular lack. Irby explains that through various relationships in schools, homes, and neighborhoods, Black youth suffer innumerable racist attacks upon their dignity, loss of human connections, and containment, all of which act to bring about feelings of being disposable, loss of place, loss of self-worth, loss of trust in others and in schooling. Boys experiencing this transformation may act out or they may be the quiet ones in the classroom. Passive boys in the classroom do not achieve academically, but they may avoid some of their other problems (e.g., substance abuse) coming to the attention of school authorities.

The two vignettes presented by Irby point to some of the ways in which STPP can be disrupted from the outset. Such disruption will not only ease the loss of African American men from the productive aspects of society but will also (and more importantly) ease the pain and suffering of African American men and African American families who lose their husbands, fathers, sons, and brothers, to prisons.

Like Chapter 2, Brenda G. Valles focuses on the experiences of those who are vulnerable to the STPP and how those experiences affected the school lives and identities of the youth. However, rather than focusing on the experiences of African American men, she focuses on the experiences of Chicano youth.

Learning from the Experiences of Chicano Youth – Valles

In Chapter 3, Valles's counternarrative focuses on the voices of Chicano boys as they describe their experiences and attempts to disrupt being pushed out of school and into the STPP. In this counternarrative, the students describe their experiences with school discipline in the state of Utah, a primarily White state characterized by "niceness." This is a White "niceness" that does not recognize other forms of culture, where school personnel act quickly to expel Chicanos whose nonviolent communication they subjectively characterize as being disobedient or disruptive to a White culture of "niceness." Two of the youths describe how they were pushed out of their high schools and into alternative schools. Being placed in alternative schools disrupted the friendships that youth had made in their own schools and acted to socialize them to become criminals. They described how they begin to lose their identity of being a student and internalize deficit stereotypes, adopting the ascribed identity of being a "f***-up." They realize that their efforts to resist were often damaging to themselves but could not readily see any other ways to resist. Upon reflection, they describe ways in which schools need to change to keep youth in their halls instead of pushing out. Most of their suggestions have to do with creating a sense of belonging for the Chicanas, what the students described as "revolutionary loving spaces." While speaking explicitly about African American and Chicano boys, many of the lessons we learned from Chapters 2 and 3 could be applied to others vulnerable to the STPP. Based on Chapters 2 and 3, some of the practices that schools can begin to implement right now include the following:

- Schools must become not only places of safety but they must also seek to embrace African American and Chicano boys holistically and provide them with a sense of belonging.
    - Include classes in Mexican American and African American culture and everyday communication practices in teacher education curricula and in teacher development workshops, which can help disrupt deficit stereotypes.
    - School leaders need to make sure that Chicano and African American culture (literature, holidays, and day-to-day practices) are reflected in the schools. In other words, schools need to create a sense of holistic belonging for Chicano students. It could begin with something as simple as a stanza from Pablo Neruda or Richard Wright is stenciled onto a highly visible wall, along with their picture.
    - Colleges of Education need to begin offering scholarships to Black and Chicano men to become teachers. With more Black and Chicano male teachers within schools at all levels, Black male students are more likely to develop a sense of belonging and possibility of their own.
    - Respect and listen to students, especially those who struggle with school culture. Encourage, respect, and care about all the students whom one sees on a regular basis.
- Faculty, staff, and school leaders need to attend to the quiet students, who are failing, as well as the ones acting out.
- Faculty and school leaders need to understand the ubiquitous aspect of racism and learn how to explicitly address it when it occurs on or off school grounds.
- Eliminate the zero tolerance policy and other school/district policies that create a punitive school environment (which is more likely to be applied to those who have endured discrimination) and create stronger links between schools and prisons.
- Provide English and Spanish classes where parents are informed of their rights as well as their children's rights as students such as, due process, should any dispute happen regarding their children in schools.

Chapters 2 and 3 described the personal experiences that African American and Chicano men had in the STPP. In Chapters 4 and 5, the authors take a slightly different approach examining the STPP from a school's perspective. We turn first to Chapter 4, where Hugh Potter, Brian Boggs, and Christopher Dunbar examine how schools construct the STPP.

Stop the Reflexive Punishment of Black and Brown Boys – Potter, Boggs, and Dunbar

In Chapter 4, Potter, Boggs, and Dunbar argue that a punitive environment (implementing a zero tolerance policy that overutilizes exclusion for subjectively determined "crimes") within a totalizing school environment leads to the STPP. This construction of STPP particularly for Black and Brown Boys is largely due to the Whiteness (the color of their skin, but more importantly, their White privileging cultural orientation, and ethnocentrism) of the teaching faculty and school leaders, who make these subjective judgments in schools. Their study of four schools in a mid-western school district found that between 73% and 93% of punishments meted out by a school unit resulted in suspension (exclusion) and the percent of exclusions that were for weapons were all less than 1%, whereas 30–60% of suspensions were based on subjective judgments. They suggest a different approach to school discipline, which would disrupt the STPP. Their suggestions resonate with those produced from the personal narratives. They suggest that in order for schools to disrupt the STPP schools need to do the following:

- Eliminate the immediate removal of students from the classroom for subjective infractions.
- Implement teaching and discipline policies that are culturally responsive to students and the backgrounds with which they arrive at schools.

While Chapters 3 and 4 describe the Whiteness of the teaching faculty as a major factor in the reproduction and maintenance of the STPP for minority boys, Garth Stahl in Chapter 5 examines how the economic class orientation of a school can coerce working-class White boys into the STPP.

Ending the Pathologization of Lower Economic Class White Boys

In Chapter 5, Stahl examines how White working-class male students in the United Kingdom are pathologized in school through the use of deficit discourses; this pathologization would eventually contribute to the students describing themselves with deficit views and would also have a negative impact on their academic achievement. Stahl interviews 23 White working-class boys aged 14–16, is the lowest performing group of all ethnic groups. Stahl uses Whiteness and power to explain how working-class Whites are constructed as "new race victims" (p. 10). By looking deeply at the discourses in school, "normative practices embedded in the 'soft structures' contribute heavily to the school-to-prison pipeline" (p. 23). But given that these students are White, and in their indigenous context, much of the racialized and classist discourse used to pathologize them has gone unrecognized. This pathologization is internalized by the boys, which leads them into increasingly deviant behavior and thus into the STPP. The study leaves us with three central implications:

- Schools must begin to recognize deficit discourses that pathologize students and communities, which ultimately lead to marginalization, poor school performance, and deviant behavior.
- Schools must find ways to combat discourses that lead to boys in lower economic classes internalization of deviancy.
- Schools must develop counter discourses for lower economic class White boys (and all ethnicities) to the ones that currently prevail in schools.

We have suggested a number of changes that schools can begin to implement in order to disrupt the STPP for minority and lower income boys based on Chapters 3, 4, and 5. Chapters 6 and 7 critically examine attempts that are currently underway to circumvent, dismantle, or in some way ameliorate the STPP.

A CRITICAL EXAMINATION OF ATTEMPTS TO DISMANTLE THE STPP

Chapter 6, by Hilary Lustick, and Chapter 7, by Joshua Bornstein, critically examine some of innovative disciplinary strategies that are being used with the idea of dismantling the STPP. Bornstein questions the use of positive discipline and Lustick examines the complexity of restorative discipline. Both found that the innovative disciplinary practices worked better at creating an orderly school than addressing the problems that have created the STPP.

"What Are We Restoring?" Black Teachers on Restorative Discipline – Lustick

In Chapter 6, Lustick focuses upon Black teachers' experience with restorative discipline. Her study demonstrates the difficult complexity of restorative practices in balancing authenticity and maintaining school order. In interviews with Black teachers at a New York City school, Lustick uncovered evidence that indicates that restorative practices did not build trust and relationships with students, as they were intended to do. Instead they restored obedience and order within the school. Framed with Du Bois's theory of Double Consciousness, Black teachers felt that administrators' use of restorative practices were motivated by the more traditional goals to maintain order and that this conflicted with restorative ideals. The teachers reported inconsistency in the practice of restorative discipline, particularly when the principal felt pressured by other building administrators to keep the school safe. The inconsistency of practice and perceived lack of caring created a lack of trust in the students; Black teachers felt they faced dual pressure to both support restorative practices and to cajole students into participating by using their positive relationships as a lever. In order to prevent the continuing racial disproportionality in school discipline practices, Lustick proposes the following:

- Evaluate restorative programs not only by the number of suspensions prevented and the number of conferences held but also by the extent to which community-building circles are successful at building trust and addressing bias, as well as by the degree of trust that students (especially those vulnerable to the STPP) have in their school.
- School staff should focus on cultural responsiveness and antibias in their practices.
- Recognize that restorative practices, while valuable for preventing exclusions of students from school, can also create collaboration by framing conflict and misbehavior as breaches of trust, rather than focusing only on mediation and reconciliation.

Like Lustick for restorative discipline, Bornstein appreciates the theoretical purpose of using positive behavior intervention and support (PBIS) but finds that in actual practice it fails to substantially address factors that create the STPP. In Chapter 7, Bornstein investigates the very purpose and function of PBIS by asking: is it meant to restore order, or justice? His multicase qualitative study highlights school principals who looked for nonexclusionary disciplinary practices, and found PBIS. But by using a

Foucauldian discourse analysis that uses DisCrit Theory, Bornstein demonstrates how leaders used PBIS to make "bad" kids into "sick" kids. In other words, the students who displayed non-normative behaviors in school were given medical designations – or medicalized – in ways that make kids officially deviant. He showed how referrals, for example, were one of many pieces of evidence used to medicalize students into a disorder. But in PBIS, the discussions about students essentially served the same purpose, and PBIS (and RTI and other similar practices) all continued the same deficit discourses that led to medicalization of students. The goal, therefore, was to create equitable and socially just environments for students, but instead, PBIS was used to maintain tight control of the environments. The effect was very similar to the pathologization of lower income White boys, in that the students were constructed as medical pathologies (deviants) rather than character deviants. Bornstein, therefore, offers several recommendations for social justice leaders:

- "Social justice leaders should not only implement culturally responsive practice, but also deconstruct the falsely scientific medicalizing discourses embedded in conventional PBIS practices" (p. 33).
- They should not "swap one deficit identity for another" (p. 33).
- And social justice leaders should shift away from deficit understandings of students and should use data to document student strengths, not deficits.

In Chapters 6 and 7, the authors critically examined innovative disciplinary strategies that were intended to disrupt or obviate factors leading to the STPP. However, in Chapter 8 Andrea Kalvesmaki and Joseph B. Tulman suggest a way to use current disability policies to disrupt the STPP.

You Can Use Disability Rights Laws to Keep Children in Schools and out of the STPP

In Chapter 8, Kalvesmaki and Tulman use systems theory to understand the STPP, explaining the leverage points, or elements of special education laws, that can disrupt the feedback loops in which the STPP flourishes. Citing clear legislative intent in special education law at ameliorating discriminatory practices, this chapter identifies key features within both legislation and case law that are useful for providing appropriate services to students rather than continuing the STPP. For example, the IDEA includes the provision for free and appropriate public education (FAPE) for special education students. FAPE governs a school district's ability to remove a special education student from the classroom and requires a school district to provide educational services in the event a student is removed for disciplinary reasons. Both the ADA and Section 504 provide additional levers to prevent discriminatory practices that result in segregation based on a person's disability. Case law indicates clear pathways for protection of special education students' rights. The *Burlington* remedy, resulting from an IDEA case, supports students' rights to transition services in preparing for postsecondary education. In the case of disengaged students who may fall victim to the STPP, the *Burlington* remedy provides a clear direction to school districts that they are responsible for providing acceptable transition services to all students, even in cases in which students have been dropped out and are disenfranchised from the system. The authors essentially suggest the following:

- Schools need to offer professional development, conducted by experts in special education law (e.g., special education attorneys), to principals and special education coordinators on how to justly utilize special education policies and mandates to serve students with disabilities.
- Parent advocacy groups that focus on families with children with disabilities should educate parents on how to advocate for their children's educational needs and rights.

Chapter 8 offers hope for yet another strategy for disrupting the STPP. We must continue to hope and continue to strive against the STPP and the destructive effects it has upon the lives of children, families, and society.

Ending the STPP and into a Better Future

The term social justice has become quite trendy in schools and in Colleges of Education. However, as the term has grown in popularity, a significant number of students continue to be funneled into the STPP, significantly Black and Brown boys as well as lower income boys of all ethnicities. We hope that Chapters 2 and 3 help readers to understand the pain that children and youth suffer as they are coerced into the STPP. We hope that Chapters 4, 5, and 6 help readers to understand some of the policies and practices that schools are enhancing to reproduce and maintain the factors that bring about that pain as well as the STPP. Chapters 7 and 8 critically examine two innovative disciplinary strategies which were meant to reduce that pain and bring about a sense of belonging and hope for the children and youth who have been experiencing the frustration, pain, and anger as they are funneled into the STPP. Nevertheless, the authors caution that the practices of restorative discipline and PBIS may be used more for maintaining order than for creating a sense of belonging and trust for all students. Finally, Chapter 8 suggests a way to use disability rights, policies, and laws to disrupt the STPP. From these chapters, we have suggested a number of policies and practices that schools and educational stakeholders can begin to implement in order to create a sense of belonging and trust for all students; to reduce pain and waste of lives; and to bring about the possibility of a better future. We have summarized these into six suggestions that we think are most important and that schools should begin immediately to implement.

(i) Eliminate zero tolerance policies.
(ii) Begin and continue principal and teacher development workshops to help them to become aware of their ethnocentricity and develop other cultural understandings.
(iii) Begin and continue principal and teacher development workshops to help teachers to teach and maintain discipline in a culturally responsive manner for Black, Brown, and lower income boys.
(iv) Combat the discourses that construct Black, Brown, and lower income boys as deviant. Construct counter discourses that construct Black, Brown, and lower income boys through positive lenses of possibility.
(v) When using innovative disciplinary strategies that are intended to circumvent, disrupt, or dismantle the STPP, be cautious that the practices are not used to "maintain order" but rather create an environment of belonging for vulnerable youth.
(vi) Begin to use disability rights and laws to disrupt the STPP but be cautious not to fall into the same pattern as was found in the studies on PBIS and the restorative discipline.

We hope this book helps readers to understand why the STPP is of such pressing concern, the factors that help to maintain the STPP, and ways in which we can continue to disrupt the STPP. But more importantly, we hope this book motivates readers to immediately begin to do what they can to make changes in their schools that help create a better future for the children who are suffering from coercion into the STPP, their families, and for society in general.

Finally, we urge that research is conducted as each of these suggestions are followed to ensure that they really are effective in ameliorating the STPP.

ABOUT THE EDITORS AND CONTRIBUTORS

Brian Boggs serves as Outreach and Development Specialist at the Office of K-12 Outreach in the College of Education at Michigan State University. His area of expertise is policy development and analysis in the area of school reform and holds a dual major Ph.D. in educational policy and administration from MSU. In addition, Brian holds a special certification in urban education from MSU and is a graduate of the Michigan Educational Policy Fellowship Program (2012–2013). With a bachelor's degree in English and history and his master's degree in English language and literature, he has taught college rhetoric and critical writing courses at the University of Michigan – Flint in addition to courses in educational policy and school administration. He has written extensively on organizational and instructional complexity. His research interests include organizational theory, policy making, sociology of education, experimental design, school improvement, and the history and politics of US education.

Joshua Bornstein is presently an Assistant Professor and Director of the Educational Leadership at Felician University. A career in public education spans numerous leadership roles in a similar broad set of communities. Dr. Bornstein has served as a Teacher, Union Leader, Principal, Staff Developer, and School Board Member. He has worked in urban, rural, and suburban communities in Maryland, New Jersey, and New York. His research centers on inclusive educational leadership that eliminates race, class, gender, disability, and first language as predictors of student success.

Felecia M. Briscoe earned her doctorate in the foundations of education from the University of Cincinnati and has spent over 20 years studying the way power works in and through schools. She has published two books, *Becoming Critical: The Emergence of Social Justice Scholars* and *The Power of Talk: How Words Change Our Lives*. She has also published numerous articles. These include "A counternarrative autoethnography exploring school districts' role in reproducing racism: Willful blindness to race disparities in school suspensions" in *Teachers College Record*; "'That racism thing:'

A critical discourse analysis of a conflict over the proposed closure of a Black high school" in *Race, Ethnicity, & Education*; "Anarchist, neoliberal, & democratic decision-making: Deepening the joy in learning and teaching" in *Educational Studies*; and ""They make you invisible": Negotiating power at the academic intersections of ethnicity, gender, and class" in *Equity & Excellence in Education*.

Christopher Dunbar is a Professor of education policy, organization, and leadership at the University of Illinois Urbana-Champaign. He received his Ph.D. from the University of Illinois-Champaign. His research has focused on alternative education for students who have been unable to successfully matriculate through traditional public school. He has authored scholarly journal articles and studies. His book *Alternative School for African American Youth* (2001) examines an alternative school designed for students perceived as disruptive. His current research examines the intersection of between school choice and educational opportunities for disruptive students, zero tolerance policy, and its impact on school administrators. Prior to coming to the University of Illinois, he was a professor of educational administration at Michigan State University.

Decoteau J. Irby is an Assistant Professor at University of Illinois at Chicago in the Department of Educational Policy Studies where he advises in the Urban Education Leadership Ed.D. and Educational Organization and Leadership Ph.D. programs. He teaches classes on educational leadership, organizational change, and school improvement using pedagogical approaches grounded in action research and team-based inquiry. He is also an affiliate faculty member with UIC's Center for Urban Education Leadership. Dr. Irby's research explores how equity-focused school leadership can be used as a lever to improve Black children and youth's academic achievement and socioemotional well-being across a range of K-12 educational settings. Specifically, he is interested in how adults make sense of and use their personal and collective influence and resources to transform educational spaces (including the self) to benefit students of color.

Andrea Kalvesmaki is a Research Associate at the Utah Education Policy Center. She holds degrees in psychology and medical anthropology and works as an evaluator in education and policy. She is currently pursuing a doctorate in educational leadership and policy at the University of Utah. Her research examines policies and practices impacting child outcomes across various contexts. Her doctoral research examines policies that contribute to the incarceration of children in the United States.

Muhammad Khalifa is an Associate Professor in educational leadership at the University of Minnesota. His research examines how urban school leaders enact culturally responsive leadership practices. He has published in top education journals, such as *Review of Educational Research*, *Teachers College Record*, and *Educational Administration Quarterly*. He is the author of the forthcoming book, *Leading with Community: Culturally Responsive School Leadership for Minoritized Youth* (Harvard Education Press). He is also a coeditor of two other books: *Handbook on Urban Educational Leadership* (Rowan & Littlefield) and *Becoming Critical: The Emergence of Social Justice Scholars* (SUNY Press). He has led equity audits in US schools as a way to reduce achievement and discipline gaps and is the first to develop and use online equity audits. He has helped school districts avoid "blind reforming" and select appropriate reforms that counter inequitable practices in school. He has also contributed to school leadership reform in African and Asian countries.

Hilary Lustick is an Assistant Professor of educational leadership and school improvement at Texas State University, the state's first and largest college of education. She teaches school leadership and research courses in educational administration. She studies issues of equity and school discipline in the urban context. Her work can be found in *International Leadership in Education*; *Race, Ethnicity, and Education* and a forthcoming volume on policy analysis by Palgrave.

Nathern S. Okilwa is an Assistant Professor of educational leadership and policy studies at the University of Texas San Antonio. His life experiences and long career as an educator in a variety of K-12 contexts – rural/urban, general/special education, alternative schooling, and international – informs his research agenda. His research interests include educational and life outcomes of disadvantaged or underserved or marginalized students (e.g., low SES, culturally and linguistically diverse, racial/ethnic minorities, and special education); school leadership in diverse school contexts; and educational policy. He is also engaged with consortiums of international school leadership researchers – International Successful School Principal Project and International School Leadership Development Network. Additionally, he is involved in local school district partnerships where he coordinates one of the master's level leadership cohort program. He teaches and advises students in the master's and doctoral programs.

Hugh Potter is a Doctoral Candidate in education policy at Michigan State University. He holds a special certificate in urban education from Michigan

State University. His area of scholarship focuses on urban education, policy implementation, and the study of inequity within educational systems. Prior to entering the doctoral program in Education Policy, Hugh earned master's degrees in both K-12 administration and curriculum and teaching. After certification in social studies education, Hugh was a classroom teacher for seven years in Michigan.

Garth Stahl (@GarthStahl) is a Lecturer in literacy and sociology at University of South Australia. He is a theorist of sociology of education. His research interests lie on the nexus of neoliberalism and sociocultural studies of education, identity, equity/inequality, and social change. Of particular interest to him is exploring counternarratives to neoliberalism around "value" and "respectability" for working-class youth. His book, entitled *Identity, Neoliberalism and Aspiration: Educating White Working-Class Boys* is now available from Routledge. He is on the editorial board of *British Journal of Sociology of Education* and *Sociological Research Online*.

Joseph B. Tulman, J.D., M.A.T., is a Professor of law at the University of the District of Columbia David A. Clarke School of Law. He directs the Juvenile and Special Education Law Clinic and the Took Crowell Institute for Youth. His research emphasizes special education advocacy on behalf of children who are enmeshed in the delinquency system or criminal system to reduce unnecessary incarceration. His practice of law has focused on delinquency defense, child welfare, and special education.

Brenda G. Valles is the Director for Research and Assessment in the Office for Equity and Diversity at the University of Utah. Valles received her doctorate in educational leadership & policy from the University of Utah. Her research interests focus on underrepresented student achievement, in particular Chicana/o students. Dr. Valles' work spans the PK-20 educational pipeline. In her current role, she examines higher education success factors for underrepresented students and teaches courses in ethnic studies.

INDEX

Printed in the United States
By Bookmasters